Illustrated MS-DOS 5.0

and All Previous MS/PC-DOS Versions

I don't sell this book - Keep for future reference!

Russell A. Stultz

Wordware Publishing, Inc.

Library of Congress Cataloging-in-Publication Data

Stultz, Russell Allen.
Illustrated MS-DOS 5.00 and all previous MS/PC-DOS versions /
Russell A. Stultz.
p. cm.
Includes index.
ISBN 1-55622-214-9 : $21.95
1. MS-DOS (Computer operating system) 2. PC DOS (Computer
operating system) I. Title.
QA76.76.063S77 1991
005'.4'436—dc20 91-8357
CIP

1506 Capital Avenue
Plano, Texas 75074

Printed in the United States of America

ISBN 1-55622-214-9

10 9 8 7 2 5 4 3 2 1
9103

All inquiries for volume purchases of this book should be addressed to Wordware Publishing, Inc.,
at the above address. Telephone inquiries may be made by calling:

(214) 423-0090

Contents

Contents (Cont.)

Recommended Learning Sequence

Recommended Learning Sequence (Cont.)

Preface

About DOS My first encounter with a microcomputer-based operating system was with Digital Research's Control Program for Microcomputers, more commonly known as CP/M. I was amazed at how simplicity and power could be combined into a relatively small command set. But I was concerned too. The commands were cryptic. Efficient computer operation required memory work. Fortunately, only a handful of commands were needed, so it did not take long to master CP/M operation.

When DOS found its way into the marketplace, I was delighted to find that it was quite similar to the old, familiar CP/M system. That meant that I would not have to memorize a new command set. Although the form of several commands changed, they were close enough to avoid the need to start from scratch.

With each new version of DOS came new, more powerful commands. Versions of DOS beginning with 2.00 introduced fixed-disk formatting and backup utilities, filter commands for redirection of input/output, a set of system configuration commands, and several enhancements to existing commands.

DOS 3.00 introduced commands that support file sharing. This version also supports the application of DOS in different countries by letting you choose different date, time, currency, decimal value, and keyboard formats.

DOS 3.30 and its derivatives were introduced with the microchannel architecture machines, such as IBM's new Personal System/2 series of microcomputers, and with Compaq's new line of 386 machines. This version of DOS introduced what is known as code page switching. This capability lets users configure their operating system for use with a number of national language character sets. Code page switching now lets users select character sets common to their local language. The characters are selected and switched under software control, resulting in a keyboard, display, and printer that is familiar to users who speak many different languages.

DOS Version 5.00 introduces a number of new, useful features including a new and improved DOSSHELL utility. The new DOSSHELL lets users switch between active applications much like Windows 3.0. DOS 5.00 also makes more efficient use of memory above 640K for PCs using 80286 and 80386 microprocessors with at least 64K of extended memory. It makes use of memory between 640K and 1024K on 80386 and 80486 PCs for loading programs, device drivers, and TSR (or pop-up) programs. DOS 5.00 is also smaller than DOS 4.01, which frees up memory below 640K on 8088-based PCs.

Other features include a new full-screen editor, called EDIT, and a new HELP command that displays information about a named DOS command. Here's a summary of what's new.

DOSKEY—Records keystrokes used at the DOS prompt that can be recalled and reused like macros.

EDIT—A full-screen editor used to create and edit documents. Includes the same editing features provided by most program editors, such as QuickBASIC.

DIR—The directory command now has a series of new parameters for searching subdirectories, sorting, displaying files having specified attributes (such as hidden or readonly), etc.

FIND—The find command now has a /I option to let you find either uppercase or lowercase strings.

FORMAT—A new, safe format command now lets you unformat disks to recover information. A /Q option lets you erase a formatted floppy diskette in less than 10 seconds.

QBASIC—QuickBASIC is now supplied with DOS 5.00 as the standard programming utility.

UNDELETE—You can now undelete files to recover them.

UNFORMAT—You can now unformat a disk that has been accidentally reformatted.

A few other enhancements include the ability to rename a directory from the DOS shell. The new enhancements are described in detail within their respective modules.

About Illustrated Books As a classroom instructor and writer of books about many kinds of microcomputer software applications, I find myself constantly searching for good, authoritative sources of information. This includes books that can help me learn and that are ready-made to help me teach others — ones that get at the "heart" of the information fast and that teach principles through practice.

The alphabetized, modular format of the Illustrated Series lets you find the area of interest quickly. A description, applications, and step-by-step examples are provided. This combination provides quick answers and contains illustrative models that are used to show you precisely how to apply software commands.

You will find the Illustrated approach goes beyond standard documentation and books that treat software theoretically or in broad and sometimes vague terms. Unlike textbooks which have little value as a reference tool, the Illustrated format guarantees the book's usefulness long after you complete the learning sequence.

To the best of my knowledge, Wordware's Illustrated books comprise the only true computer book series on the market today. The organizational approach, presentation style, and examples are predictably consistent and reliable. Rigid author guidelines have been constructed for Wordware's Illustrated book authors to guarantee a reliable, consistent format between books in the series. Technical audits are conducted to ensure that operational procedures and source listings work. Screen illustrations are captured during the technical audit process to assure that you see exactly what the software displays.

These extra steps have placed books in the Illustrated series in hundreds of universities and colleges around the world. In addition, technical schools, corporate learning centers, and computer dealers are using Illustrated books for training purposes. Many dealers use the *Illustrated MS-DOS* book as their standard DOS reference manual in place of the one supplied with the software.

I hope readers continue to enjoy the use of this series of books as much as I've enjoyed contributing to it.

Russell A. Stultz
President and C.E.O.
Wordware Publishing, Inc.

Rom Bios - read only memory, Basic input/output system.
Bio Com -
Boot - start up
Boot up - loading the operating system into the computers memory
Command Com -
Dos Com
Con - console = Keyboard
Contiguous = having ajoining boundries

Module 1
ABOUT THIS BOOK

INTRODUCTION

This book describes the Microsoft® Disk Operating System (MS-DOS). It describes how you can use the various versions of MS-DOS, including versions 1.00 through 5.00, to get the most out of your microcomputer. Each module title in this book includes a number, within parentheses, to designate the DOS version in which the subject command was introduced.

The terms MS-DOS, PC-DOS, and DOS are used interchangeably by many users. This book uses the names DOS and MS-DOS. What is DOS? In simple terms, a disk operating system provides a predictable linkage (one following established rules) between your computer's electronic circuitry (hardware) and the software programs you use, such as word processors, electronic spreadsheets, database managers, and accounting programs.

In addition to providing the software-to-machine interface, DOS features a host of handy "housekeeping tools." For example, there are special utilities for preparing new disks, listing the contents (or filenames) of a magnetic disk on the display screen or to your printer, creating, copying, deleting, and combining files, and much more. These features are described in this book.

This book is designed for a broad range of users. It is for beginners who wish to learn DOS from scratch. It provides intermediate and advanced users a quick reference that contains commands that work and serve as useful examples. And, finally, it serves the classroom instructor as an instructionally designed DOS textbook.

The DOS program is sophisticated; it often appears intimidating because its commands are cryptic. DOS does not display a series of friendly menus from which to make a selection. To the contrary, it displays a letter and a blinking cursor. Although it is not apparent, this is the DOS prompt, where a prompt invites you to type a command from the keyboard.

Therefore, it is necessary for you to memorize a few fundamental DOS commands, where commands are instructions recognized by DOS. English-speaking computer users are fortunate, because most DOS commands are English derivatives. For example, the DIR command displays a directory (or list) of filenames on the screen. The FORMAT command is used to format (or prepare) a new magnetic storage diskette for use with your microcomputer.

One nice thing about DOS is that it tries to stay out of your way unless you call on it by entering one of its special commands. Of course, you can ignore DOS by running packaged applications programs. But learning the ins and outs of DOS is strongly recommended if you are to exploit the full power of your microcomputer.

If you are a beginning user who is not afraid to "mess around" with DOS commands, you will discover that DOS is easy to use within a matter of minutes. You can do useful things by learning a half-dozen or so commands. The more you use DOS, the richer it becomes. After a brief exposure, you will begin to feel like a veteran computer user, because the utility of DOS lets you get down to the nuts and bolts of file creation and management.

To prove to yourself how easy DOS can be, you may want to jump over to Module 2 and go through the sample session with your computer. The sample session lets you do useful things, and you quickly see how you can have DOS working for you in a matter of minutes. Once you develop an appreciation for its usefulness, you should have the incentive to explore DOS even further.

ORGANIZATION

This book is organized into compact, easy-to-read, example-packed modules. In order to best fit the broad range of users that it addresses, literally hundreds of examples and illustrations are presented in the description, applications, and typical operation sections of the modules. These show how DOS is used to solve practical, everyday problems.

Working examples that let you experiment with DOS commands take the mystery out of what might otherwise be difficult to appreciate. In addition to conducting "hands-on" experimentation, you will probably find yourself having a lot of fun, because learning by doing is a rewarding experience.

WITHIN THE MODULES

This module provides information about the book, and it briefly describes what kind of equipment is used with DOS. It also tells you what you should know before moving on to subsequent modules.

With the exception of modules 1 through 3, most of the modules in this book contain information that pertains to specific DOS commands, functions, or families of commands or functions.

Module 2 introduces you to DOS. As you experiment with several of the more commonly used DOS utilities, you will see how responsive DOS is, as well as being relatively easy to use. If you are the kind of person who likes to "dive in," you will enjoy the sample DOS session in Module 2. You will discover not only how DOS commands are used, but how you can follow the sample session on your computer.

This is a preview of things to come, because this book is designed to let you follow along on your computer.

Module 3 introduces ways in which DOS and your keyboard interact. In addition, you will learn about internal and external DOS commands, hidden files, and several important new terms. A DOS command summary also is provided as a handy quick reference.

Modules 4 through 68 describe and illustrate the many DOS commands. These commands are arranged in alphabetical order, as in a dictionary, for easy reference.

If you are learning DOS, be sure to follow the recommended learning sequence at the front of this book. This sequence rearranges the commands, which are alphabetized for easy reference, into a simple-to-complex order. This organization is designed specifically for learning (or teaching) commands and has been used by thousands of self-taught users and classroom teachers. As you work your way through this book, you can check off the modules you have completed.

TERMS AND DEFINITIONS

Appendix A contains a list of terms and definitions that are used in this book. Although many terms are defined when first encountered, there may be a few that slipped in without explanation. If you encounter such a term, check Appendix A for a definition.

DOS PRACTICE EXERCISES

Appendix B is provided for both classroom and self-teaching situations. It contains DOS exercises. If you are a classroom instructor, you may wish to include these exercises in student assignments. If you are learning DOS on your own, the exercises are a good way to see what you have learned about a command. If you can answer the questions, you are ready to move on to the next module in the learning sequence.

HARDWARE AND SOFTWARE REQUIREMENTS

The various versions of DOS operate with Intel's 8086, 8088, 80186, 80286, 80386, and 80486 family of microprocessors. DOS-based computers are being used around the world by an estimated fifty million people for perhaps a hundred thousand applications. This includes hundreds of computer models ranging from desktop to laptop computers from nearly as many manufacturers.

With a growing base of complex software programs, the need for larger amounts of memory is increasing. Today, it is not uncommon to find DOS-based microcomputers sporting from one to sixteen megabytes (million characters) of memory. Your ability to take advantage of large amounts of memory depends on the specific programs you use and the way you configure your computer. However, most computers using 8086 through 80286 microprocessors cannot address more than 640 kilobytes (thousand characters) of memory at a time.

To get around the 640-kilobyte barrier, a technique called *bank switching* is used. This lets the software move from one 640-kilobyte partition of memory to another, and then back again, giving the user operational continuity. Remember, your hardware, software, and system configuration will vary the amount of available memory and the way it is used.

Within the past few years, extended and expanded memory specifications have been developed to let 80286 through 80486 class microcomputers load greater amounts of executable code and data into memory.

This capability achieves greater execution speeds that rival those attained by many minicomputers, giving rise to a new breed of super microcomputers.

Until the advent of DOS 4.01 and a series of 80386-based microcomputers from Compaq Computer Corporation, DOS-based microcomputers were unable to address more than a 32-megabyte partition of disk space. With the elimination of the 32-megabyte barrier, users have the ability to manage huge amounts of data on a modern-technology microcomputer.

In addition, higher disk density technology is reducing the cost of hard disks and other storage media, yielding greater storage capacities at lower costs. This is putting microcomputers within the financial reach of users who operate within even the smallest businesses.

A key to good system usage is your ability to use DOS. You can set up virtual disks, called memory or RAM disks, to take advantage of extra memory in your system. You can also use memory-resident programs, including programs like Borland International's Sidekick, Lightning, and others.

WHAT YOU SHOULD KNOW

As a minimum, you should be familiar with computer connection and turn-on procedures. If you have a printer, you should know how to connect it to your computer, set switches, and load paper and ribbon. You should also be familiar with your system's monitor type, keyboard, available memory, and storage subsystem. In particular, you should check the version of DOS you are using. Many commands have been added with recent DOS releases; if you have an old version, some commands will not be available for your use.

Finally, you should be familiar with your keyboard. If the keys on your keyboard are engraved with special symbols instead of words, use the following table to see how they are named in this book.

Symbol	*Key*
↵	Return or <CR>
←	Backspace
⇆	Tab
⇑	Shift
→	Right Arrow
←	Left Arrow
↑	Up Arrow
↓	Down Arrow
	Spacebar
[F1]-[F12]	Function key F1 through F12

If you have not already done so, move to Module 2 to experience a hands-on sample session with DOS.

Module 2
A SAMPLE SESSION WITH DOS

INTRODUCTION

This module provides information about your computer's disk drives, diskette storage and handling, and diskette construction. Then it takes you on a tour through a set of commonly used DOS commands. Because the intent of this module is to give you some hands-on experience, you will not find in-depth explanations of the DOS commands here. If, while using one of the commands, you become curious, check the module that describes that command in depth. When you finish your tour, move on to Module 3, which reveals additional information about the structure of DOS, special DOS operations, and how your keyboard interacts with DOS.

Your Computer's Disk Drives

Your computer is equipped with one or more diskette drives or a combination of diskette drives and a fixed (or hard) disk drive. DOS assigns different letter designations to disk drives. If you have a system with two diskette drives, the left-hand disk is normally logical disk A, while the right-hand disk is logical disk B. On some machines the disk drives are stacked. Check with the manufacturer to determine which is A and which is B.

This book assumes that the disk containing DOS is either a fixed disk (drive C) or a floppy diskette (drive A). Because most systems have fixed disks, drive C is most frequently used. If you have a floppy-disk system, substitute A: for C: in the practice activities.

Although many use the term diskette to refer to a removable, flexible (or floppy) diskette, and disk to refer to a fixed disk, the term disk is used in this book to refer to both disks and diskettes. When a fixed disk is specifically referenced, the terms fixed or hard disk are used.

Disk Handling and Storage

Flexible disks are delicate and should be handled accordingly. This is particularly true with the popular 5.25-inch diskette. The 3.5-inch diskette configuration is encased in a hard plastic shell and is less susceptible to physical damage. Some suggestions for the handling and storage of flexible diskettes follow.

1. Never touch the exposed magnetic surfaces; always hold disks by their protective jackets.

2. Never expose disks to:
   a. Magnetic fields (magnets, motors, heavy metal objects)
   b. Extreme heat or cold
   c. Direct sunlight
   d. Moisture or oil
   e. Abrasive materials or dust
3. Take care not to scratch, score, or prick the disk or its protective cover.
4. Never eat, drink, or smoke in areas where disks are in use or being stored.
5. Use a soft felt-tip marker when writing on disk labels, and write lightly; do not use pencils, ball-point or nylon-tip pens.
6. Store disks in a flat diskette case or box to avoid bending or folding.

Following these simple suggestions minimizes the possibility of damage to your valuable programs and stored information (or data).

DISK CONSTRUCTION

The various parts of standard 5.25- and 3.5-inch disks are contained in Figure 2-1. A description of each part is also provided.

1. Write protect notch—When covered, prevents information from being recorded on the disk; when uncovered, information can be recorded.
2. Temporary label—An adhesive-backed label allowing the contents of a disk to be identified.
3. Permanent label—When used, contains disk manufacturer and capacity information.
4. Exposed recording surface—Metal oxide surface used to magnetically record data. Do not touch!
5. Protective jacket—Houses magnetic disk; provides protective cover.
6. Diskette envelope (sleeve)—Used to store disks; prevents accidental contact with exposed surface.
7. Protective slide—Protects magnetic media surface; slides open when inserted into a diskette drive (only on 3 1/2-inch diskettes).

USING DOS

Your tour of DOS includes a description of the DOS installation process. The guided tour assumes that DOS is properly installed and ready to use. This book assumes you have a hard disk drive system and at least one removable (or floppy) disk drive. Your hard disk drive is probably designated C, but any other letter may be substituted for C, such as D or E. Floppy drives are designated A and B. You will have at least a drive A.

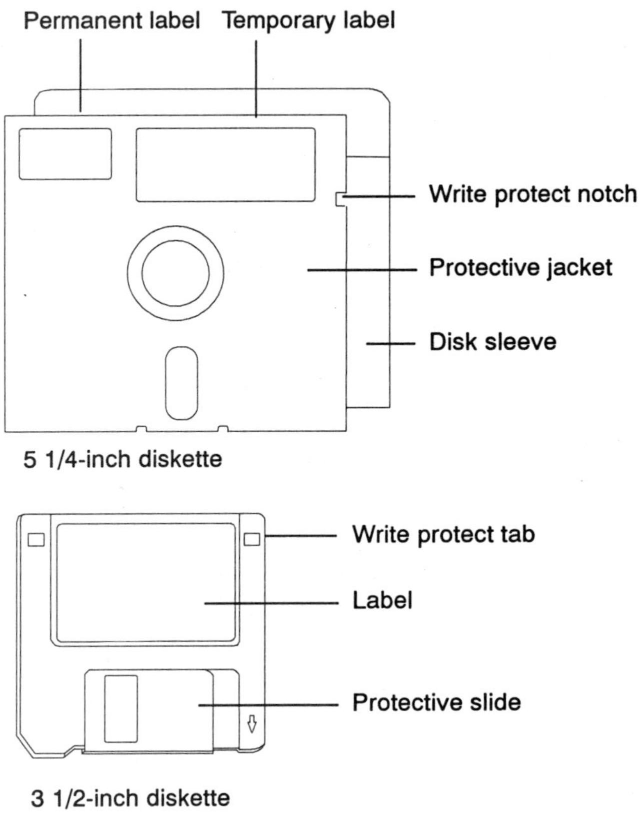

Figure 2-1 The Parts of a Floppy Disk

INSTALLING/UPGRADING DOS If you purchased your computer from a computer store or obtained it from a corporate MIS organization, DOS should have been properly installed by the supplier. Therefore, if DOS is already installed on your system, do not attempt to install it again. Neither should you attempt to partition or format a hard disk drive using the FORMAT or FDISK commands. This will cause the loss of important configuration files, programs, and data.

If you bought your computer from an individual or built it yourself using "off-the-shelf" parts, then you may have to perform the installation process yourself.

If You Must Install DOS 3.3 Or Earlier: If you intend to install DOS 3.3 or earlier on either a hard or floppy drive, the drive must be formatted in accordance with the information in modules 27 and 30, which cover the FDISK and FORMAT commands.

If You Must Install DOS 4.01 If you are installing DOS 4.01 on a machine containing DOS 3.3 or earlier, skip this paragraph and move on to the FIXED DISK USER NOTE. Otherwise, read the next four paragraphs to prepare your DOS 4.01 working disk.

If you are using DOS 4.01, you must have an 80286, 80386, or IBM PS/2 microcomputer. Otherwise, you must use DOS version 3.3 or earlier. When installing DOS 4.01 on one of the above mentioned systems, use the SELECT program to create a working system diskette or to write DOS directly to your fixed disk. This program displays an easy-to-follow series of menus that guide you through the installation process. Once a working DOS diskette is created, you can use the FORMAT command to prepare additional DOS diskettes.

If your system uses 3.5-inch 720 KB diskettes, you should have two DOS distribution diskettes labeled Install and Operating. If you are using 5.25-inch 360 KB diskettes, you have five diskettes labeled Install, Select, Operating 1, Operating 2, and Operating 3. The SELECT program is found on the 3.5-inch diskette labeled Install. As you might imagine, the SELECT program is on the 5.25-inch diskette labeled Select.

Before installing DOS 4.01 on a diskette for the first time, you should have a set of the following diskettes, depending on the disk drives installed on your computer.

Installing DOS 4.01 On:	*Number Required*
1.44 MB Diskette Drive	1
720 KB Diskette Drive	2
1.2 MB Diskette Drive	2
360 KB Diskette Drive	4
Fixed Disk	0*

*You can install DOS 4.01 directly on a fixed disk system using the original distribution diskettes.

The SELECT program restricts installation of DOS 4.01 to either drive C (fixed disk) or drive B (floppy disk). However, if you are using a working version of DOS 4.01, you can install the system on any drive, as with earlier versions of DOS.

Once DOS 4.01 is installed on either your fixed or floppy disk, restart your computer with the DOS 4.01 system in either drive A or on your fixed disk. If the DOS Shell is automatically displayed, select exit to display the DOS command line (or prompt A> or C>).

FIXED DISK USER NOTE:

If you have a fixed disk system with DOS installed on a DOS subdirectory or on the root directory, substitute C: (or C:\DOS) for A:. Use A: in place of B: as the working data diskette.

If You Must Install or Update DOS 5.00 The DOS 5.00 installation disks make use of a self-running installation/updating program named SETUP. SETUP checks your hardware as well as any previous version of DOS that may be present. If you are installing or updating DOS 5.00 on a hard drive, SETUP creates the subdirectory C:\DOS and copies all necessary files to it. It also creates two UNINSTALL diskettes that can be used to remove version 5.00 from your hard disk and restore the original version of DOS. If you intend to keep DOS 5.00 on your hard disk, a CLEANUP utility is provided to remove all old DOS files. Do not use CLEANUP if you ever intend to restore your original DOS version. When using floppy disks, SETUP creates several DOS disks.

FIXED DISK INSTALLATION:

1. Turn on your computer and wait for the DOS prompt display.
2. Format two floppy diskettes and label them UNINSTALL #1 and UNINSTALL #2. This is achieved by putting a blank disk in drive A. Then type **FORMAT A:** and press **Return.** Wait for the format operation to finish. Format the second disk by making the appropriate response to the displayed prompts.
3. Set the floppy disks aside for later use. These diskettes let you uninstall DOS 5.00 so you can restore any prior version of DOS.

NOTE

If updating your DOS system, you should make a copy of your CONFIG.SYS and AUTOEXEC.BAT files to ensure that important commands are available. This is recommended as the DOS 5.00 SETUP utility modifies these files. Make copies of these using step 4. Otherwise, proceed directly to step 5.

4. If updating your version of DOS, rename your CONFIG.SYS and AUTOEXEC.BAT files as follows:
    a. Type **COPY C:\CONFIG.SYS C:\CONFIG.OLD** and press **Return.**
    b. Type **COPY C:\AUTOEXEC.BAT C:\AUTOEXEC.OLD** and press **Return.**
5. Insert DOS 5.00 Disk 1 in drive A and close the load lever. Then type **SETUP** and press **Return.**
6. Follow the screen prompts, exchanging disks as often as necessary, until the installation program is done.

FLOPPY DISK INSTALLATION:

1. Turn on your computer and wait for the DOS prompt display.
2. Collect either seven 5.25-inch or four 3.5-inch floppy disks and label them according to the following table. The DOS 5.00 SETUP program automatically formats these disks for you. You can even use disks that contain obsolete files.

Disk Type	*Number*	*Disk Label Names*	
5.25-inch	7	STARTUP	BASIC/EDIT
360K		SUPPORT	UTILITY
		SHELL	SUPPLEMENTAL
		HELP	
3.5-inch	4	STARTUP/SUPPORT	
720K or 1.4M		SHELL/HELP	
		BASIC/EDIT/UTILITY	
		SUPPLEMENTAL	

3. Set the labeled floppy disks in a convenient location.
4. Insert DOS 5.00 Disk 1 in drive A and close the load lever. Then type **SETUP** and press **Return**.
5. Follow the screen prompts, exchanging disks as often as necessary, until the installation program is done.

NOTE

You should type PROMPT pg and press Return to set your DOS prompt display. Then type PATH C:\;C:\DOS and press Return to provide access to your DOS commands. If you wish, put the following lines in an AUTOEXEC.BAT file (see Module 7).

```
PROMPT $p$g
PATH C:\;C:\DOS
```

FORMATTING AND COPYING DOS TO A WORKING DISK Begin your tour by performing the following procedure.

1. Check to see that your computer is connected properly and plugged into a wall outlet.
2. If you are using a floppy disk system, insert your original DOS disk in drive A and close the load lever as shown in Figure 2-2. If you are using a fixed disk system, your system should "boot" (start) automatically.

NOTE

If your computer is equipped with a clock-calendar option, skip to step 6.

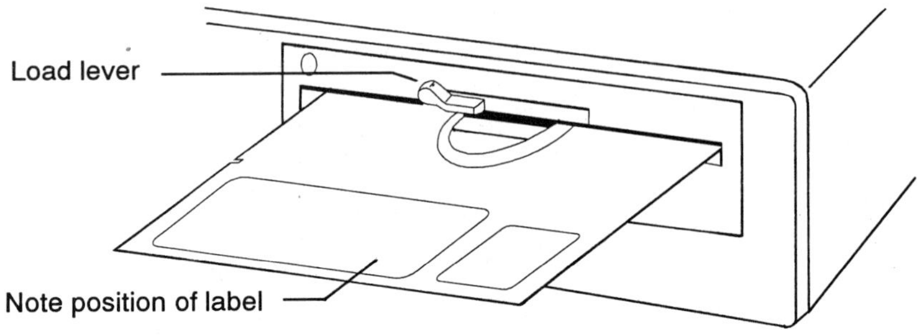

Figure 2-2 Inserting a Flexible Disk into a Disk Drive

3. Turn on your computer and wait for the Date prompt display; your display screen should resemble the following illustration.

```
Current date is mm-dd-yy
Enter new date:_
```

4. Type the date in the form **11-15-91** and press **Return** (or Enter on many keyboards; Return is used throughout this book). Notice the time prompt:

```
Current time is hh:mm:ss
Enter new time:_
```

5. Type the time in the form **09:15** and press **Return**. Notice that the DOS prompt is redisplayed.

NOTE

If the date and time are not important, you can press Return twice without typing the date and time. However, if you create or revise any new files during your computer session, they will not be labeled with the current time and date. The procedure assumes that your computer is not equipped with a clock-calendar device.

NOTE

In the following steps, if you are using a fixed disk system, your DOS files are on drive C and your working diskette is in drive A. Therefore, substitute drive C for A and drive A for B. When formatting or copying files from drive C, be sure to log the subdirectory containing your DOS files. This subdirectory is normally designated C:\DOS and is accessed by typing CD\DOS and pressing Return at the C> prompt. The subdirectory name \DOS may vary with the person who set up your system. Review Module 19 for an understanding of the DOS directory commands and how to use them.

6. Insert a blank disk into drive B (the right-hand drive on a two-floppy-drive PC) and close the load lever.

NOTE

In steps 7 through 11, the FORMAT and COPY commands are used to format the new disk and then to copy the contents of your DOS disk to the new disk in drive B.

7. Type **FORMAT B:/S** and press **Return**; notice the display.

```
A:\>FORMAT B:/S
Insert new diskette for drive B:
and press ENTER when ready...
```

8. Press any key (like Spacebar) and notice that the display indicates the formatting process. Early versions of DOS display the word "Formatting... ." Later versions display head and cylinder status, which identifies defective regions of a disk when encountered.

   Upon completion of the formatting process, a message similar to the following is displayed.

```
Volume label (11 characters, ENTER for none)?

   1457664 bytes total disk space
    117760 bytes used by system
   1339904 bytes available on disk

       512 bytes in each allocation unit
      2617 allocation units available on disk

Volume Serial Number is 346D-10FF

Format another (Y/N)?
```

NOTE

The amount of disk space, bytes used, and bytes available varies with the version of DOS and the type of disk you are using. A byte is roughly equivalent to a text character.

9. Type **N** and press **Return** and notice that the system redisplays the DOS A> prompt.
10. Type **COPY *.* B:/V** and press **Return**. Notice that a list of filenames is displayed as each file is copied from the disk in drive A (the source disk) to the disk in drive B (the target disk). The /V "verifies" successful copies.
11. List a directory of the filenames on drive A by typing **DIR** and pressing **Return**. Your display should resemble the following illustration.

```
ANSI     SYS      8868 12-13-90   4:09a
AUTOEXEC BAT       128 02-20-91   9:22p
COMMAND  COM     46246 12-13-90   4:09a
CONFIG   SYS       165 02-21-91   9:42a
DISPLAY  SYS     15682 12-13-90   4:09a
DOSKEY   COM      5693 12-13-90   4:09a
DRIVER   SYS      5384 12-13-90   4:09a
FORMAT   COM     32285 12-13-90   4:09a
HIMEM    SYS     11120 12-13-90   4:09a
MEM      EXE     22104 12-13-90   4:09a
SMARTDRV SYS      8005 12-13-90   4:09a
SYS      COM     13200 12-13-90   4:09a
UNDELETE EXE     13666 12-13-90   4:09a
HLPFILES     <DIR>     01-01-91  10:20a
       14 file(s)     183682 bytes
                       91588 bytes free

A:>
```

12. List a directory of the files on drive B by typing **DIR B:** and pressing **Return**. Your display should resemble the following illustration.

```
ANSI     SYS      8868 12-13-90   4:09a
AUTOEXEC BAT       128 02-20-91   9:22p
COMMAND  COM     46246 12-13-90   4:09a
CONFIG   SYS       165 02-21-91   9:42a
DISPLAY  SYS     15682 12-13-90   4:09a
DOSKEY   COM      5693 12-13-90   4:09a
DRIVER   SYS      5384 12-13-90   4:09a
FORMAT   COM     32285 12-13-90   4:09a
HIMEM    SYS     11120 12-13-90   4:09a
MEM      EXE     22104 12-13-90   4:09a
SMARTDRV SYS      8005 12-13-90   4:09a
SYS      COM     13200 12-13-90   4:09a
UNDELETE EXE     13666 12-13-90   4:09a
       13 file(s)     183674 bytes
                     1198644 bytes free

A:>
```

NOTE

The following step applies to a diskette-based system.

13. When the DOS prompt is redisplayed, remove the original DOS distribution disk from drive A and store it in a safe place.
14. Take the new working disk from drive B, insert it into drive A, and close the load lever.

NOTE

In the following step, you create a new file by copying the contents of the console (keyboard and screen), designated CON, to drive A.

15. Create a new file as follows:

NOTE

The notation Ctrl-X designates pressing and holding the Ctrl key while typing a second key (X). This is like pressing and holding the Shift key to type a capital letter. You may type commands in either uppercase or lowercase.

   a. Type **COPY CON A:MYFILE** and press **Return**.
   b. Type the following two lines of text, ending each line by pressing **Return**.

```
This is my first file.
I am going to save it.
```

   c. Press **Ctrl-Z** and then press **Return**. (Ctrl-Z insertes an end-of-file marker.)
   d. Notice the display screen; it should resemble the following illustration.

```
A:\>COPY CON A:MYFILE
This is my first file
I am going to save it.
^Z
        1 file(s) copied

A:\>
```

16. Display your new file (MYFILE) on the screen by typing **TYPE MYFILE** and pressing **Return**.
17. Make a copy of MYFILE called MYFILE.#2 by typing **COPY MYFILE MYFILE.#2** and pressing **Return**.
18. Combine the files MYFILE and MYFILE.#2 into a file called MYFILE.#3 by typing **COPY MYFILE+MYFILE.#2 MYFILE.#3** and pressing **Return**.

19. Display a directory of the three new files by typing **DIR MYFILE** and pressing **Return.**
20. Notice the display screen; it should resemble the following illustration.

```
A:\>DIR MYFILE

 Volume in drive A has no label
 Directory of A:\

MYFILE                  47 02-22-91   10:07a
MYFILE    #2            47 02-22-91   10:07a
MYFILE    #3            95 02-22-91   10:09a
         3 file(s)           189 bytes
                          165888 bytes free

A:\>
```

21. Display the file named MYFILE.#3 on the screen by typing **TYPE MYFILE.#3** and pressing **Return.**
22. Notice the display screen; it should resemble the following illustration.

```
A:\>TYPE MYFILE.#3
This is my first file
I am going to save it.
This is my first file
I am going to save it.

A:\>
```

23. Rename the file MYFILE.#2 to MYTWO.TXT by typing **REN MYFILE.#2 MYTWO.TXT** and pressing **Return.**
24. Display a directory of filenames beginning with "MY" by typing **DIR MY*.*** and pressing **Return.**
25. Notice the display screen; it should resemble the following illustration.

```
A:\>DIR MY*.*

 Volume in drive A has no label
 Directory of A:\

MYFILE                  47 02-22-91   10:07a
MYFILE    #3            95 02-22-91   10:09a
MYTWO     TXT           47 02-22-91   10:07a
         3 file(s)           189 bytes
                          165888 bytes free

A:\>
```

26. Delete the file MYFILE by typing **DEL MYFILE** and pressing **Return.**

27. Display a directory of filenames beginning with "MY" by typing **DIR MY*.*** and pressing **Return**.
28. Notice the display screen; it should resemble the following illustration.

```
A:\>DIR MY*.*

 Volume in drive A has no label
 Directory of A:\

MYFILE   #3          95 02-22-91  10:09a
MYTWO    TXT         47 02-22-91  10:07a
        2 file(s)        142 bytes
                      166912 bytes free

A:\>
```

29. Open the disk drive load lever, remove your new working disk, put it in its protective envelope, and store it in a safe place for later use.
30. Turn off the power to your computer equipment.

As a result of this practice session, you can now perform the following DOS operations:

- Format a blank disk and transfer the DOS system
- Copy all files from one disk to another
- Display a directory of all filenames on the logged disk
- Display a directory of filenames on the disk in drive B
- Replace the master disk in drive A with the new working disk from drive B
- Create a file
- Display (type) the new file on the screen
- Make a copy of the new file
- Combine two files to create a third
- Display a directory of selected filenames on the disk in drive A
- Rename a file
- Delete a file

As you can see, DOS performs a number of important tasks. However, these are just a few of the DOS operations available to you. You will learn many other equally powerful and useful DOS operations as you work your way through the rest of this book.

If you are following the learning sequence, turn to Module 3. There, information about a number of DOS characteristics is provided including:

- The structure of DOS
- A DOS command summary
- The names that DOS uses for different input/output devices
- The way your keyboard interacts with DOS

Module 3
SYSTEM OVERVIEW

INTRODUCTION

This module provides an overview of DOS and the DOS commands described in this book, specifically, information about the following subjects:

- The structure of DOS
- A DOS command summary
- The names that DOS uses to address the different computer input/output devices
- The way that your keyboard interacts with DOS

WHAT IS DOS?

Your disk operating system (DOS) performs a number of essential jobs. These include:

1. Controlling the way various application programs, such as word processors, electronic worksheets, database managers, accounting programs, etc., operate with your computer. DOS creates an environment that lets these programs "talk" to your computer and its input and output devices (printers, modems, display screen, keyboard, disk drives, etc.). Keyboard- and program-generated information is read, interpreted by DOS, and transferred to the selected computer device. Data being returned by your computer is again translated by DOS into useful information and written to an output device, such as your display screen, printer, or disk.
2. Providing "housekeeping" and file management utilities that perform useful tasks such as:
   - Disk preparation (formatting, copying, etc.)
   - File operations (creating, displaying, copying, combining, renaming, deleting, etc.)
3. Automating repetitive tasks through automatic execution, or batch, files which have the extension .BAT.
4. Controlling the way certain information is displayed on the screen.
5. Controlling the way your computer interprets certain commands.

Figure 3-1 contains a simplified diagram of the way DOS interacts between your computer programs and computer (hardware). Notice the BIO.COM and ROM BIOS (read-only memory basic input/output system). The BIO.COM is a software module that contains hardware initialization and device drivers. Hardware initialization includes preparing various parts of the hardware, such as memory, communication ports, etc., for operation. BIO.COM also loads DOS from the disk and transfers control to the user. Device drivers are small programs that accept calls from DOS to perform the appropriate hardware operation.

The ROM BIOS is actually a hardware device that contains a series of unalterable computer control programs (hence the term read-only). The ROM BIOS intercepts and processes instructions from BIO.COM. When instructions are received, the ROM BIOS handles the operation of the computer's hardware devices. Returning control information passes through ROM BIOS, BIO.COM, DOS, and back to the program being used. It is essential that your version of DOS is compatible with the ROM BIOS of your computer.

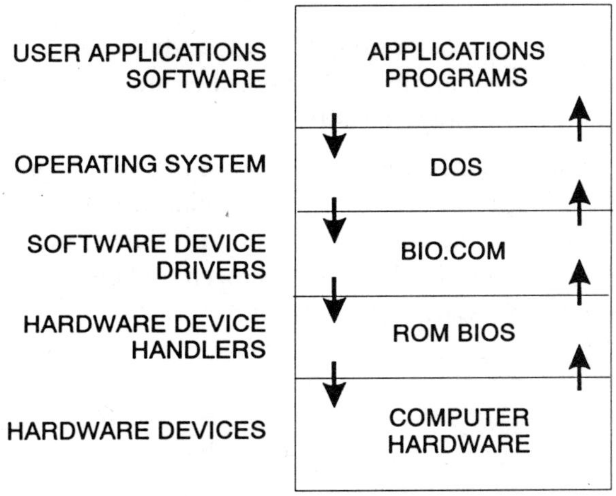

Figure 3-1 DOS and Your Computer, Simplified Diagram

DOS AND DISKS

The care and storage of disks (or diskettes) is described at the beginning of Module 2. Here, a description of the construction and organization of a typical disk is provided.

CONSTRUCTION Almost everyone is familiar with audio recording tape. The tape is a long, flexible acetate or mylar strip coated with ferrous oxide. This coating, which is a powdered iron-like substance, is affected by magnetic fields. Tape recorders are equipped with record and playback heads. The record head places magnetic patterns on the tape. These patterns may be a derivative of voice, music, or even audible computer data. The playback head detects the recorded patterns, which then are amplified several thousand times. The amplified signal is finally reproduced by a speaker.

A disk is similar to a recording tape in substance. Flexible (floppy) disks are also made of ferrous oxide-coated mylar material. Fixed (or hard) disks are made of a more rigid material, but still have the ferrous oxide coating.

The playback and record heads on a disk drive are called read and write heads, although they perform the same functions as their tape recorder counterparts.

Prerecorded tape cassettes containing valuable music programming are protected with a plastic tab. This tab prevents tape recorders from recording over (erasing) the audio information. Flexible disks also can be write protected to keep you from accidentally writing over valuable programs or stored data. Any time you have a valuable program or data disk, be sure to place an adhesive-backed write protect tab or tape over the write protect notch on the disk sleeve.

ORGANIZATION Figure 3-2 is a diagram of a disk. Because the 5.25-inch double-sided, double density disk is most common, it is illustrated. Other disk formats vary in tracks, sectors, and data storage density.

Notice that the disk is organized into concentric tracks instead of one continuous track (like the groove in a phonograph record). The tracks are further subdivided into wedge-shaped sectors. Tracks and sectors are not produced in the manufacturing process. They are created magnetically (*soft sectored*) when a disk is formatted in your computer using the DOS FORMAT command.

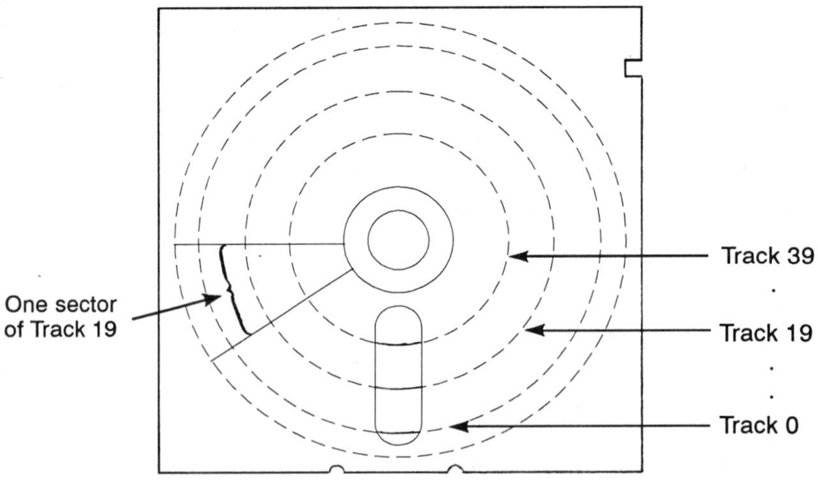

Figure 3-2 Disk Organization

There are 40 tracks on each side of a double-sided flexible disk. These tracks are numbered zero though 39 on side zero (the first side). Track numbers 40 through 79 are located on side one (the "flip" side) of a double-sided diskette.

Track number zero is reserved for disk directory information. The other tracks are available for program and file information. You can think of the disk directory as a post office, because it maintains name, address, and other important information about every file stored on the disk. Directory information includes:

- The file address (where a file begins and ends by track and sector location)
- The filename (assigned by programmers and computer users)
- The total size of the file in bytes (or characters)
- The date the file was last saved
- The time the file was last saved

NOTE

Before continuing, a few definitions are in order. The term "byte" represents a single computer character. A kilobyte (or KB) is 1,000 bytes. A megabyte (or MB) is one million bytes.

Each sector (or track-sector) on a standard double-density disk stores 512 bytes of information. DOS versions 1.00 through 1.25 have eight sectors per track, while versions 2.00, 2.10, and 2.11 have nine sectors per track. DOS version 3.00 offers both the eight- and nine-sector-per-track disk configuration in addition to a high-capacity disk that contains 15 sectors per track.

The 3.5-inch diskette format was first adopted by a number of laptop computers and then moved to the desktop variety. This storage device was initially rated at 720K capacity. With the introduction of the IBM Model 50 Personal System/2, a 1.44MB format was offered. Table 3-1 shows total formatted storage capacities. Unless otherwise noted, diskettes are the 5.25-inch variety.

Table 3-1 Approximate DOS Storage Capacities

Description	*Tracks*	*Sectors*	*Bytes/Sector*	*Capacity*
DOS 1.00 - 1.25				
1-Sided	40	8	512	161 K bytes
2-Sided	80	8	512	322 K bytes
DOS 2.00, 2.10, 2.11				
1-Sided	40	9	512	181 K bytes
2-Sided	80	9	512	362 K bytes
2-Sided 3.5-inch	80	9	1024	720 K bytes

Description	*Tracks*	*Sectors*	*Bytes/Sector*	*Capacity*
DOS 3.00				
1-Sided	40	9	512	181 K bytes
2-Sided	80	9	512	362 K bytes
High capacity	80	15	1024	1.2 M bytes
DOS 3.30 - 5.00				
2-Sided 3.5 inch	80	9	1024	720 K bytes
2-Sided 3.5 inch	80	18	1024	1.44 M bytes
DOS 5.00				
2-Sided 3.5 inch	80	36	1024	2.88 M bytes

DOS PROGRAMS

Knowing a few things about DOS may help further your understanding of how DOS works, making you a more skilled DOS user. This section includes information about:

- System control programs
- Internal and external commands
- DOS program summary
- Device designations (or names)

SYSTEM CONTROL PROGRAMS There are four essential programs associated with the control of your computer and the way it interacts with: 1) programs; 2) your keyboard and display screen; and 3) attached devices like disk drives, printers, and modems. These are:

- Boot Record
- BIO.COM
- DOS.COM
- COMMAND.COM

Only the COMMAND.COM program is displayed when you view a directory of filenames located on a disk. You can see the BIO.COM and DOS.COM programs if you have DOS version 2.00 or later and enter the CHKDSK command followed by a /V. The /V option is not available on earlier versions of DOS. Each program is described in the following paragraphs.

The Boot Record The term *boot* or *bootstrap*, when used with computers, means start or start-up. When you boot your computer, you are turning it on and loading the operating system into your computer's memory. This includes reading the boot record into memory, which passes control to DOS. Next, DOS checks for the presence of BIO.COM and DOS.COM. If these files are found, the DOS prompt is displayed on your screen. This prompt, normally an A>, B>, or C>, depending on which disk drive is active, invites you to type a command. If BIO.COM and DOS.COM are not found, an error message is displayed.

Your computer will not boot without a *boot record.* Instead, an error message is displayed telling you to insert a system disk. The boot record is located on track 0, sector 1, side 0 of your formatted DOS disk. If you have a hard disk, the boot record is located on the first sector of the first cylinder of the DOS partition.

The BIO.COM Program This program, called *IBMBIO.COM* on IBM's DOS version, interacts between your computer's ROM BIOS (read-only memory basic input/output system) and calls from the DOS.COM program described next. At start-up, BIO.COM resets the disk system and initializes attached devices. BIO.COM always contains at least five device drivers, which are used to control the operation of your keyboard, screen, printer, disk controller, and system clock. Other device drivers that often are included control large, external hard disks, serial communications, joy sticks, and mouse devices.

The final task performed by BIO.COM is to load the *command processor program,* COMMAND.COM. The BIO.COM file is programmed by the manufacturer of your computer system. Therefore, the specific type and number of device drivers vary between computers.

The DOS.COM Program This program, called *IBMDOS.COM* on IBM's DOS version, interacts directly with applications programs and the BIO.COM program described above. You can think of this program as the bridge between applications programs and BIO.COM, as it intercepts program calls for printing, data storage or retrieval, information display, and so on, and routes these calls to the BIO.COM program, which responds to the request with the appropriate reaction.

The COMMAND.COM Program The COMMAND.COM program is called the *command processor*, because it reads commands from the keyboard and executable command files. These files have the filename AUTOEXEC.BAT or the file extensions .COM and .EXE. COMMAND.COM also produces the DOS disk prompt (A>), performs error checking, and displays error messages when system errors are detected.

INTERNAL AND EXTERNAL COMMANDS There are two kinds of DOS commands. These are called internal and external. The internal commands are loaded into memory when DOS is booted. Internal commands are always available for your use, although they are not seen when you display the disk directory of filenames on your screen. Some internal commands are:

COPY	copies files
DEL or ERASE	deletes files
DIR	lists a directory of filenames on the logged disk
PROMPT	changes the form of the system prompt

REN	renames files
TYPE	displays a named file on the screen

External commands are conventional program files. These files can be deleted, copied, and even renamed. Their filenames are displayed when DIR lists a directory on the screen. Some examples of frequently used external commands are:

CHDIR	change directory — DOS versions 2.00 and higher
CHKDSK	check the available space on the selected disk
CLS	clear screen
COMP	compare files
DISKCOMP	compare disks
DISKCOPY	make verbatim copies of the source disk
DOSSHELL	display file management menus — DOS version 4.01 and 5.0
FORMAT	organize new disks for use with DOS

DOS PROGRAM SUMMARY Table 3-2 is a summary of DOS commands. In addition to command names and descriptions, the DOS version number and the type of command are listed. In the Version column, 3.+ designates version 3.00 or higher. In the Type column, I represents internal, and E is used for external. These commands are described in the modules of this book which include working examples.

Table 3-2 DOS Command Summary

Command	*Ver.*	*Type*	*Description*
APPEND	3.+	E,I	Appends file paths to the currently logged directory to enable the direct use of files in the appended file path without having to designate the file drive or directory.
ASSIGN	2.+	I	Reassigns the specified disk drive designations.
ATTRIB	3.	E	Sets “read-only” file attribute.
BACKUP	2.+	E	Copies files from a fixed disk to flexible disks; produces “insurance” copies of working files and programs.
BREAK ON/OFF	2.+	I	Instructs DOS to check for a Ctrl-Break from the keyboard during program operation.
BUFFERS=nn	2.+	I	Allocates a number of disk buffers in memory equal to nn, which are activated at system turn-on. The value nn is a number between one and 99. The buffers command is contained in a file named CONFIG.SYS, which is automatically read at turn-on.
CHKDSK	1.+	E	Checks disk space, showing space occupied by files and space remaining for use.
CHDIR	2.+	I	Changes DOS directory in use; short form is CD.
CHCP	3.3+	I	Changes to specified national language code page; NLSFUNC must be run prior to use.

Command	*Ver.*	*Type*	*Description*
CLEANUP	5.+	E	Removes all obsolete files associated with a prior version of DOS after DOS 5.00 is installed.
CLS	2.+	E	Clears screen from DOS prompt.
COMP	1.+	E	Compares designated files.
CONFIG	1.+	E	Selects communications parameters.
COPY	1.+	I	Copies and combines files.
COUNTRY	3.	E	Selects the date and time format in a configuration file used at system turn-on.
CTTY	2.+	I	Assigns console control to a remote device.
DATE	1.+	I	Sets the system date.
DEBUG	1.+	I	Provides facility for displaying and modifying program files.
DEVICE	2.+	I	Entered as a command line within the CONFIG.SYS file to specify the name of a file containing a device driver. The device driver is loaded upon system turn-on.
DIR	1.+	I	Lists a directory of filenames on the designated disk to the display screen.
DIRCMD	5.+	I	Sets the way the DIR command operates. Often used in the AUTOEXEC.BAT file.
DISKCOMP	1.+	E	Compares the contents of two disks; used to verify that a diskcopy operation has been performed properly.
DISKCOPY	1.+	E	Makes a duplicate copy of a disk.
DOSKEY	5.+	E	Memory-resident utility that maintains a list of previously used DOS commands; use Up/Down Arrow or PgUp/PgDn keys to move to recall DOS commands.
DOSSHELL	4.+	E	Displays a menu-driven file manager; updated in DOS 5.00.
EDIT	5.+	E	Full-screen editor first supplied with DOS 5.00. Useful for creating and editing files.
EDLIN	1.+	E	Used to create and edit files; a simple line editor that is provided as a standard DOS utility.
ERASE (or DELETE)	1.+	I	Deletes (or erases) files from a disk.
EXE2BIN	1.+	I	Used to convert program files into executable DOS programs.
FASTOPEN	3.3+	E	Stores a specified number of file addresses in memory to increase access speed.
FCBS	3.	E	Specifies the number of files that can be open at the same time. Prevents files from being automatically closed by an active program.

Command	*Ver.*	*Type*	*Description*
FDISK	2.+	E	Used to divide a fixed disk into two or more partitions. Allows two or more operating systems to be used on the same fixed disk.
FILES=nn	2.+	I	Allows up to 99 files, specified by *nn,* to be simultaneously opened during program operation. The default value is eight.
FIND	2.+	E	Finds and displays or writes all lines from a specified filename containing a specified text string.
HELP *command*	5.+	E	Displays information about the named DOS command.
HIMEM	5.+	E	Used with CONFIG.SYS to make use of extended memory on 80286, 386, and 486-based computers.
INSTALL	4.+	E	Used with CONFIG.SYS to load commands for DOS startup activity.
JOIN	3.1+	E	Creates a file path and joins files on a specified disk drive to give access to those files as if they existed in the newly created file path.
LABEL	3.	E	Used to create, change, or delete disk volume name (or label).
LASTDRIVE	3.	E	Used to specify the number of disk drives available to your system.
LOADFIX	5.+	E	Loads programs that may not operate properly with extra memory freed by MS-DOS 5.00.
MEM	4.+	E	Displays the amount of used and available memory and a list of the programs in use.
MIRROR	5.+	E	Produces undelete and disk partition information files that are used when a disk is unformatted by the UNFORMAT command.
MKDIR	2.+	I	Creates a new directory branch. Short form is MD.
MORE	2.+	E	Reads data, such as a displayed directory, pauses output to the display screen when a full-screen condition is detected, and displays the message "--More--." Pressing any key resumes output until the next full-screen condition is detected, at which time "--More--" is displayed again.
MODE	2.+	E	Sets output parameters to output devices including printers, display units, and asynchronous communications devices (modems).
NLSFUNC	3.2+	E	Activates National Language Support for code page switching, which selects alternate character sets that correspond to selected national languages.
PATH	2.+	E	Searches specified directories for executable program (or batch) files that are not found in the current directory.

Command	Ver.	Type	Description
PRINT	2.+	E	Queues from one to ten specified data files for printing. The queued files print from a special memory buffer, allowing you to perform other tasks on your computer during printing. Sometimes called a print spooler.
PROMPT	2.+	I	Modifies the form of the DOS prompt.
RECOVER	2.+	E	Recovers defective files.
RENAME	1.+	I	Renames an existing disk file.
REPLACE	3.1+	E	Replaces (or updates) all existing files on a target disk with matching files from a source disk.
RESTORE	2.+	E	Reads backup files from flexible disks and writes them to a fixed disk.
RMDIR	2.+	I	Removes a directory from a disk. The short form is RD.
SELECT	3.	E	Used to set date, time, currency, and decimal formats for different countries. Discontinued with DOS 5.00.
SET	2.+	I	Displays the computer's environment; lets you enter changes to the setting from the keyboard.
SETUP	5.+	E	Installs a minimum MS-DOS system (SETUP /M).
SETVER	5.+	E	Allows use of one or more programs that are compatible with earlier versions of DOS.
SHARE	3.	E	Reserves disk space for multiuser control information.
SHELL	2.+	I	Used by system programmers to specify the name and location of a command processor to be used in place of the standard DOS command processor (COMMAND.COM).
SMARTDRV	5.+	E	Used with CONFIG.SYS to allocate disk cache in extended or expanded memory.
SORT	2.+	E	Sorts designated filenames or disk directories in alphabetical order.
SUBST	3.1+	E	Substitutes a disk drive designation in place of a file path name.
SWITCHES	4.+	E	Used with the CONFIG.SYS program to provide compatibility with programs that are incompatible with enhanced keyboards.
SYS	1.+	E	Transfers DOS to the designated disk.
TIME	1.+	I	Sets the system time.
TREE	2.+	E	Displays a hierarchy of disk directories.
TYPE	1.+	I	Displays a designated file on the screen.
UNDELETE	5.+	E	Undeletes one or more recently deleted files.
UNFORMAT	5.+	E	Unformats a safe formatted disk.

Command	Ver.	Type	Description
VDISK	3.	E	Establishes a memory disk; added to DOS at system turn-on.
VER	2.+	I	Displays the version of DOS being used.
VERIFY	2.+	E	Verifies the integrity of copied data.
VOL	2.+	E	Displays the volume name of the designated disk.
XCOPY	3.2+	E	Copies files selectively.
XMAEM	4.0+	E	A device driver used in the CONFIG.SYS file to emulate the IBM PS/2 80286 Expanded Memory Adapter/A. Only used with 80386-based systems like the IBM PS/2 Model 80.
XMA2EMS	4.0+	E	A device driver used in the CONFIG.SYS file to support the LIM Expanded Memory Specification.

DEVICE DESIGNATIONS A device designation is a reserved abbreviation, followed by a colon, which stands for different computer devices. For example, the device designations for disk drives A and B are A: and B:. The device designation for your keyboard and screen, referred to as the console, is CON:. Like DOS commands, device designations can be typed in either uppercase or lowercase. So the designation "con:" is interpreted by DOS as "CON:." Table 3-3 is a list of DOS device designations and their meanings.

Table 3-3 Device Designations

Designation	Description
A: through G:	Disk drive designations A through G. Modified with the LASTDRIVE command introduced in DOS version 3.00.
CON:	The console, or keyboard and screen, designation. Used when copying keyboard/screen information to a file or other device. Ctrl-Z (or F6) is used to mark the end of a file.
COM1: or AUX:	Communications Port 1 or the serial communications or printer designation.
COM2: through COM4:	Communications Ports 2 through 4 or the second, third, and fourth serial communications connectors (or ports).
LPT1: or PRN:	First parallel printer port.
LPT2:, LPT3:	The second and third parallel printer ports.
NUL:	A dummy device used when testing a command. Input operations encounter an immediate end-of-file condition. Output operations are simulated without actual data transfer.

DOS AND YOUR KEYBOARD

Keyboards vary with the brand of computer. However, almost all computer keyboards have similarities. This section describes the categories of keys used by computer keyboards.

KEYBOARD LAYOUT The keyboard layout of a typical personal computer is shown in Figure 3-3.

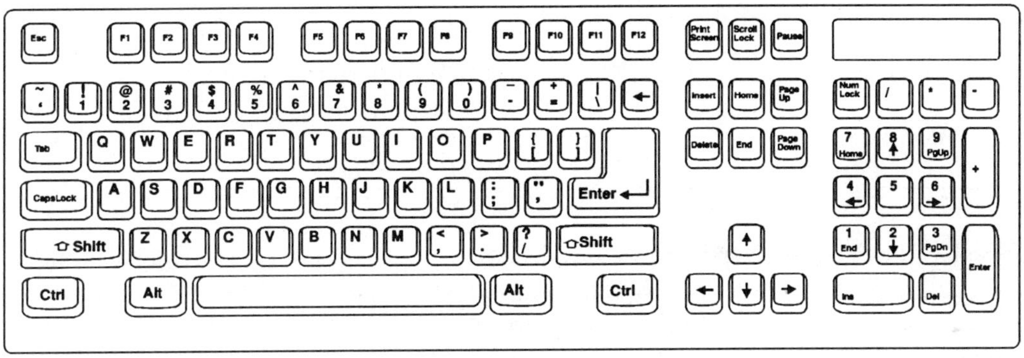

AT type keyboard

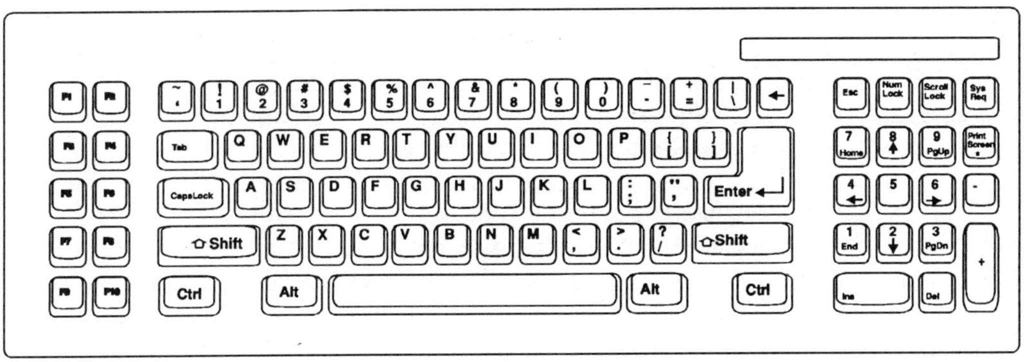

XT type keyboard

Figure 3-3 Typical Keyboard Layouts

STANDARD TYPING KEYS The standard typing keys are the same as those used on a conventional typewriter. These include letter and number keys, the Tab key, and the Shift keys. The Shift key is used to type uppercase letters and the symbols above the upper row of number keys, just as on a typewriter. The Caps Lock key lets you type in uppercase without pressing a Shift key. When the Caps Lock is on, pressing Shift produces lowercase characters. There are also several special character keys available to you on the computer keyboard, such as the vertical bar, back slash, tilde, and grave (accent mark) symbols:

Description	*Symbol*	*Description*	*Symbol*
Vertical Bar	|	Less Than	<
Back Slash	\	Open Bracket	[
Tilde	~	Close Bracket	]
Grave	`	Open Brace	{
Greater Than	>	Close Brace	}

SPECIAL CONTROL KEYS Special control keys send special codes to your computer. These codes are used frequently to perform special operations. For example, the Arrow keys are used to move the cursor (flashing bar or block) left, right, up, or down. Some programs use the Ins and Del keys to insert and delete characters.

Expressions like Ctrl-X and Alt-X, where X is any keyboard character, indicate that the Ctrl or Alt key is pressed and held while the indicated character key is typed. This is done in the same way that capital letters are typed using the Shift key. Keystrokes that you press or type in procedures are boldfaced as in **Ctrl-KB** or **Return**.

The ↵ key is used like a carriage return key on a typewriter to end a line or complete a command. "Return" is used throughout this book.

There are also function keys F1 through F12, and other keys, such as Ins, Del, Num Lock, the Arrow keys, and more.

FUNCTION KEYS Because each program reacts differently with special control keys, it is necessary to learn what each does when you begin using a new software product. DOS uses the function keys, F1 through F6, in addition to several other keys. A list of functions and corresponding keys is contained in Table 3-4.

Table 3-4 DOS and the Keyboard

Function	*Key(s)*
Complete command or end a line	Return or Enter
Move down one line to continue typing	Ctrl-Return
Backup cursor to blank text or retype	Backspace
Discard typed command so you can retype it correctly	Esc
Discontinue or cancel program operation	Ctrl-Break or Ctrl-C
Pause scrolling of text on screen; press any key to resume scrolling	Ctrl-Num Lock or Ctrl-S

Function	*Key(s)*
Print displayed screen	Shift-PrtSc
Print characters that are typed or displayed on the screen	Ctrl-P or Ctrl-PrtSc
Type capitals	Shift-(letter/number key)
Lock capitals on/off	Caps Lock
Shifts numeric keypad between numbers and function keys	Num Lock
Type numbers with Num Lock on, use cursor and special control keys with Num Lock off	Numeric Keypad
Reset (warm boot) your computer	Ctrl-Alt-Del
Used with character keys to perform special operations	Ctrl

NOTE

Previously typed DOS commands are stored in a temporary memory location called a buffer. The following keys are used to reuse and modify the stored command line. This may vary slightly depending upon your microcomputer.

Copy one character from the buffer.	F1
Copy all characters from the buffer up to the character *x*.	F2 *x*
Copy all remaining characters from the buffer, beginning at the present position to the end of the line.	F3
Skip all characters up to the character x.	F4 x
Use the last edited line for further modification.	F5
Insert one or more characters in a line.	Ins
Delete the next character from the buffer.	Del
Cancel this line and start over; does not change contents of the buffer.	Esc
Type End-of-file marker.	F6 or Ctrl-Z

RESTARTING WITH Ctrl-Alt-Del

Pressing the Ctrl, Alt, and Del keys simultaneously restarts your computer system. This process is called a *warm boot*, reset, or reinitialization. If your computer "hangs" (or *crashes*) for some reason, it may be necessary to reset with Ctrl-Alt-Del to get it going again. You should do this only as a last resort. If the Ctrl-Alt-Del key sequence has no effect, it means that the codes being sent from your keyboard are no longer being received and interpreted by your computer. If this happens, you must turn the power off, wait several seconds, and turn the power back on again to resume operation. If you have a fixed disk, you should wait until disk rotation stops before turning your computer back on.

If you are following the learning sequence, turn to Module 17. This is the first module dealing with a specific DOS command.

Module 4
APPEND (3.30+)

DESCRIPTION

The APPEND command is similar to the PATH command in that it causes DOS to search directories (or file paths) other than the current directory for a specified file. The current directory is always searched first. Then DOS searches for the specified file in those directories that you have appended using the APPEND command. Although the searched file may have any extension, executable files having the extensions .COM, .EXE, and .BAT are the ones most frequently involved.

APPEND command is an external command when first called. Once loaded, it becomes an internal command as it resides in memory. As with the PATH command, you can specify multiple file paths by separating each subdirectory name with a semicolon. Forms of the APPEND command and clarifying examples are presented in the following list.

APPEND A:\BAS;C:\DB	Appends the file paths A:\BAS and C:\DB.	
APPEND	When used alone, APPEND returns a list of appended file paths.	
	APPEND No Append	Indicates that APPEND is inactive
	APPEND APPEND=A:\BAS;C:\DB	Indicates file paths A:\BAS and C:\DB are presently appended
;	When a semicolon is used by itself, it cancels APPEND paths. Also used to separate file path names when multiple file paths are appended.	
APPEND;	Cancels existing APPEND paths	
APPEND A:\BAS;C:\WP	Separates file paths	
/PATH:ON	This is the default value of the APPEND command following its entry. While on, files are searched for within the specified drives and directories.	
APPEND /PATH:ON	Resets PATH to on	

APPEND /PATH:OFF	This form of the APPEND command prevents DOS from searching for a specified file outside the current drive and directory. When used, the drive and directory designation is ignored.

DOS 4.01+

APPEND /X:OFF	Used to turn off searches for and processing of executable files (such as those having the extensions .COM, .EXE, or .BAT).
APPEND /X:ON (or /X)	Causes APPEND to operate like the PATH command in searching for and executing a specified file.
APPEND /E	Stores APPEND paths within the DOS environment ("E" stands for environment). This is similar to the PATH command, causing calls to files to search all appended file paths. You can view and change the path values using either the APPEND or SET commands. The /E parameter is used only with the first use of the APPEND command. When /E is not used, the path string remains part of the APPEND command; file paths are only viewed or changed using the APPEND command. The use of an alternate command processor changes the environment, losing the APPEND paths. If you use an alternate command processor, do not use the /E parameter if you wish to retain established APPEND relationships.
APPEND /E /X	Following APPEND path(s) placed in the DOS environment and then searched as necessary; a specified file is executed when found in the searched file path.
APPEND C:\DB	Appends file path C:\DB, which is searched as necessary

The preceding two command lines achieve the same result as the following three command lines, which combine the APPEND and PATH commands.

PATH C:\DB	Sets C:\DB as the file path to search
APPEND /E	Following APPEND paths placed DOS environment
APPEND C:\DB	Appends file path C:\DB

CHANGING THE APPEND COMMAND You can change the current APPEND values by entering a new APPEND command. Searching begins in the current directory and moves to the directories included within the last APPEND command entered.

FILES OF THE SAME NAME You should be aware that if you are trying to execute a program file in an appended file path and one of the same name exists in the currently logged directory, the search ends when the first file is found, even if it not an executable file. For example, you may have a source file named MENU.PRG in the current directory.

Another, named MENU.EXE is in an appended file path. The MENU program does not run because DOS finds MENU.PRG first, which is not an executable file.

READING AND WRITING FILES When a file is read from an appended file path and then rewritten to disk, the saved version of the file is stored on the current directory, leaving the original version of the file unchanged.

USING APPEND WITHIN .BAT FILES Although the APPEND command can be entered from the DOS command line, it is often entered within relationships between program operation and those file paths used by the program.

APPLICATIONS

The APPEND command is normally used with a fixed disk, although you can append a subdirectory in a floppy diskette drive. Although there are several similarities between the APPEND and PATH commands, the PATH command searches only for executable files having the extension .BAT, .COM, or .EXE. The APPEND command lets you use any file type, including data files. For example, you can use the DOS TYPE command to display a text file on the screen in an appended file path. This is not achievable with the PATH command.

The APPEND command lets you access both executable and data files on any file path available to your system. This eliminates the need to place utilities or reference files on multiple directories.

By placing the APPEND command in a .BAT file that starts an applications program, you can start the program and search one or more file paths in an automatic fashion. This saves the "hassle" associated with continually logging a variety of file paths to find your working files and programs.

TYPICAL OPERATION

In this activity you enter the APPEND command and then use the DOS TYPE command to display a file, located in another directory to the screen. Begin at the root directory (C:\). If you are using a floppy system, substitute A: for C:.

1. Type **COPY CON NEWFILE** and press **Return**. Now type the following lines of text, pressing **Return** at the end of each line. Press **Ctrl-Z** and **Return** at the end of the last line to copy the file to disk.

```
10 CLS
20 FOR I=1 TO 10
30 PRINT I
40 NEXT I
50 END^Z
```

2. Create a temporary subdirectory named TEMP by typing **MD TEMP** and pressing **Return**.
3. Change to the new directory by typing **CD TEMP** and pressing **Return**.
4. Type **APPEND C:** and press **Return** to append the root directory to the currently logged directory (C:\TEMP).
5. Type **TYPE NEWFILE** and notice that the file is displayed on your screen; the root directory is appended.
6. Type **APPEND** and press **Return** to display the APPEND file paths. Notice the "APPEND=C:\" display.
7. Type **CD** and press **Return** to move back to the root directory.
8. Type **RD TEMP** to remove the TEMP directory.
9. Type **DEL NEWFILE** and press **Return** to delete the practice file.
10. Turn to Module 48 to continue the learning sequence.

Module 5
ASSIGN (2.00+)

DESCRIPTION

The ASSIGN command is an external DOS command available on version 2.00 and later. It tells DOS to look at an assigned disk, rather than on the disk that is normally used by programs. For example, if you have a program on the disk in drive B and the logged drive is A, you can type the command: ASSIGN A=B. Although you may be logged to drive A, typing the program name causes it to run. Why? Because the ASSIGN command rerouted the command to the disk in drive B. To cancel the ASSIGN command, just type ASSIGN and press Return and everything returns to normal.

If you have a computer with three disk drives, you can use a command like ASSIGN A=C B=C. This tells DOS to look on the disk in drive C for all programs and files. Even if you type DIR A:, the ASSIGN command causes DOS to list a directory of drive C.

There are a few commands that ignore ASSIGN. These include DISKCOPY and DISKCOMP. However, most commands honor the ASSIGN setting. Therefore, you should always remember when ASSIGN is in use. Otherwise, unpredictable things may happen when you use common DOS commands. In particular, never use the ASSIGN command when the PRINT command (Module 47) is active.

APPLICATIONS

Often, programs are written to use two or more disks on a floppy system. In these cases, the program "looks" for files on specific disk drives other than the one on which the program is actually located. This is often the case when a program is put on a hard disk system. Here, you can use ASSIGN to redirect calls to the hard drive. The command ASSIGN B = C does the job.

TYPICAL OPERATION

In this activity you use the ASSIGN command to temporarily designate drive B as the active drive. Begin at the DOS prompt.

1. Insert a formatted data disk containing files into drive B.
2. Type **ASSIGN A=B** and press **Return**.

3. Now, with the A prompt displayed, type **DIR** and press **Return** to display a file directory. Notice that the file directory is that of the disk in drive B.
4. Type **ASSIGN** and press **Return** to return to normal.
5. Now type **DIR** and press **Return**. Notice that the DIR command now displays a directory of the disk in drive A.
6. Turn to Module 36 to continue the learning sequence.

Module 6
ATTRIB (3.00+)

DESCRIPTION

The ATTRIB command is an external command that is used to change the attribute of a file. That is, you can use ATTRIB to make a file "read-only," which prevents the file from being written over (or changed). DOS version 3.20 added the ability to set the *archive bit*, which is set to one when a file is created or changed. This bit is used by the BACKUP and XCOPY commands to determine if new or changed files exist. These two commands provide a time-saving option that updates only those files that require updating.

ATTRIB uses +R and –R to set and remove the read-only attribute. The +A and –A options were added to DOS 3.20 to give you control over the archive attribute. Study the following examples.

First, you can use ATTRIB to determine the attribute status of a file by typing ATTRIB, the filename, and pressing Return.

To make MYFILE1.TXT a read-only file, type

```
ATTRIB +R MYFILE1.TXT
```

To cancel the read-only status, type

```
ATTRIB -R MYFILE1.TXT
```

Similarly, to set the archive attribute (change it to one), type

```
ATTRIB +A MYFILE1.TXT
```

To reset the archive bit back to zero, type

```
ATTRIB -A MYFILE1.TXT
```

APPLICATIONS

Being able to make a file read-only avoids damage from modifying it accidentally. This is particularly important if your system is in a networking environment, where many users have access to valuable programs. By making the programs read-only, the programs can't be modified by network users.

Resetting the archive attribute is sometimes desirable when using BACKUP and XCOPY. For example, if you discover that a damaged file was copied to your archive diskette or tape, you can change the file attribute in order to recopy it during the backup process.

TYPICAL OPERATION

In this activity you use ATTRIB to make the CHKDSK.COM program read-only. After you check it, you then change it back to read/write. Begin at the DOS prompt.

1. Type **ATTRIB +R CHKDSK.COM** and press **Return** to make the CHKDSK program read-only.
2. Check the attribute of the file by typing **ATTRIB CHKDSK.COM** and pressing **Return**. Notice the resulting display.

```
A:\>ATTRIB CHKDSK.COM
  A    R      A:\CHKDSK.COM

A:\>
```

3. Change the attribute back to normal by typing **ATTRIB –R CHKDSK.COM** and pressing **Return.**
4. Turn to Module 52 to continue the learning sequence.

Module 7
AUTOMATIC FILE EXECUTION (BATCH FILES)

DESCRIPTION

All versions of DOS let you create and store a series of DOS commands that are acted upon (or "executed") automatically one line at a time in the order entered. The file containing the series of DOS commands is called a *batch file*. These files must have the extension .BAT and contain legitimate DOS commands on each line.

If the batch file is given the special filename AUTOEXEC.BAT, it is executed automatically when you first start your computer. If the batch filename is given another name, like LIST.BAT, you must type LIST and press Return for the commands in the batch file to run.

If you have DOS version 2.00 or later, here is an example of a batch file you might want to use at system start-up. It asks for the time and date, configures your DOS prompt, and clears the screen. Do not type the remarks.

```
                        Remarks
@ECHO OFF               Turns off batch processing dialogue.
TIME                    Displays the time prompt.
DATE                    Displays the date prompt.
PROMPT $p$g             Displays the active directory path.
SET DIRCMD=o/:-GN/P     Alphabetized DIR displays with files first
                        followed by directories (DOS 5.00 only).
```

You can use EDLIN or the COPY command to create the file. If you have DOS 5.00, use the EDIT program. With COPY, the file is created by typing the following lines from the DOS prompt. End each line by pressing Return.

```
COPY CON: AUTOEXEC.BAT
@ECHO OFF
TIME
DATE
PROMPT $p$g
^Z        (Use Ctrl-Z or press F6 to insert the ^Z character.)
```

All versions of DOS let you create, save, and use batch files. However, beginning with DOS version 2.00, some new batch file commands were added. The following table lists special DOS batch commands, summarizes their use, and indicates the DOS version in which they operate. You should know that batch files are often referred to as BAT files.

Batch File Commands

Command	*Version*	*Description*
Ctrl-Break or Ctrl-C	(all versions)	Stops batch file operation and displays the message: `Terminate batch job (Y/N)?` Type Y to display the DOS prompt; N resumes batch file operation.

%0-%9	(all versions)	Lets you substitute from one to ten character strings in a batch file command line. The strings are substituted in the order encountered when the %n (where n is a number from 0 to 9) is encountered in a command line. Look at the following examples.
		`CD %1`
		`TYPE %2`
		If the batch filename is CDSHOW.BAT (for "change directory and show a file"), you can type
		`CDSHOW WP MOMS.LTR`
		to cause the following commands to be executed.
		`CD WP`
		`TYPE MOMS.LTR`
		Notice that %1 is replaced with "WP" and %2 is replaced with "MOMS.LTR." If a filename contains a %, use a double % ("%%") to represent a literal percent sign.

CALL	(4.01+)	Runs a second batch file and returns to the batch file from which it was called.
		`ECHO INSERT DISK 2 OF 2 IN DRIVE A`
		`PAUSE`
		`CALL AUTOEXE1`
		`CLS`
		`ECHO FILES COPIED SUCCESSFULLY...`

ECHO	(2.00+)	Turns screen display off and on during batch file operation. If off, the command ECHO followed by a message displays that message. This lets you display specified messages even when ECHO is OFF.
		`ECHO OFF              (Turns batch file display off)`
		`ECHO Insert Disk 1     (Displays message)`
		`ECHO ON               (Turns batch file display on)`

FOR	(2.00+)	Used to perform an operation on a set of filenames that follow the FOR %%variable expression. The entire expression might be `FOR %%f IN (FILE1.TXT FILE2.TXT) DO TYPE %%f` This command line uses the TYPE command (following the DO expression) to type FILE1.TXT and FILE2.TXT automatically.

Command	*Version*	*Description*
GOTO	(2.00+)	Transfers batch file operation to the line following a label name. The label name is always "flagged" with a preceding colon. For example, :FLAG1 might be used as a label. The expression

```
GOTO FLAG1
```

transfers batch file operation to the line following the label :FLAG1.

IF	(2.00+)	Lets you set conditions for executing batch file commands. If the following condition is met, the following command (see examples) is executed. If not, batch file operation moves to the next command line. There are two forms of the IF command. You can use either IF or IF NOT to test one of three conditions:

```
EXIST filename
```

Checks to see if the filename exists in the condition string. If the filename exists, the condition is considered "true." Look at the following examples.

```
IF EXIST MOMS.LTR GOTO FLAG1
ECHO File not found
CLS
GOTO FLAG2
:FLAG1
TYPE %1
  :
  :
:FLAG2
```

Here, if the file MOMS.LTR exists, the GOTO FLAG1 command is acted upon. If it does not exist, then control moves to the next line, which displays the message "File not found."

```
string1==string2
```

Checks to see if string1 is an exact match with string2, including a match of uppercase and lowercase. If an exact match exists, the condition is met and the following batch file command is executed. If the condition is not met, batch file control moves to the next line. Look at the following example.

```
IF NOT %1 == uncles.ltr GOTO FLAG2
COPY %1 WP\%1
CD WP
GOTO FLAG1
:FLAG2
CD WP
WP %1
:FLAG1
```

<table>
<tr><th>Command</th><th>Version</th><th>Description</th></tr>
<tr><td>IF (cont.)</td><td></td><td>If the first string in the command line does not match "uncles.ltr," then the CD WP command (change directory to the WP subdirectory) is executed; otherwise, control skips to the next batch file command line.

<code>ERRORLEVEL number</code>

Checks to see if the program in use exits with an error number. If the error number is equal to or greater than the one designated, the condition is met, and the command line is executed. If it is not, execution skips to the next command line in the batch file. Look at the following example.

<code>IF ERRORLEVEL 1</code>
<code>REM Program failure, check for overlay file.</code>

This example "traps" a program error level of 1 or greater. If an error occurs, the remark "Program failure... " is displayed, and batch file operation is discontinued.</td></tr>
<tr><td>PAUSE</td><td>(all versions)</td><td>Pauses batch file operation and displays the message "Strike any key when ready..." on the next line. You can add a message following the word PAUSE.

<code>PAUSE Insert your program disk in drive A.</code>
<code>Strike any key when ready...</code></td></tr>
<tr><td>REM</td><td>(all versions)</td><td>Displays remark lines when encountered within a batch file. Remarks can be up to 123 characters long. REM without following text displays a blank line during batch file execution.

<code>REM Transferring files...</code></td></tr>
<tr><td>SHIFT</td><td>(2.00+)</td><td>Lets you shift the relationship between character strings and substitution parameters (%0 through %9) one number to the left. For example, assume the following relationships between strings and substitution numbers 0% through 3%:

<code>0% ONE.LTR</code>
<code>1% TWO.LTR</code>
<code>2% THREE.LTR</code>
<code>4% FOUR.LTR</code>

Having SHIFT on a line in a batch file changes the relationships as shown.

<code>0% TWO.LTR</code>
<code>1% THREE.LTR</code>
<code>2% FOUR.LTR</code>
<code>4%</code>

The file ONE.LTR is no longer associated with the command string. This adds space for an additional substitution string.</td></tr>
</table>

The last command line in a batch file is sometimes the name of another batch file. This lets you run multiple batch files. DOS "remembers" where it started, and when batch file operation is finished, it takes you back to the original directory.

The balance of this section provides an example of a series of batch files that display menus, execute commonly used programs, and return to the top level directory and automatically redisplay your menu.

By typing the batch file names, you can perform many convenient tasks if:

1. You have a hard disk with ample space for the program files used in the batch file.

   NOTE
   Even if you have a floppy disk system, you can use the principles demonstrated in these examples.

2. You are using DOS version 2.00 or later.
3. The following subdirectories exist:

   DBASE <DIR> Contains dBASE III Plus; typing DBASE *filename* starts this program. The filename is optional.

   WP51 <DIR> Contains WordPerfect; typing WP *filename* starts this program. The filename is optional.

   QPRO <DIR> Contains QuattroPro; typing Q *filename* starts this program. The filename is optional.

   LOTUS <DIR> Contains Lotus 1-2-3; typing LOTUS starts this program.

4. The batch file AUTOEXEC.BAT is typed as follows using either DOS 5.00 EDIT, EDLIN, the COPY command, or a word processor that produces an ASCII text file.

```
DATE
TIME
ECHO OFF
CLS
PATH C:\;C:\DOS
PROMPT $p$g
MENU
^Z
```

Next, a MENU.BAT program is created.

```
CLS
ECHO.
ECHO.
ECHO.
ECHO                                  *** Program Menu ***
ECHO                                ============================
ECHO                                   To Run         Enter
ECHO                                ----------------------------
ECHO                                WordPerfect ..... WP
ECHO                                dBASE III Plus .. DB filename
ECHO                                Quattro Pro ..... Q filename
ECHO                                Lotus 1-2-3 ..... LOTUS
ECHO                                ============================
ECHO                                Note: "filename" is optional.
^Z
```

Next, it is necessary to type individual batch files that act on the commands WP, DB, Q, and LOTUS. These commands change to the appropriate subdirectory and then start the program. Then they return to the root directory and redisplay the menu. Those commands that can use filenames require substitution characters (%1). The DB.BAT and the LOTUS.BAT batch files are shown. The WP.BAT batch file is similar to the LOTUS.BAT batch file, while the Q.BAT and DB.BAT files are similar as both programs accept filenames at start-up.

DB Batch File DB.BAT:

```
CD \DBASE
DBASE %1
CD\
MENU
```

LOTUS Batch File LOTUS.BAT:

```
CD \LOTUS
LOTUS
CD\
MENU
```

If you are using a DOS version earlier than 2.00, you can replace ECHO with REM and eliminate the CLS, PATH, and PROMPT commands to produce a batch file that provides similar results.

APPLICATIONS

As you can see by the above examples, batch files are extremely powerful tools. They let you minimize the keystrokes required to perform a series of DOS operations. You can pack hundreds of commands into one or more batch files. The batch files can be executed with just a few simple keystrokes, saving time and minimizing the potential for typographical errors.

The AUTOEXEC.BAT and MENU.BAT batch files are excellent for automatically starting a program when you turn on your systempower. This lets inexperienced computer operators use programs without having to know how to use DOS commands or program start-up sequences.

TYPICAL OPERATION

In this activity you create and use a batch file. Begin at the DOS prompt.

1. Use EDLIN, DOS 5.00 EDIT, or the COPY command to create the following AUTOEXEC.BAT file. The example shows COPY being used. Type the indicated lines, ending each by pressing **Return**. (Press Ctrl-Z to enter ^Z.)

```
A:\>COPY CON: AUTOEXEC.BAT
ECHO OFF
DATE
TIME
PROMPT $p$g ^Z
        1 file(s) copied

A:\>
```

2. Execute the AUTOEXEC.BAT file by typing **AUTOEXEC** and pressing **Return**.
3. Notice the following display; respond to the DATE and TIME prompts by pressing **Return**.

```
A:\>AUTOEXEC

A:\>ECHO OFF
Current date is Thu 02-28-1991
Enter new date (mm-dd-yy):
Current time is 10:32:01.98a
Enter new time:

A:\>
```

4. If you wish, you can delete the file with the DEL command. Otherwise, you may wish to use the AUTOEXEC command on a regular basis.
5. Type **PROMPT pg** and press **Return** to restore the A:\> prompt.
6. Turn to Module 14 to continue the learning sequence.

Module 8
BACKUP (2.00+)

DESCRIPTION

The BACKUP command is used with fixed disk systems using DOS versions 2.00 and later. BACKUP is an external command used to copy files automatically from a fixed disk to floppy disks. BACKUP lets you copy selected files, all files in a specified directory path, or every file on the fixed disk. It also lets you copy only those files that have been changed or saved after a specified date.

If the files being copied exceed the capacity of the target floppy disk, BACKUP prompts you to change disks and then to continue the process. Files can be divided between floppy disks. The BACKUP command automatically tags each backup disk in the sequence used. Later, you can use the RESTORE command (Module 53) to copy the files back to the fixed disk. Having each disk numbered helps you restore the fixed disk in the right order.

The general form of the BACKUP command is:

```
BACKUP C:\path A:
```

This form copies all files in the specified directory path to the disk in drive A. There are a number of parameters available with the BACKUP command. These are:

/S Causes all files in subdirectories of the specified path to be copied.

```
BACKUP C:\ A:/S
```

This form of the BACKUP command copies all files in all subdirectories from the fixed disk to floppy disks in drive A.

/M Copies only those files that have been modified since the last backup operation.

```
BACKUP C:\WP\*.TXT A:/M
```

Copies all files in the WP directory having the filename extension TXT that have been saved since the last time BACKUP was used. The files are copied from drive C to drive A.

/A Adds files to those that already reside on the target disk. When /A is not used, BACKUP erases all files on the target disk and replaces them with those being copied.

```
BACKUP C:\DB\*.PRN A:/A
```

Copies all files in drive C with the directory path DB and the extension PRN to the disk in drive A. This does not erase any files that presently exist on the disk in drive A.

/D Lets you copy those files saved on or after a specified date (in the DATE command format mm-dd-yy).

```
BACKUP C:\ A:/S/D:07-01-90
```

Copies all files on drive C (in all subdirectories) that have been saved on or after 07-01-90 to the disk(s) in drive A.

/T Lets you copy those files saved on or after a specified time (in the TIME command format hh:mm:ss).

```
BACKUP C:\ A:/S /D:07-08-90 /T:12:00
```

Copies all files on drive C (in all subdirectories) that have been saved on or after the specified date and time to the disk(s) in drive A.

/L Creates a backup log containing the date and time of the backup, diskette numbers, and the full path and filename of each backed up file. The default filename, BACKUP.LOG is assigned unless you specify a filename using the following format.

```
BACKUP C:\ A:/S /L:MARYBU.LOG
```

/F The /F parameter was introduced with DOS 3.00. It lets you format the target disk before transferring files. In DOS version 4.01, the BACKUP command formats the target disk automatically before backing up the files.

Before using BACKUP, you should format several floppy diskettes or have a tape backup device available. On versions of DOS after 3.00, you can use the /F parameter to format the diskettes during the backup process. Version 4.01 automatically formats the target disks, eliminating the need to preformat floppy disks. If you are using floppy diskettes, plan on using as many as 28 to 30 floppy diskettes for each 10 megabytes of fixed disk capacity. As files are backed up, filenames are displayed on the screen. As each target diskette fills up, you are prompted to insert the next disk. This process continues until the last file is copied.

Although BACKUP tags each disk with a number, you should also write a sequential number on your disks, beginning with 1, as they are removed from the floppy drive. This lets you stack your diskettes in the right order when you must restore files to your fixed disk.

APPLICATIONS

Having a backup copy of the files on your hard disk is the best insurance you can have. Although it isn't necessary to back up the entire disk, it's always a good idea to back up new files as they are created and stored. For example, you might wish to back up your files or individual directories two or three times a week. In the case of big, irreplaceable files, you should back them up as soon as they are filed.

If you ever encounter a fixed disk failure, you'll thank your lucky stars for your backup copies. If you haven't backed up, you're likely to start talking to yourself in an uncomplimentary way.

TYPICAL OPERATION

In this activity you use the BACKUP command to back up all files on your root directory. The procedure assumes you have a fixed disk designated drive C. If the drive is E, then substitute E for C. Begin at the DOS prompt.

1. Assuming you have a fixed disk system, place a formatted scratch disk in drive A.
2. Type **BACKUP C: A:** and press **Return**.
3. Notice a prompt similar to the following illustration.

```
C:\>BACKUP C: A:

Insert backup diskette 01 in drive A:

WARNING! Files in the target drive
A:\ root directory will be erased
Press any key to continue . . .
```

4. Press any key and watch the filenames appear on the screen as they are copied.
5. Notice the "Backup is complete" message after all files are copied.
6. Save your backup disk for use in the Typical Operation activity of Module 53 (RESTORE).
7. Turn to Module 53 to continue the learning sequence.

Module 9
CHCP (3.30+)

DESCRIPTION

The CHCP command, which is an internal DOS command, was introduced in DOS version 3.30 for use with code page switching. The form of the CHCP command is

```
CHCP nnn
```

where *nnn* is a code page number. If a code page number is not included in the command, the current operating system code page number is displayed.

Before CHCP takes effect, execution of the NLSFUNC (*National Language Support Function*) command is required (see Module 44). In addition, the preparation of code pages is required using the MODE command (see Module 42).

When everything is properly loaded, the CHCP command uses the COUNTRY.SYS file, which contains a set of country information tables. If the file is not accessed by CHCP, a "File not found" message is displayed.

APPLICATIONS

The CHCP command lets you change code pages for all devices and their corresponding code pages. However, it is necessary that all devices have been properly prepared using the MODE command, and that the NLSFUNC command precedes use of the CHCP command. The CHCP command lets you switch code pages without having to resort to a series of MODE CP SELECT commands.

TYPICAL OPERATION

There is no activity required for this command, as its use relies on a series of events associated with code page switching. For more information about associated commands, refer to modules 12, 14, 37, 42, and 44. These modules describe code page switching, configuration files and device drivers, and the MODE, NLSFUNC, and KEYB commands. Turn to Module 56 to continue the learning sequence.

Module 10
CHKDSK (1.00+)

DESCRIPTION

The CHKDSK command, available on all versions of DOS, checks the status of a selected disk. It is an external DOS command, and it displays several important items of information. These include:

- The total disk space
- The total disk space occupied and the number of files
- The total disk space either lost or considered unusable by the system
- The amount of disk space available for use
- The total amount of memory available in your computer
- The amount of memory occupied by the operating system and memory-resident programs
- The amount of memory available for use

DOS Version 4.01 also displays the volume serial number, if one exists, and disk and memory allocation information. The general form of the CHKDSK command is:

```
CHKDSK D:
```

where D: is the drive letter holding the disk to be checked. For example, the command CHKDSK B: performs a disk check of the disk in drive B. If no disk drive is specified, the logged disk drive is assumed, as is the case with most DOS commands.

THE GENERAL FORM When CHKDSK is typed and the Return key pressed, a message similar to the following is displayed.

```
A:\>CHKDSK
Volume Serial Number is 0F66-14F7

    362496 bytes total disk space
     71680 bytes in 2 hidden files
      1024 bytes in 1 directories
    193536 bytes in 16 user files
     96256 bytes available on disk

      1024 bytes in each allocation unit
       354 total allocation units on disk
        94 available allocation units on disk

    655360 total bytes memory
    605392 bytes free
```

DOS version 3.00 and later display directory information. DOS 4.01 provides disk allocation information as shown in the following screen illustration. The number of bytes in each allocation unit varies with the disk format. For example, a 1.2 MB floppy diskette has 512 bytes in each allocation unit.

```
  33449984 bytes total disk space
     73728 bytes in 3 hidden files
     83968 bytes in 27 directories
  25513984 bytes in 1202 user files
   7690240 bytes available on disk

      2048 bytes in each allocation unit
     16333 total allocation units on disk
      3755 available allocation units on disk

    655360 total bytes memory
    544288 bytes free

C:\DOS>
```

The "hidden files" are your DOS system files. These show up on all DOS disks. "User files" are those that are listed when the DIR command is used.

The amount of available disk space is perhaps the most important line in the report. This tells you if you have enough space on a disk for continued work. If the amount of space is limited, it may be time to use another disk, delete obsolete files to recover disk space, or copy inactive files to another disk and then delete them from the current one.

Notice that the CHKDSK command also gives you a report on your computer's memory. The total amount of memory and the amount of free memory is displayed. In the first sample report, the system is using 49,968 bytes (or characters) of memory space. This is often called system overhead. The second example shows a substantial amount of memory in use by DOS and other memory-resident programs. Here, it is probably advisable to deactivate memory-resident programs if you must run a large application program. As a precaution, memory-resident programs should be turned off in the reverse order of turn-on. Otherwise, you are likely to experience a system "crash."

CHKDSK WITH DOS 2.00 AND LATER With the introduction of DOS 2.00, a few new CHKDSK parameters became available. A /V parameter (you can think of V for view) displays the directories and files as they are checked. If errors are encountered, additional information is displayed.

A /F (for fix) parameter is also available to recover lost clusters within chains, which are sections of disk that have been inadvertently misallocated in the directory. If lost clusters are found by the CHKDSK operation, you might see a message similar to the following:

```
C:\DOS>CHKDSK

Volume DISK1_VOL1  created 08-22-1989 3:23p
Volume Serial Number is 1458-047A
Errors found, F parameter not specified
Corrections will not be written to disk


   43 lost allocation units found in 2 chains.
Convert lost chains to files (Y/N)?
```

Type N and press Return to display information similar to the following:

```
     88064 bytes disk space would be freed

  33449984 bytes total disk space
     73728 bytes in 3 hidden files
     83968 bytes in 27 directories
  25530368 bytes in 1204 user files
   7673856 bytes available on disk

      2048 bytes in each allocation unit
     16333 total allocation units on disk
      3747 available allocation units on disk

    655360 total bytes memory
    544288 bytes free

C:\DOS>
```

To recover the lost disk space, enter CHKDSK /F. The lost data is recovered and placed in a file having the name FILE0000.CHK. You can examine this file by displaying it on the screen with the TYPE command (Module 62), EDLIN (Module 25), or with a text editor. If it is garbage, you can delete it from the disk with the DEL (ERASE) command (Module 26). If it is important data, you may wish to use an editor to perform necessary repairs.

CHECKING FILES WITH CHKDSK The CHKDSK command also determines how one or more files are scattered across the geography of a disk. For example, when a file occupies adjacent sectors, disk input/output operations are relatively quick. As files are edited, new portions often "leap frog" over other files on the disk to find available disk space. This creates what is called a noncontiguous file, or one that is scattered across two or more blocks of space. To check a file named LETTER1.TXT on disk B, you can type CHKDSK B:LETTER1.TXT and press Return. A display similar to the following appears.

```
A:\>CHKDSK B:LETTER1.TXT
Volume Serial Number is 3168-16D4

   1457664 bytes total disk space
       512 bytes in 1 directories
      2048 bytes in 4 user files
   1455104 bytes available on disk

       512 bytes in each allocation unit
      2847 total allocation units on disk
      2842 available allocation units on disk

    655360 total bytes memory
    544288 bytes free

All specified file(s) are contiguous

A:\>
```

If you want to determine if there are files on disk B having discontinuity, you can type CHKDSK B:*.* and press Return. This presents a display similar to the following:

```
A:\>CHKDSK B:*.*
Volume Serial Number is 3168-16D4

   1457664 bytes total disk space
       512 bytes in 1 directories
      2048 bytes in 4 user files
   1455104 bytes available on disk

       512 bytes in each allocation unit
      2847 total allocation units on disk
      2842 available allocation units on disk

    655360 total bytes memory
    544288 bytes free

B:\LETTER1.TXT
  Contains 2 non-contiguous blocks.
B:\LETTER2.TXT
  Contains 3 non-contiguous blocks.
```

SUMMARY Because several forms of the CHKDSK command are available, a summary of these command forms is presented for your convenience.

All versions of DOS:

CHKDSK or CHKDSK B:	Checks the total disk space, the amount of disk space occupied by files, the amount of disk space available for use, the amount of total memory, and the amount of memory space free for use.

Versions 2.00 and later:

CHKDSK /V	Displays each directory and file as it is encountered by the program. Also displays disk error information.
CHKDSK /F	Used to recover (or fix) disk space that has been misallocated in the directory. Places recovered disk space into files and assigns filenames beginning with FILE0000.CHK, FILE0001.CHK, and so on.
CHKDSK filename	Checks the designated file for continuity in the way it is arranged on the disk. Displays a message telling whether the file blocks used are contiguous.
CHKDSK *.*	Checks all files on the designated disk for continuity. Lists the names and number of noncontiguous blocks for all files having more than one contiguous block.

APPLICATIONS

The CHKDSK command is one of the more frequently used DOS utilities. You can use it to determine whether or not there is enough file space available on a disk to continue using it. It also tells you whether or not enough free memory exists to run certain applications programs.

You should run CHKDSK on each disk that you use to ensure the integrity of the file structures. If you detect a problem, move your files to another diskette as soon as possible. Otherwise, you may lose valuable data or programs.

The additional CHKDSK command options offered by DOS versions 2.00 and later let you perform many helpful functions. In particular, the CHKDSK /V option lets you view all directories and all files, helping you quickly find a misplaced file (when you forget which directory contains the file).

If file access time starts to get annoyingly long, it is probably because the file has been scattered randomly across the disk's "geography." When this happens, the read/write heads of your disk drive must move to different parts of the disk to read and write parts of the file. You can see just how badly a file is broken up by using the CHKDSK FILENAME form of the command. If the file resides in several noncontiguous blocks, you can use the COPY command to copy it to a new disk, which gathers the file into a continuous block.

TYPICAL OPERATION

In this activity you use the CHKDSK command to check the amount of disk space on your DOS diskette. Begin at the A prompt.

1. Type **CHKDSK** and press **Return**; notice the display. (This a DOS 5.0 CHKDSK display.)

```
A:\>CHKDSK
Volume Serial Number is 0F66-14F7

    362496 bytes total disk space
     71680 bytes in 2 hidden files
      1024 bytes in 1 directories
    193536 bytes in 16 user files
     96256 bytes available on disk

      1024 bytes in each allocation unit
       354 total allocation units on disk
        94 available allocation units on disk

    655360 total bytes memory
    544288 bytes free

A:\>
```

NOTE

If you are using DOS version 2.00 or later, perform the following steps. If you are using an earlier version of DOS, ignore the following steps and move on to Module 66.

2. Type **CHKDSK *.*** and press **Return**; notice a display similar to the following.

```
A:\>CHKDSK *.*
Volume Serial Number is 0F66-14F7

    362496 bytes total disk space
     71680 bytes in 2 hidden files
      1024 bytes in 1 directories
    193536 bytes in 16 user files
     96256 bytes available on disk

      1024 bytes in each allocation unit
       354 total allocation units on disk
        94 available allocation units on disk

    655360 total bytes memory
    544288 bytes free

All specified file(s) are contiguous.

A:\>
```

3. Turn to Module 66 to continue the learning sequence.

Module 11
CLS (2.00+)

DESCRIPTION

The CLS command clears the display screen and redisplays the DOS prompt at the upper left-hand corner of your screen. This command is an internal command available on DOS versions 2.00 and later. The form of the CLS command is

```
CLS
```

APPLICATIONS

The primary application of the CLS command is to remove unwanted clutter from the display screen, or to start commands at the top of the screen. When automatic execution (*batch files*) are used, the last command is often a CLS to remove confusing clutter and to display the cursor at the top of a "clean slate." If you want to dump a directory from your screen to your printer using Shift-PrtSc, you may want to clear your screen, display the directory, and then do the printing. Here again, CLS removes unwanted text from your screen.

TYPICAL OPERATION

In this activity you use the CLS command to clear information from your screen. Begin at the DOS prompt.

1. Type **DIR** and press **Return** to display a disk directory to the screen.
2. Type **CLS** and press **Return**; notice that your screen is clear.
3. Turn to Module 62 to continue the learning sequence.

Module 12
CODE PAGE SWITCHING

DESCRIPTION

Code page switching, introduced in DOS 3.30, lets you select various character sets that are unique to a variety of countries. When loaded, the characters displayed, printed, or entered from the keyboard satisfy the requirements of a number of languages.

If you have DOS version 4.01, you are given installation choices when using the SELECT program. Here, you can specify a desired code page number. These numbers are included in this module and in others that describe commands used with code page switching.

The default character set of U.S.-built microcomputers is called the *hardware code page*. To select an alternate code page, you must enter the appropriate command lines into your CONFIG.SYS and AUTOEXEC.BAT files. These lines load device drivers that change the input/output environment (or the way that keystrokes are interpreted and characters are displayed or printed).

Each code page set contains 256 characters. Most of the characters within code pages are common with the exception of a few that are unique to the selected language. If you have the proper hardware, you can examine the effect of each code page by experimenting with the code page switching commands.

Each code page has a unique number. These are

Language	*Code Page Number*
English	437
Multilingual	850
Portuguese	860
French (Canada)	863
Nordic	865

The multilingual (850) code page is used for the following countries:

Australia	Germany	Sweden
Belgium	Italy	Switzerland (French and German)
Canada (English and French)	Latin America	United Kingdom
Denmark	Netherlands	United States (English)
Finland	Norway	
France	Portugal	
	Spain	

If you are a new DOS user, use code page 850 as it is common to most European and American languages. If you find that an application does not operate satisfactorily with code page 850, exit the application program. Then select another code page, restart the program, and verify that the newly selected code page operates satisfactorily.

The following hardware devices are supported by code page switching. The corresponding DOS support files and device drivers are listed. These files are selected from lines within the CONFIG.SYS file.

Device	*Support File*	*Device Driver*
Enhanced Color Adaptors (EGA)	EGA.CPI	DISPLAY.SYS
IBM 4201 Proprinter family	4201.CPI	PRINTER.SYS
IBM 5202 Quietwriter III	5202.CPI	PRINTER.SYS
Added to DOS 4.01:		
IBM PS/2 Display Adapter 8514/A	EGA.CPI	DISPLAY.SYS
IBM PS/2 Family Displays	EGA.CPI	DISPLAY.SYS
IBM Convertible LCD	LCD.CPI	DISPLAY.SYS
IBM 4202 Proprinter XL	4201.CPI	PRINTER.SYS
IBM 4207 Proprinter X24	4208.CPI	PRINTER.SYS
IBM 4208 Proprinter XL24	4208.CPI	PRINTER.SYS

The precise format of command lines within the CONFIG.SYS file is presented in the configuration files module.

CODE PAGE SWITCHING SOFTWARE A number of device drivers and commands are used to prepare, select, and change code pages. These commands are included in your CONFIG.SYS file or in your AUTOEXEC.BAT file. Some commands are entered from your keyboard at the DOS prompt. The DOS programs and files that interact with code page switching are

DISKCOPY	COM	DRIVER	SYS
FORMAT	COM	DISPLAY	SYS
GRAFTABL	COM	KEYBOARD	SYS
KEYB	COM	PRINTER	SYS
MODE	COM	EGA	CPI
SELECT	COM	LCD	CPI
XCOPY	EXE	4201	CPI
NLSFUNC	EXE	4202	CPI
COUNTRY	SYS	4208	CPI
INSTALL	COM	5202	CPI

The INSTALL program is supplied with the DOS 4.01 distribution diskette and is generally not copied to working DOS 4.01 system disks.

Your CONFIG.SYS file may include one or more of the following commands.

COUNTRY — Includes a specific country number followed by the appropriate code page number. The following table on the next page lists country (nnn) and code page (xxx) numbers; also included are keyboard code numbers (yy). The KEYB command, described in Module 37 and alluded to later in this module, includes the country (nnn) and keyboard (yy) codes. Keyboard codes are used only with enhanced keyboards. Because some countries have more than one enhanced keyboard, the keyboard ID let you switch to the keyboard you want to use.

DOS Versions 3.00+				*DOS Versions 3.30+*			
Country	*nnn*	*xxx*	*yy*	*Country*	*nnn*	*xxx*	*yy*
United States	001	437	US	Arabic	785	850	None
Canada (Eng)	001	850	US	Australia	061	850	US
France	033	863	FR	Belgium	032	850	BE
Spain	034	850	SP	Canada (Fr)	002	863	CF
Italy	039	850	IT	Denmark	045	850	DK
United Kingdom	044	850	UK	Finland	358	850	SU
Germany	049	850	GR	Hebrew	972	850	None
				Latin America	003	850	LA
				Netherlands	031	850	NL
				Norway	047	865	NO
				Portugal	351	860	PO
				Sweden	046	850	SV
				Switzerland (Fr)	041	850	SF
				Switzerland (Gr)	041	850	SG

DOS Versions 4.01+			
Country	*nnn*	*xxx*	*yy*
Japan	081	932 437	None
Korea	082	934 437	None
Traditional Chinese	088	938 437	None

DEVICE — Specifies certain compatible printer and/or display device drivers. (See DISPLAY.SYS and PRINTER.SYS in the Configuration Command module.)

Your AUTOEXEC.BAT file may include one or more of the following commands. Each of these commands are described in their respective modules.

NLSFUNC	Loads national language support from the COUNTRY.SYS file.
KEYB	Loads keyboard support for the selected language.
MODE	Prepares, selects, or refreshes selected devices for code page use.

There are four categories of commands that control the effect of the DOS code page switching facility. Each is described in the following four paragraphs.

Code Page Information (CPI) Files These files have the extension .CPI and are called from your CONFIG.SYS file. Their purpose is to prepare your computer for use with a designated printer or display device. Two command lines, one that sets up your system for use with a IBM Proprinter II Model 4201 and another that sets it up for an enhanced graphics adapter (EGA) display, are

```
DEVICE=PRINTER.SYS LPT1=(4201,437,3)
DEVICE=DISPLAY.SYS CON=(EGA,437,2)
```

Note that the command lines use the PRINTER and DISPLAY device driver files supplied with DOS 3.3. Code page number 437 (English) is specified in each of the command lines. The precise syntax of command lines is presented in the configuration files module (Module 14).

System Code Page Commands There are three system code page commands used to prepare or change the active code page. These commands are

CHCP	This command is an internal DOS command that is entered from the keyboard. Literally, it means "CHange Code Page." When used, it changes or displays the active code page for all devices, i.e., printers and displays, that have been prepared in the CONFIG.SYS file. The NLSFUNC command is always entered prior to CHCP. An example of the CHCP command that changes to code page 860 is CHCP 860. Remember, however, that code page 860 must have been prepared using the appropriate MODE command and device driver within your CONFIG.SYS file.
COUNTRY	The COUNTRY command is included as a line in the CONFIG.SYS file. It inputs the code page number corresponding to the country of your choice. This changes such things as date and time formats that correspond to the code page number. For example, the command line COUNTRY=033,850 selects the multilingual code page for the French language.

NLSFUNC	The "National Language Support FUNCtion" is used to load national language support from the COUNTRY.SYS file included with DOS version 3.30. Remember that the COUNTRY command prepares your computer for use with a specified language and code page. It is included in the CONFIG.SYS file. NLSFUNC finishes the job by loading national language support specified by COUNTRY.SYS. The NLSFUNC command is usually included in the AUTOEXEC.BAT file. This ensures the automatic installation of code page switching upon system turn on. However, you can enter the NLSFUNC command directly from your keyboard. The NLSFUNC command is always used prior to the CHCP command.
INSTALL	Although not a system code page command, DOS 4.01 introduced the INSTALL program, which lets you configure your system at start-up. You can use the NLSFUNC and KEYB commands with INSTALL.

Device Code Page Commands Device code page commands set up code pages for use with compatible printer and display devices. Device-specific code page commands are described in the following list.

DEVICE=PRINTER.SYS	This CONFIG.SYS file command line prepares the specified printer for the selected code page.
DEVICE=DISPLAY.SYS	This CONFIG.SYS file command line prepares the specified display for the selected code page.
MODE	The MODE command, normally included in the AUTOEXEC.BAT file, prepares, selects, and restores the printer or display device specified in the CONFIG. SYS file. It is also used to display the active code page status. Some MODE command examples follow:
MODE CON CP PREP= ((437,850)EGA.CPI)	Prepares code pages 437 and 850 for an EGA display device.
MODE PRN CP PREP= ((437,850,865)4201.CPI)	Prepares code pages 437, 850, and 865 for use with an IBM Proprinter II Model 4201.
MODE CON CP SEL=850	Selects code page 850 for use with the console (display).
MODE LPT1 CP PREP= ((850)4201.CPI) MODE LPT1 CP REF	This combination of MODE commands refreshes (or restores) the designated LPT1 (parallel printer) device.

The number of software code pages prepared for any device with the MODE command is never greater than the number specified in the corresponding CONFIG. SYS file DEVICE command.

Commands Using Code Page Switching The following commands interact with code page switching by using established parameters.

GRAFTABL	The GRAFTABL command is used to display graphics characters above 127. The specific characters are compatible with the selected code page. The characters are displayed when the computer is in the graphics mode. The GRAFTABL command is usually included in your AUTOEXEC.BAT file.
KEYB	The KEYB command, which is also most often included in your AUTOEXEC.BAT file, loads keyboard support for a specified language. The result is a changed keyboard layout that corresponds to the selected code page.
SELECT	The SELECT command in versions of DOS prior to 4.01 is used to install DOS on a new diskette. This command automatically transfers the code page setup, including creation of an AUTOEXEC.BAT file with the appropriate KEYB command and a CONFIG.SYS file containing the appropriate COUNTRY command.
DISKINIT	The DISKINIT command performs the same code page setup as SELECT, i.e., the AUTOEXEC.BAT and CONFIG.SYS files are prepared as with the SELECT command.
SORT	The SORT command honors the country-specific sorting hierarchy that corresponds to the selected code page.

APPLICATIONS

Code page switching is used when you wish to configure your display, keyboard, and printer for use with one or more languages other than English. The selected code page overlays the default hardware code page (number 437) with the one selected. It is placed in your computer's memory.

If you are using multiple languages, you can prepare multiple code pages with the MODE command. The printer and display device drivers should be loaded into your CONFIG.SYS file for compatibility with printer and display devices that take advantage of various character sets. These devices include IBM Model 4201 Proprinters, Model 5201 Quietwriters, Enhanced Graphics Adapters, and LCD displays.

By using the SELECT command and then adding the appropriate device driver lines to the CONFIG.SYS file, you can prepare a library of system disks. Each can be used to configure your computer for a different language. All that is required is for you to insert the language disk of your choice and turn on your system.

TYPICAL OPERATION

In this activity you create a CONFIG.SYS file and enter the appropriate commands to create a disk for use with an computer equipped with an EGA monitor, an IBM Model 4201 Proprinter, and the Spanish language. This activity assumes that you are using DOS version 3.30 or higher and have a two-floppy drive system (drives A and B). If you are using a system with a fixed disk, use C in place of B in the following steps.

1. Place your DOS system disk in drive B and a blank floppy disk in drive A.
2. Log drive B by typing **B:** and pressing **Return.**
3. Format the blank disk by typing **FORMAT A:/S** and pressing **Return.**
4. After the disk is formatted, use the COPY command to create and save the following lines in a CONFIG.SYS file on the disk in drive A. End each line by pressing **Return**. After typing **BUFFERS=20**, press **Return Ctrl-Z Return.**

```
COPY CON A:CONFIG.SYS
COUNTRY=034,850
DEVICE=PRINTER.SYS LPT1=(4201,850,2)
DEVICE=DISPLAY.SYS CON=(EGA,850,2)
FILES=20
BUFFERS=20
^Z
```

5. Create the following AUTOEXEC.BAT file on the disk in drive A by typing the following lines. End each by pressing **Return**; end the last line by pressing **Ctrl-Z Return.**

```
COPY CON A:AUTOEXEC.BAT
ECHO OFF
PATH \;
KEYB SP 034
MODE CON CP PREP=((850,437)EGA.CPI)
MODE LPT1 CP PREP=((850,437)4201.CPI)
NLSFUNC
CLS
DATE
TIME
^Z
```

6. Use the COPY command to copy the following files to the disk in drive A.

4201	CPI	KEYBOARD	SYS
DRIVER	SYS	MODE	COM
EGA	CPI	NLSFUNC	EXE
GRAFTABL	COM	PRINTER	SYS
KEYB	COM	COUNTRY	SYS

7. The disk is now ready for use with EGA graphics, a Model 4201 Proprinter, and the Spanish language.
8. To use the disk, place it in drive A and turn on your computer. If it is already on, press **Ctrl-Alt-Del** to reboot your system.
9. Turn to Module 54 to continue the learning sequence.

Module 13
COMP (1.00+), FC (3.30+)

DESCRIPTION

Both the COMP and FC commands are external DOS commands that compare the contents of two specified files. Because these commands perform similar operations, they are grouped together for convenience.

COMP The COMP command compares the contents of two files a byte at a time to determine if they are identical. In versions of COMP prior to the release of DOS 5.00, the command was used in the form:

```
COMP file1 file2
```

DOS 5.00 added several parameters to the COMP command. These are summarized in the following list.

COMP *file1 file2*	Compares the two files and returns differing character values in ASCII decimal notation. The *OFFSET* position of each differing character in the file is also displayed in hexadecimal format. The offset of the first character in the file is 0, the second character is 2, and so on.
COMP *file1 file2* /A	This command is identical to the preceding one except the differing character values are displayed in ASCII format, i.e., an X is displayed as X instead of decimal 58.
COMP *file1 file2* /D	Displays the character values in hexadecimal format, as well as the offset value.
COMP *file1 file2* /L	Display line numbers instead of offset positions.
COMP *file1 file2* /C	Ignore upper and lowercase in the comparison of two files.
COMP *file1 file2* /N:100	Compare the first 100 lines of the specified files.

You can also run the COMP command by typing COMP and pressing Return. The program prompts you for two filenames and options, i.e., /A, /L, etc. Press Return to begin the comparison.

FC Sometimes called FILECOMP, this command compares the contents of files and lists the differences. The listing differs from that produced by the COMP command. The Typical Operation activity demonstrates the differences. Following are different forms of the FC command.

FC *file1 file2*	Compares files in ASCII mode and lists the offset and decimal values of the differing characters.
FC /A *file1 file2*	Abbreviates the listed output by displaying only those lines that begin a set of differences.
FC /B *file1 file2*	Performs a byte-by-byte binary comparison of the specified files.
FC /C *file1 file2*	Ignores upper and lowercase by treating all characters as uppercase.
FC /L *file1 file2*	Compares files in the ASCII mode, which is the default mode.
FC /N *file1 file2*	Lists line numbers when comparing ASCII files.
FC /T *file1 file2*	Treats a tab as a single character instead of expanding it to eight spaces, which is how tabs are normally treated by the file comparison options.
FC /W *file1 file2*	Compresses white space produced by tabs and spaces during the comparison process. Multiple tabs and spaces are treated as a single character.
FC /LB200 *file1 file2*	Sets the internal line buffer to 200 lines. The default value is 100 lines. When the number of consecutive lines exceeds the line value, file comparison is canceled.
FC /1000 *file1 file2*	Specifies the consecutive number of file lines that must match after a difference between files is found. If the number of matching lines is less than the specified number, matching lines are displayed as differences.

APPLICATIONS

The most notable use of the COMP command is to compare one or more copies of a file to the original file to verify an exact reproduction. This is the quickest way to ensure a good quality file copy. If you suspect copy problems, you may wish to use COMP or FC each time you make a copy of a file just to be safe.

You can also use the COMP and FC commands to locate differences in ASCII text files. This lets you go directly to the area of change for a visual comparison.

TYPICAL OPERATION

In this activity you use the COPY command to create a four-line file. Next, you copy and modify it using EDLIN. Finally, you use both COMP and FC to determine the changes. Begin at the DOS prompt.

1. Type **COPY CON TEMP1.TXT** and press **Return**. Then type the following lines ending each with **Return**. Press **Ctrl-Z** or **F6** on the last line.

```
The city of Munich is in southeast Germany.
Hamburg is in the north.
Amsterdam is below sea level.
Dover overlooks the English Channel.
^Z
```

2. Type **COPY TEMP1.TXT TEMP2.TXT** and press **Return**.
3. Type **EDLIN TEMP2.TXT** and press **Return**.
4. Type **1** and press **Return**. Change line 1 to read:

   The *town* of Munich is in southeast Germany.

5. Type **4** and press **Return**. Change line 4 to read:

   Dover is *beside the* English Channel.

6. Type **E** and press **Return** to save the file.
7. Type **COMP TEMP1.TXT TEMP2.TXT** and press **Return**. Notice your display. Type **N** and press **Return** to continue.
8. Type **FC /n TEMP1.TXT TEMP2.TXT** and press **Return**. Compare the results of the two commands.
9. Turn to Module 29 to continue the learning sequence.

Module 14
CONFIGURATION COMMANDS

DESCRIPTION

The configuration file was introduced with DOS version 2.00. Since then, new versions of DOS have added configuration capabilities and corresponding configuration commands.

The configuration file must have the name CONFIG.SYS. A configuration file is created using EDLIN, the DOS 5.00 EDIT program, the COPY command, or an ASCII word processor. The SELECT command is also used to create CONFIG.SYS files in DOS versions 3.30 and 4.01. SELECT was discontinued in DOS 5.00.

Configuration files contain one or more lines of commands like the DOS command lines in batch files (Module 7). When your computer is turned on, DOS checks for the CONFIG.SYS file and adjusts the system configuration accordingly.

CONFIG.SYS commands are summarized in the following list. Expanded descriptions are provided in the balance of this section.

BREAK=on
or BREAK=off (The default is off.)

BUFFERS=*n* *n* is a number from 1 to 99 (The default is 2.)

DEVICE=*filename* The *filename* is that of a *device driver,* such as:

```
DEVICE=ANSI.SYS
DEVICE=DRIVER.SYS
DEVICE=VDISK.SYS
```

NOTE

Many configuration commands load named device driver files. For a device driver to be loaded, it must be in the root directory of the boot disk, or the filepath containing the device driver be specified in the CONFIG.SYS command line. The command DEVICE =C:\DOS\ANSI.SYS is used if the ANSI.SYS file is in the \DOS directory.

FILES=*n* *n* is a number from 1 to 99 (The default is 8.)

SHELL=*filename* The *filename* is that of a special command processor.

COUNTRY=*nnn*	*nnn* is a three-digit country code (The default is 001; introduced in DOS version 3.00.)
FCBS=*m,n*	*m* is the number of files that can be opened at any given time, ranging in value from 1 to 255 (The default is 4; introduced in DOS version 3.00.). *n* is the maximum number of files that may remain open at any given time, ranging in value from 0 to 255. (The default is 0.)
LASTDRIVE=*x*	*x* is a character from A to Z (Introduced in DOS version 3.00.)

DOS version 3.30 introduced the following device drivers, which are used with code page switching, which is explained in Module 12. For now, it should suffice for you to know that code page switching is used to access non-U.S. character sets on certain keyboard, display, and printer devices.

DEVICE=DISPLAY.SYS
DEVICE=KEYBOARD.SYS
DEVICE=PRINTER.SYS

DOS 4.01 introduced the following four device drivers.

DEVICE= XMA2EMS.SYS	This device driver supports the Lotus, Intel, Microsoft (LIM) Expanded memory Specification (EMS) 4.0 when DOS 4.01 is in use. EMS is used when the XMA2EMS.SYS device driver and a hardware adapter capable of using the EMS is installed in your computer.
DEVICE=XMAEM.SYS	This device driver is used with IBM PS/2 systems equipped with 80386 microprocessors, such as the PS/2 Model 80. It is used to establish emulation of the IBM Personal System/2 80286 Expanded Memory Adapter/A.
INSTALL= *filename/parameter*	The *filename/parameter* is a valid DOS command, such as FASTOPEN.COM, KEYB.COM, NLSFUNC.EXE, or SHARE.EXE.
SWITCHES=/K	/K prevents the system from using extended keyboard functions normally available on an extended keyboard.

DOS 5.00 introduced device drivers designed to make more efficient use of extended and expanded memory.

DEVICE= SMARTDRV.SYS *n* /A	*n* is a number between 256 and 2048, which allocates the amount of memory to use for disk cache, which speeds up program execution. The /A parameter is used if you have expanded memory; /A is not used when your computer uses extended memory. Use the MEM command to display your memory configuration.

DEVICE= C:\DOS\HIMEM.SYS	When loaded, certain programs can make use of extended memory. If you want DOS 5.00 to load in extended memory, use DOS=HIGH to conserve program memory below 640K.
DEVICE=C:\DOS\ SETVER.EXE	The SETVER command is used to reassign the DOS version so that a program that is compatible with an earlier version of DOS may be run.

Each of the commonly used commands and corresponding examples are presented to familiarize you with their use and syntax.

BREAK The BREAK ON command causes DOS to check for the Ctrl-Break (or Ctrl-C) sequence before performing any program operation. When BREAK OFF is active (which is the default value) operation is interrupted only when an input operation from, or output operation to, a standard device (LPTn, COMn, CON, AUX, etc.) occurs. If your CONFIG.SYS file includes the command line BREAK=ON, then you can press Ctrl-Break to interrupt program operation and return to the DOS prompt. To check the status of BREAK, you can type BREAK and press Return.

BUFFERS In general, a *buffer* is a 528-character (or byte) block of computer memory temporarily used to store data that is either read from or written to your disk. The general form of the BUFFER command is:

```
BUFFERS=n,m/X
```

where *n* is the number of buffers from 1 to 99.

m is called the *look ahead* buffer because it sets the maximum number of sectors read prior to processing input operations. The value of *m* may range from 1 to 8. This parameter increases data throughput for applications that read and write sequentially, such as database files. This parameter was introduced in DOS 4.01.

/X is an optional parameter that loads buffers in expanded memory to save space in low memory for applications programs. This parameter was introduced in DOS 4.01.

A buffer is used only when the data is less than a "block" of disk space (528 bytes). By temporarily storing small segments of data in memory, disk read/write activity, and therefore data access time, is reduced. The default buffer value is 2. With DOS 4.01, the default buffer value changes with disk and memory capacities as follows

Diskette drive greater than 360 KB	BUFFERS=3
Memory size greater than 128 KB	BUFFERS=5
Memory size greater than 256 KB	BUFFERS=10
Memory size greater than 512 KB	BUFFERS=15

In addition, DOS 4.01 buffers use slightly more space. Each additional *n* buffer occupies 532 bytes, while the *m* buffer occupies 512 bytes. Too many buffers may cause an application to run slower.

With the release of DOS 5.00, Microsoft established the following recommendations based on the size of the hard drive in use.

Hard Drive Capacity	*Command*
Less than 40 MB	BUFFERS=20
40 through 79 MB	BUFFERS=30
80 through 119 MB	BUFFERS=40
More than 120 MB	BUFFERS=50

When buffers are used, the program searches them, instead of a disk, for stored data. However, if too many buffers exist, the search time may exceed the time saved by avoiding disk operations. In addition, buffers reduce the amount of memory available to your program. With each buffer, you lose 528 bytes of memory; 50 buffers occupy 26,400 bytes of memory. A loss of memory may increase disk input/output activity by your program, again increasing time instead of reducing it.

Because the most efficient number of buffers corresponds to the kind and size of program in use, there's no pat answer for how many buffers are best. You can try numbers between 10 and 50. If you want a configuration file that establishes 30 buffers, it must contain the line BUFFERS=30.

If you are using DOS 4.01, the following command establishes 20 disk buffers and 8 look ahead buffers and places buffer processing in expanded memory.

```
BUFFERS=20,8 /X
```

You can also use SMARTDRV.SYS, described later in this module, as a secondary cache. This driver is particularly useful for database programs and language compilers, and speeds program loading.

COUNTRY The COUNTRY command was introduced with DOS version 3.00. The form of the COUNTRY command is:

```
COUNTRY=nnn
```

where *nnn* is a country code equal to one of the following:

Country	*nnn*	*Country*	*nnn*
United States	001	Denmark	045
Netherlands	031	Sweden	046
Belgium	032	Norway	047
France	033	Germany	049
Spain	034	Australia	061
Italy	038	Finland	358
Switzerland	041	Israel	972
United Kingdom	044		

DOS 4.01 introduced the following country codes:

Country	*nnn*
Japan	081
Korea	082
Traditional Chinese	088

COUNTRY sets the DATE and TIME format, the currency symbol, and the decimal character. However, it does not translate the language used in DOS prompts.

DEVICE The DEVICE command lets you specify the name of a file that contains what is called a "device driver." A device driver is a program that does such things as structuring the data used during communications or printing. At system start-up, DOS loads the device driver file into memory where it resides as an active part of DOS.

Some versions of DOS are supplied with ready-made device driver files. These files often have the extension .DEV or .SYS. For example, if you see the filename RAMDISK.DEV, you probably have a device driver that creates a logical disk drive in memory.

The ANSI.SYS Driver The ANSI.SYS device driver is supplied with most versions of DOS. Available on DOS version 2.00 and higher, it provides extended screen and keyboard control features. Documentation supplied with programs requiring the ANSI.SYS driver usually tells you to load the ANSI.SYS driver in your CONFIG.SYS file. Some programs do not operate properly without it or require the ANSI.SYS driver on non-IBM branded microcomputers. For example, programs compiled with Nantucket's Clipper Compiler require the ANSI.SYS driver to operate properly on some AT&T microcomputer models.

DOS 4.01 added three new parameter to ANSI.SYS:

/X Adds new key values to keys having extended values.

```
DEVICE=ANSI.SYS /X
```

/L Retains the number of lines displayed on the screen as set with the MODE command; this prevents the display from being changed back to the standard 25-line display by an application program.

```
DEVICE=ANSI.SYS /L
```

/K Uses conventional keyboard functions (or values) in place of extended keyboard functions when an extended keyboard is in use by your computer.

```
DEVICE=ANSI.SYS /K
```

DOS 5.00 added the /screensize: (row,col) parameter, which is used to set the physical screen size.

When the DEVICE=ANSI.SYS line is contained in the CONFIG.SYS file, you use the Esc key with extended key values for control. You can:

- Reassign the value that a key produces
- Control screen attributes (foreground and background colors)
- Erase the screen or a line
- Set the display mode (screen size, type, and resolution)
- Control and/or determine the cursor position

Reassigning Keys You can reassign the value of one key with that of another. For example, you can:

- Assign Q to the A key and A to the Q key (transpose key values 81 and 65 decimal)
- Assign the F10 function key (00 68) the value "DIR" <CR>
- Assign CLS <CR> to the grey Home key on an enhanced keyboard

To make these reassignments, use an editor capable of capturing the extended value for Esc and perform the following steps.

1. Create a file containing Esc, open bracket, and the decimal values of a key and its replacement in the form:

   ```
   Esc[original key value;new key value
   ```

   You can assign a string value like "DIR" to a key. Note that strings are entered within quotes. If the first character is a 0 (null), the first two characters are counted for the key value. This is true of function keys F1 through F12.

2. Save the file to disk.
3. Use the TYPE command to "execute" the file.

You can also enter the key values from the DOS prompt using the PROMPT command, or embed the key values in a batch (.BAT) file using the PROMPT command. The PROMPT command is used because it lets you enter the Esc key value as $e directly from the keyboard. Once entered, you can use the PROMPT command again to reestablish the original DOS prompt. Remember, the ANSI.SYS device driver must have been installed using the CONFIG.SYS command before these key values take effect.

In the following example you can use EDLIN or the COPY command to create the KEYS.BAT file. For simplicity, the COPY command is used. The remarks to the right of each line are not part of the file.

1. Type COPY CON KEY.BAT and press Return.
2. Type the following five lines, pressing Return after each. (Do not type the remarks.)

```
                                Remarks
PROMPT $e[81;65p            Assigns Q to the A key
PROMPT $e[65;81p            Assigns A to the Q key
PROMPT $e[0;68;"DIR";13p    Assigns DIR <CR> to F10
PROMPT $e[224;71;"CLS";13p  Assigns CLS <CR> to Home
PROMPT $p$g
```

3. Press Ctrl-Z and Return to write the file to disk.
4. Type KEY and press Return. Notice that the commands within the KEY.BAT file are displayed on the screen.
5. Test the A, Q, F10, and Home keys.
6. You can reboot your system or reassign the original key values using

```
                                Remarks
PROMPT $e[81;81p            Assigns Q back to Q
PROMPT $e[65;65p            Assigns A back to A
PROMPT $e[0;68;0;68p        Assigns F10 back to F10
PROMPT $e[224;71;224;71p    Assigns Home back to Home
```

Controlling Display Attributes (Setting the Graphics Rendition) The following list of Esc codes is used to set display attributes, sometimes called the Graphics Rendition. These codes are entered in the same way as key values. They are changed by entering a subsequent code. Note that the "m" is entered in lowercase as the last character on the Esc code line.

Esc[	*Character Attr.*	*Esc[*	*Foreground Attr.*	*Esc[*	*Background Attr.*
0m	Normal (white on black)	30m	Black	40m	Black
1m	Bold (high intensity)	31m	Red	41m	Red
4m	Underline (mono only)	32m	Green	42m	Green
5m	Blink	33m	Yellow	43m	Yellow
7m	Reverse video	34m	Blue	44m	Blue
8m	Canceled (invisible)	35m	Magenta	45m	Magenta
		36m	Cyan	46m	Cyan
		37m	White	47m	White

The preceding codes are often used in combination. For example, to alter both the foreground and background colors to high intensity white on a blue background, use

```
Esc[1;37;44m
```

Erasing the Screen or a Line The following Esc codes erase the screen or a specified line.

```
                  Remarks
Esc[2J        Erases the screen (similar to the CLS command)
Esc[K         Erases from the cursor to the end of the line
```

Screen Display Modes The following Esc codes (called Set Mode codes) control screen width or type.

Esc[	*Mode*	*Esc[*	*Mode*
=0h	40X25 black and white	=7h	Line wrap at right edge
=1h	40X25 color	=14h	640X200 color
=2h	80X25 black and white	=15h	640X350 mono
=3h	80X25 color	=16h	640X350 color
=4h	320X200 color	=17h	640X480 mono
=5h	320X200 black and white	=18h	640X480 color
=6h	640X200 black and white	=19h	320X200 color

There is also a series of Reset Mode Esc codes identical to the values of the preceding Set Mode codes except that they terminate with a lowercase L. For example Esc[141 resets 640X200 color. When Reset Mode code 7 is used (Esc[=7l), the line wrap function is suppressed. Characters beyond the right edge of the screen are discarded.

Cursor Control You can use Esc codes to position the cursor or to return its position. The following Esc codes are available to perform cursor-related operations.

Code	*Operation*
Esc[*r*;*c*H or Esc[*r*;*c*f	Moves cursor to the specified row and column positions, where *r* and *c* are row and column numbers.
Esc[H or Esc[f	Moves cursor to upper left-hand corner of screen.
Esc[*n*A	Moves cursor up *n* rows.
Esc[*n*B	Moves cursor down *n* rows.
Esc[*n*C	Moves cursor right *n* columns.
Esc[*n*D	Moves cursor left *n* columns.
Esc[*r*;*c*R	Reports the cursor position through a standard input device, where *r* is the row number and *c* is the column number.
Esc[6*n*	Outputs the cursor position report upon receipt of device status report. Never use this Esc code as part of a PROMPT command line, as your system may enter a continuous loop, which is only exited upon a system reset.
Esc[s	Saves the current cursor position.
Esc[u	Restores the saved cursor position (saved with Esc[s).

The DRIVER.SYS Driver This driver is used to establish floppy disk drive parameters. It is particularly useful if you add a third floppy drive to your system. MS-DOS has a built-in device driver that automatically controls two floppy disk drives. The form of the command is:

```
DEVICE=DRIVER.SYS /D:n [/T:n] [/S:n] [/H:n] [/C] [/N] [/F:n]
```

where: /D:*n* specifies a drive designator between 0 and 255.

The numbers 0, 1, and 2 are the first, second, and third physical diskette drives. The numbers 128 and 129 are the first and second physical fixed (or hard) disks.

The following DRIVER.SYS options are discretionary:

/T:*n*	Tracks per side, from 1 to 999; default = 80
/S:*n*	Sectors per track, from 1 to 99; default = 9
/H:*n*	Heads per drive, from 1 to 99; default = 2
/C	Requires changeline support (Only applies to IBM PC AT.)
/N	Specifies a nonremovable device, such as a fixed disk
/F:*n*	Designates drive type and form factor; default = 2 Values for *n* are: 0 = 160, 180, 320, and 360KB 1 = 1.2MB 2 = 720KB 7 = 1.44MB

Typical switch settings are summarized in the following table.

Drive	*/F*	*/H*	*/S*	*/T*
360K	0	1 or 2	8 or 9	40
1.2MB	1	2	15	80
720K	2	2	9	80
1.44MB	7	2	18	80
2.88MB	7	2	36	80

To set up a 720KB external disk drive on a PC-XT having drives A and C, use

```
DEVICE=DRIVER.SYS /D:2/F:2
```

Note that the /F:2 is the default value and is not required.

To copy files from one 1.2MB diskette to another in a PC AT equipped with one hard drive, one 1.2MB drive, and one 360KB drive, use the following DRIVER.SYS command:

```
DEVICE=DRIVER.SYS /D:0 /T:80 /S:15 /H:2 /F:1
```

The new logical drive (/D:0) is D, with 80 tracks per side (/T:80), 15 sectors per track (/s:15), two heads (/H:2), and a drive form factor of 1 (/F:1) for the 1.2MB drive. Note that /T:80 and /H:2 could have been omitted as these are default values.

The SETVER Command This command was introduced in DOS 5.00. It is used to specify a previous version of DOS with which a specific program is compatible. For example, assume the PSPRINT.EXE program uses DOS 3.31 or 4.01. You can issue the command: SETVER C: PSPRINT.EXE 4.01. Now version 4.01 is reported back to the PSPRINT program, which satisfies operational requirements. Some switches that are available with SETVER are:

/delete or /D — Deletes the version entry and program name.

```
SETVER C:\MYPATH\PSPRINT.EXE /D
```

/quiet — Suppresses screen message during entry deletion.

```
SETVER C:\MYPATH\PSPRINT.EXE /QUIET
```

You can list the contents of the current setver table with SETVER C:.

The VDISK.SYS Driver The VDISK.SYS file, also called RAMDISK.SYS in some renditions of DOS, was introduced with DOS version 3.00. These drivers let you establish a *virtual disk*, or *RAM disk* in memory. The line in the CONFIG.SYS file that establishes your virtual disk is:

```
DEVICE=VDISK.SYS nnn sss ddd /E
DEVICE=VDISK.SYS nnn sss ddd /X or /A
```

where: *nnn* is the virtual disk size (64K default)

sss is the sector size (128, 256, or 512) in bytes (128 default)

ddd is the number of directory entries (2 to 512); (64 default)

/E makes use of extended memory at or above 1 megabyte

/X (introduced in DOS 4.01) or /A (in DOS 5.00) makes use of expanded memory.

The /E and /X or /A parameters leave your system's low memory free for use by applications programs.

The line:

```
DEVICE=VDISK.SYS
```

establishes a 64K virtual disk with 128-byte sectors and 64 possible directory entries.

```
DEVICE=VDISK.SYS 256 512 128
```

establishes a 256K virtual disk with 512-byte sectors and 128 possible directory entries.

```
DEVICE=VDISK.SYS 256 512 128 /E
```

This command establishes the virtual disk described above in extended memory.

You can have multiple virtual disks by placing multiple VDISK command lines in your CONFIG.SYS file. The first virtual disk drive letter assumes the next letter following the highest one in use. For example, a system with physical drives A and B uses C as the first virtual drive, D as the second, and so on.

The DISPLAY.SYS Driver This command enables code page switching with LCD, EGA, and the IBM Personal System/2 displays. The command line has the following form:

```
DEVICE=DISPLAY.SYS CON:/type,xxx,n,m
```

where: *type* is either LCD, EGA, MONO, or CGA.

xxx is one or more code page numbers including 437, 850, 860, 863, and/or 865.

n is the number of additional code pages that can be supported. Neither MONO nor CGA support additional code pages; this requires that n =0.

m is an optional entry used to specify the maximum number of subfonts, which are alternate characters called with Alt and Shift key sequences for certain code pages.

When the *m* value is omitted from the command line, the maximum number of subfonts revert to a default value. The EGA and Personal System/2 displays have a default value of 2; The *m* value for an LCD display is 1.

The command line DEVICE=DISPLAY.SYS CON:=(EGA,850,1) sets up your system for use with an Enhanced Graphics Adapter using the multilingual code page (850). The n value of 1 provides for the addition of one more code page. A value of n=0 prevents the preparation of additional code pages. In this example, the EGA.CPI file is used to configure the display adapter.

The DOS 4.01 DISPLAY.SYS driver checks for the type of display adapter in use if the display adapter type is omitted within the command.

The KEYBOARD.SYS Driver The KEYBOARD.SYS driver operates with the KEYB program, which is used to load keyboard drivers in support of non-U.S. English keyboards. It is called with the SELECT command. See Module 37 for more information about the KEYB command.

The keyboard code used within the KEYB command selects a table within the KEYBOARD.SYS file. These tables load an ASCII character set that corresponds to a prepared code page. You can reenter the KEYB command using new parameters to change to a different code page. The parameters (or code page number) must match one that has been prepared with the MODE command. You should be aware that the version 3.30 KEYB command is not compatible with earlier versions of DOS.

The PRINTER.SYS Driver The PRINTER.SYS device driver file is loaded by your CONFIG.SYS file with the line:

```
DEVICE=PRINTER.SYS LPTn:=(type,xxx,n)
```

where: LPT*n* is a printer device name such as LPT1 or LPT2.

type is either 4201 or 5202 to correspond to the IBM Model 4201 Proprinter or Model 5202 Quietwriter III.

xxx is one or more code page numbers, including 437, 850, 860, 863, or 865.

n represents the number of additional code pages that can be supported.

DOS 4.01 added additional printer support. The supported printers are listed in Module 12.

The SMARTDRV.SYS Driver (DOS 5.00+) This driver is a standard DOS 5.00 utility that installs cache memory in extended or expanded memory, which speeds program execution by loading and executing programs in memory rather than on disk. SMARTDRV is particularly useful with Windows 3.0, as Windows can adjust the size of cache memory as necessary.

Extended memory is assumed by SMARTDRV.SYS unless you use the /A parameter at the end of the SMARTDRV.SYS command line to specify expanded memory. If you have both extended and expanded, use extended. You can assign the amount of memory used by SMARTDRV. Values between 256 and 2048 are recommended, with the largest possible number recommended. Values below 256 and above 2048 diminish the effectiveness of SMARTDRV. When installed, SMARTDRV uses about 15K of conventional memory, i.e., program memory below 640K. The following command line in the CONFIG.SYS file installs SMARTDRV.SYS, allocating 1024 bytes of extended memory.

```
DEVICE=C:\DOS\SMARTDRV.SYS 1024
```

To load SMARTDRV.SYS in extended memory, put the following commands at the beginning of your CONFIG.SYS file.

```
DEVICE=C:\DOS\HIMEM.SYS
DEVICE=C:\DOS\SMARTDRV.SYS 1024
```

Add /A at the end of the line to load SMARTDRV.SYS in expanded memory.

HIMEM.SYS Extended-Memory Manager The HIMEM.SYS driver makes extended memory available to applications that make use of extended memory, like Ventura Publisher. This SYS driver is used with computers having 80286, 80386, and 80486 microprocessors. It is not used with 8086- or 8088-based computers. HIMEM.SYS also lets DOS 5.00+ load in extended memory, leaving more memory below 640K for the execution of your programs. Use the command line DOS=HIGH following the HIMEM.SYS command line. When these commands are used, they should be the first two lines in your CONFIG.SYS file. The form of the command is:

```
DEVICE=C:\DOS\HIMEM.SYS
DOS=HIGH
```

DOS=HIGH is optional but recommended when using DOS 5.00.

FCBS The FCBS command was introduced in DOS version 3.00. FCBS lets you specify the number of file control blocks (FCBs) that can be open at the same time. It also prevents a program from closing files automatically when it attempts to have more than a specified number of files opened. The form of the FCBS command is:

```
FCBS=m,n
```

where: *m* is the total number of files that can be opened at the same time; m can be a number from 1 to 255 (The default is 4.)

n is the number of files that can remain open; this value is used to prevent a program from closing files automatically during operation. The value of n is a number from 0 to 255 (The default is 0.)

FILES This command lets you change the number of files that can be opened at the same time. The default value is commonly FILES=8, providing five predetermined DOS "handles" for standard device drivers (input, output, error, auxiliary, and standard printer). This leaves three for program use.

Every open file requires a file control block (FCB), referred to as a "handle," as in keeping a handle on the file. This FCB contains vital information about the file and its whereabouts on the disk. Each FCB uses 39 bytes of memory. Normally, you won't use this command unless an error message complaining about "insufficient handles" is displayed.

INSTALL The INSTALL command is a configuration command that was introduced with DOS version 4.01. It is used within the CONFIG.SYS file to load the following programs at system turn on.

FASTOPEN.EXE
KEYB.COM
NLSFUNC.EXE
SHARE.EXE

Four typical examples of the command are shown in the following series. Notice that each command line requires the use of the file extension. Each provides an example of one of the above programs.

```
INSTALL=FASTOPEN.EXE C:=30
INSTALL=KEYB.COM FR,437,C:\DOS\KEYBOARD.SYS /ID:189
INSTALL=NLSFUNC.EXE
INSTALL=SHARE.EXE /F:4096 /L:30
```

For more information about what each of these commands does, see the individual command modules.

LASTDRIVE The LASTDRIVE command was introduced with DOS version 3.00. LASTDRIVE establishes the number of drives you can use by letting you specify the last drive designator. While the default is E, you can use any character from A to Z. The command form is:

```
LASTDRIVE=D
```

where *D* is a character from A to Z.

SHELL The SHELL command lets you use a special command processor in place of DOS' standard command processor program COMMAND.COM. The SHELL command should not be needed unless you are a system programmer or have been supplied with an alternate command processor.

SWITCHES The SWITCHES command was introduced in DOS 4.01. SWITCHES lets you use conventional keyboard functions when an enhanced keyboard is installed on your system. The form of the command is:

```
SWITCHES=/K
```

When this line is included in your CONFIG.SYS file, it prevents your system from using extended keyboard functions, forcing it to use conventional keyboard functions instead. A /W parameter was added to DOS 5.00 to provide a way to move the WINA20.386 from the root directory to a different file path. This command applies to Windows users. The Windows SYSTEM.INI file must include the line: DEVICE= C:\path\WINA20.386.

Many users never use configuration files. Others find them valuable in speeding up the performance of their computer. This is particularly true of users who have versions of DOS that include device driver files to control things like printer and ram disk operation. You may wish to create a configuration file containing the BUFFERS command to speed up operation of your computer. The procedure for doing this is included in the following Typical Operation section.

TYPICAL OPERATION

In this activity you create a CONFIG.SYS file containing the FILES and BUFFERS configuration commands. If you are using a hard drive, add the INSTALL= FASTOPEN line. If your computer has extended memory and you are running DOS 5.00, add the indicated lines. The FILES command used lets you open as many as 20 files at the same time. The BUFFERS command may speed up the performance of your computer. Begin at the DOS prompt.

1. Create the following file using COPY command as follows:
   a. Type **COPY CON: CONFIG.SYS** and press **Return**.

      NOTE

      If you are using DOS 5.00 and your computer has 1 megabyte or more of extended memory, perform steps 1.b and 1.c. Otherwise, move directly to step 1.d.

   b. Type **DEVICE=C:\DOS\HIMEM.SYS** and press **Return**.
   c. Type **DOS=HIGH** and press **Return**.
   d. Type **FILES=20** and press **Return**.
   e. Type **BUFFERS=20** and press **Return**.

      NOTE

      If you have a hard disk, perform step 1.f. Otherwise, move to step 1.g. The FASTOPEN value should correspond to the size of your hard disk in megabytes, i.e., use 40 if you have a 40-megabyte disk.

   f. Type **INSTALL C:\DOS\FASTOPEN C:=40** and press **Return**.
   g. Press **Ctrl-Z** and press **Return**.

2. Use the DIR command to verify that the CONFIG.SYS file is present.
3. Turn to Module 58 to continue the learning sequence.

Module 15
COPY (1.00+)

DESCRIPTION

The COPY command is an internal DOS command that is available on all versions of DOS. It is used to:

1. Copy one or more specified files to another disk with the same filename, date, and time information.
2. Copy one or more specified files to the same or to another disk with a different filename.
3. Copy one or more specified files to the same or to another disk with the current system date and time.
4. Concatenate (or combine) two or more files into a single file.
5. Create a new file by copying what is typed on the screen (CON:) to a designated file.

The general form of the COPY command is

```
COPY sourcefile targetfile
```

Notice that a space separates the two filenames. The *sourcefile* is the filename of the file being copied. The *targetfile* is the filename of the file created by the COPY command. If no target filename is given, the source filename is used automatically. You can also use disk drive designators (like A: or B:) and, if you are using DOS version 2.00 or later, pathnames. Here is an example of the COPY command with disk and pathnames:

```
COPY C:\FORMS\FORM.LTR A:\MAIL\JOHNBOY.LTR
```

This command copies a file named FORM.LTR from directory pathname FORMS on disk C to a new file named JOHNBOY.LTR in directory pathname MAIL on disk A.

It is only necessary to specify a target filename if you want to change the filename. Otherwise, the existing filename is used. There are a number of variations to the COPY command. The following list presents most of the useful forms.

All DOS versions:

COPY OLDNAME NEWNAME	Makes a copy of the file OLDNAME on the active disk drive. The copied file is given the new filename NEWNAME.
COPY OLDNAME B:	Makes a copy of the file OLDNAME on the active disk drive and places it on the disk in drive B. The copy retains the original name, date, and time information.
COPY OLDNAME B:/V	Makes a copy of the file OLDNAME on the active disk drive and places it on the disk in drive B as in the previous example. The /V parameter verifies the integrity of the data as it is copied. Although verification is rarely needed, you can use /V when you suspect copy problems, or in cases where you want to avoid the risk of data errors.
COPY B: MYWORDS.TXT A:	Makes a copy of the file MYWORDS.TXT, which is located on the disk in drive B, and copies it to the disk in drive A with the original filename, date, and time. The A: is optional, as the default (or active) disk drive is assumed by DOS.
COPY OLDNAME B:NEWNAME	Makes a copy of the file OLDNAME, which is located in the active disk drive, and places it on the disk in drive B with the filename NEWNAME.
COPY STUFF.TXT+ THINGS.TXT COMBO.TXT	Combines the files STUFF.TXT plus THINGS.TXT into a new file named COMBO.TXT. The new file COMBO.TXT is given the current date and time. You can concatenate several files this way.
COPY FIRST+ SECOND+THIRD+ FOURTH	Adds (sometimes called appends) the named files to the end of the first file. The result is copied to the FIRST file.
COPY OLDNAME+,,	Updates the date and time to the file OLDNAME, which is located in the active disk drive.
COPY *.TXT ALL.TXT	Copies all files having the .TXT extension into one file named ALL.TXT.
COPY *.TXT+*.LTR LTR&TXT.ALL	Copies all files having the .TXT and .LTR extensions into one file named LTR&TXT.ALL.
COPY HANDY.TXT+ *.TXT	Adds all files (except HANDY.TXT itself) having the .TXT extension to the end of the file HANDY.TXT.
COPY TEXT.ONE+ B:PROG.COM/B+ B:TEXT.TWO/A COMBO.A&B	Combines ASCII (standard text) and binary (program) files into a single file named COMBO.A&B. Notice that three files are combined: TEXT.ONE, which is an ASCII file located on the default disk; PROG.COM, which is a binary

file located on the disk in drive B; and TEXT.TWO, which is another ASCII file located on the disk in drive B. The "/B" and "/A" parameters let you combine binary and ASCII file types. When either /B or /A are used, they apply to the previous file and all following files until another /B or /A is encountered. Dissimilar file types (ASCII and binary) cannot be combined without using the /A or /B parameter.

COPY CON: NEWNAME (typed text) Ctrl-Z	This combination of two or more lines copies what is typed on the screen (or console) to the named file. The last character must be a Ctrl-Z (or F6), which is recognized by DOS as an end-of-file marker. Each line in the typed file is completed by pressing the Return key.
COPY CON: LPT1:	Copies the contents of the screen to your parallel printer.
COPY FILE1 CON:	Copies (or displays) FILE1 to the screen.
COPY LETTER.ONE NUL:	Used for testing. NUL is a dummy device name.

DOS versions 2.00 and later:

COPY \PATH1\ LETTER.ONE \PATH2	Makes a copy of the file LETTER.ONE in directory PATH1 on the active disk drive and places it in directory PATH2. The copy retains the original name, date, and time information.
COPY *.* \TEXT	Copies all files in the active directory to the directory having the pathname TEXT. You can substitute a period for the *.*. The period represents all filenames in the current path. If you use a double period, all files in the parent directory are copied.
COPY *.* \	Copies all files in the active directory to the parent directory.

APPLICATIONS

The many forms of the COPY command allow a substantial amount of flexibility in copying and combining files on the same disk or from one disk to another. In addition to copying, using reserved device names with the COPY command lets you create, display, and print files. The NUL device name lets you test COPY command operations. Finally, the /A and /B (ASCII and binary) parameters let you combine dissimilar files. All of these functions offer you an extensive repertoire of file-handling utilities.

TYPICAL OPERATION

In this activity you use the COPY command to create, copy, and combine files. Begin at the DOS prompt. If you are using a hard disk system with a single floppy drive, substitute drive A for B in the following procedure.

1. Place a formatted scratch disk in drive B and close the load lever.
2. Type **COPY CON: B:FILE1** and press **Return**.
3. Type the following text, ending each line with **Return**. Press **Ctrl-Z** and then press **Return** on the last line to obtain the ^Z character.

```
This is file number one.
It contains three lines.
This is the last line.
^Z
```

4. Type **COPY B:FILE1 CON:** and press **Return**; notice that your new file is displayed on the console (screen) similar to the following.

```
A:\>COPY B:FILE1 CON:
This is file number one.
It contains three lines.
This is the last one.
        1 file(s) copied

A:\>
```

5. Type **COPY B:FILE1 B:FILE2** and press **Return**.
6. Type **DIR B:FILE*** and press **Return** to display a directory of your newly created files. Your display should resemble the following.

```
A:\>DIR B:FILE*

 Volume in drive B has no label
 Volume Serial Number is 3168-16D4
 Directory of B:\

FILE1                  75 02-26-91   5:40p
FILE2                  75 02-26-91   5:40p
        2 file(s)          150 bytes
                       1456128 bytes free

A:\>
```

7. Type **COPY B:FILE1+B:FILE2 B:FILE3** and press **Return**.

8. Type **COPY B:FILE3 CON:** and press **Return**; notice that your new combined file is displayed on the console (screen).

```
A:\>COPY B:FILE3 CON:
This is file number one.
It contains three lines.
This is the last one.
This is file number one.
It contains three lines.
This is the last one.
        1 file(s) copied

A:\>
```

9. Type **DIR B:FILE*** and press **Return** to display a directory of your newly created files. Your display should resemble:

```
A:\>DIR B:FILE*

 Volume in drive B has no label
 Volume Serial Number is 3168-16D4
 Directory of B:\

FILE1                75 02-26-91   5:40p
FILE2                75 02-26-91   5:40p
FILE3               151 02-26-91   5:43p
        3 file(s)         301 bytes
                      1455616 bytes free

A:\>
```

10. To preserve disk space, you can delete your experimental files by typing **DEL B:FILE*** and pressing **Return**.
11. Turn to Module 21 to continue the learning sequence.

This did not work as wanted

C:DOS\>	CD\	change directory to C:
C:\>	~~copy~~ ~~MKDIR(MD)~~ MKDIR TEMP	Make directory called temp on Hard drive
C:\>	copy A:*.* TEMP	Copy disk A everything to temp file on C
C:\>	copy Temp*.* A	Copy Temp file on C everything to file A
C:\>	Del Temp*.*	Delete temp file everything
C:\>	RMDIR TEMP	Remove Directory Called temp

Module 16
CTTY (2.00+)

DESCRIPTION

The CTTY command is an internal command that is available on DOS versions 2.00 and later. This command reassigns control of your keyboard and screen (console) devices to a communications port, such as COM1 or COM2. For example, if you have a remote terminal and wish to take control of your computer through your serial communications port (COM1), you can use the CTTY command. Although the command form is shown below, do not type it unless you have a terminal connected. Otherwise you will lose control of your computer and have to turn the power off and back on again to regain control.

The command form to reassign console control to a device attached to your serial communications port is

```
CTTY COM1
```

To reassign control back to your computer, you can type CTTY CON and press Return at the terminal.

APPLICATIONS

The CTTY command is superb for assigning control to remote devices. In fact, you can control your computer by telephone if you have a computer and communications equipment. The following diagram illustrates a typical setup for remote control.

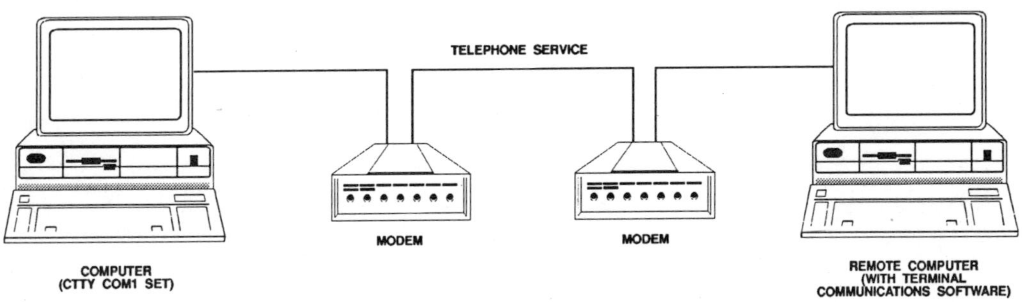

TYPICAL OPERATION

Because the CTTY command requires an auxiliary control device, a practice activity is not provided. Turn to Module 7 to continue the learning sequence.

Module 17
DATE (1.00+)

DESCRIPTION

The DATE command is an internal DOS command; therefore, you do not see the DATE command file when a directory of your DOS files is displayed. The DATE command is run automatically when you insert the DOS disk and turn on your computer. You can also run the DATE command by typing DATE and pressing Return from the DOS prompt. In either case, a screen similar to the following is displayed.

```
A:\>DATE
Current date is Tue 02-26-1991
Enter new date (mm-dd-yy):
```

Respond by typing the date notation for the national language in use. For example, if you are configured for the U.S., type the current month, day, and year in the form 09-01-90 or 10/21/91 and press Return. The date is recorded by DOS. If the date is not important to you, you can respond to the DATE prompt simply by pressing Return.

You can also enter the date by typing DATE followed by the proper date. This inputs the date on a single line without displaying the date prompt.

APPLICATIONS

Why enter the date when it is so much easier simply to press the Return key? There is a valid reason. When you enter the current date, files that are saved to disk are tagged with the current date. This lets you examine a directory to determine which files are most current.

There are a number of programs that use the system date to tag files and display calendar information. Although it may seem like a lot of trouble to enter the date, it is recommended for these reasons.

If entering the date becomes a nuisance, you can buy a clock-calendar option board to eliminate the need to type the date and time every time you turn on your computer. These boards use a battery to maintain clock and calendar operation, even when the computer is turned off or disconnected from a power source.

TYPICAL OPERATION

In this "hands-on" activity you use the DATE command to enter the current date. Check to see that your computer is properly connected and that a DOS diskette is inserted in drive A. If you have a fixed disk system equipped with a clock-calendar option, by-pass the option by booting from a floppy diskette.

1. If your computer is turned on and the DOS prompt is displayed, go to step 3 below. Otherwise, insert your DOS disk and turn on your computer.

NOTE

In the following step, you normally respond to the DATE and TIME prompts at system turn-on. However, to illustrate use of the DATE prompt by itself, ignore these prompts for the time being.

2. Press **Return** twice in response to the DATE and TIME prompts. The DOS prompt is now displayed.
3. Type **DATE** and press **Return**; notice the DATE prompt.

```
A:\>DATE
Current date is Tue 02-26-1991
Enter new date (mm-dd-yy):
```

4. Type the current date in the indicated form (separate day, month, year with hyphens or slashes) and press **Return**.
5. The current date is now recorded. To verify the current date, you can repeat step 3 above. If you do not want to change the date, press Return to redisplay the DOS prompt. Pressing Return leaves the system date unchanged.
6. Turn to Module 60 to continue the learning sequence.

Module 18
DEBUG (1.00+)

DESCRIPTION

The DEBUG program is a programmer's diagnostic utility that is available on all versions of DOS. However, versions 2.00 and later added several DEBUG enhancements including the Assemble option. DOS 5.00 added four new DEBUG commands dealing with expanded memory.

In this module, you are introduced to the DEBUG program and some of its common options. In fact, just so you know how to use it, you can follow along with the examples to see how they work. However, because DEBUG is primarily an assembly language programmer's tool, no attempt is made to provide examples for every DEBUG option. Also, if you are not an assembly language programmer and are not familiar with the 8086/8088 microprocessor architecture and its instruction set, many of the options will have no meaning to you.

STARTING DEBUG To start DEBUG, be sure that the DEBUG program is available on one of your disks. Some versions of DOS place DEBUG and LINK on a Supplemental Program disk, while others place it on the same disk as other DOS utilities. Assuming the DEBUG program is in the default drive, you can start DEBUG by typing

```
DEBUG filename
```

DEBUG OPTIONS A list of DEBUG options and descriptions follows. You can use this list for quick reference. The spacing used between DEBUG commands may vary with personal preference. The commands:

```
d cs:100 200
d,cs:100,200
dcs:100 200
```

are the same. Spaces or commas are required between two hexadecimal values.

Option	*Description*
Address	Entering a memory address (a one- to four-character number) moves DEBUG's pointer to that memory location, where subsequent options take effect. `1D3`
Assemble	Assembles assembler statements directly into memory beginning at the specified memory address. `A100`
Compare	Compares the contents of two specified ranges (or lists) of memory beginning at two designated memory addresses. `C 1C4L10 3AF` Compares 16 bytes beginning at addresses 1C4 and 3AF

Dump	Displays up to 128 continuous bytes of memory beginning at the specified memory address. The display is in hexadecimal and ASCII. If no address is specified, it displays the memory contents beginning at the present memory location.
	`D (Display the next block of memory.)`
	`D100 (Display a block of memory beginning at 0100.)`
	`D210 218 (Display the memory contents from memory addresses 210 to 218.)`

Enter	Exchanges the current memory contents with what you enter from your keyboard. `E100` Pressing Spacebar lets you jump to the next memory address to continue examining or entering memory contents. Pressing Return ends the Enter operation. Pressing - backs up to the preceding address.

Fill	Fills the specified memory addresses with the designated list of values.
	`F 100 L 3 41 42 43`
	`F 100 L 3 "ABC"`
	Either of the preceding examples places the three hexadecimal values for A, B, and C (41, 42, and 43) in memory addresses 100, 101, and 102. The "*L 3*" designates a list of 3 bytes.

Go	Causes the program in memory to execute. It is used by programmers to test their programs before they save them to disk.
	`G`
	`G=15B`
	`G=1CA 23F`

Option	*Description*
Go (cont.)	The first example executes the program beginning at the present location (determined by the contents of the 8086/8088 CS and IP registers). The second example begins program execution at memory address 15B. The third example shows a program breakpoint at memory address 23F. Up to 10 breakpoints can be used. The message "Program terminated normally" is displayed when program execution is finished.

Hexarithmetic	Adds two hexadecimal values and then subtracts the second value from the first.
	`H 03 0A`
	`1D 07`
	The sum and difference are shown on the second line.

Input	Inputs and displays the hexadecimal value found at the specified port.
	`I 2F8`
	`5F`

Load	Loads a file or specified diskette sectors into the designated memory address.
	`L 200`
	
	`N filename`
	`L`
	
	`L 100 0 00 0F`
	The first example loads the file named at DEBUG start-up beginning at memory address 200. The second example shows how the Name option is used to first specify a filename before the Load option is used. If no memory address is specified, the file loads at memory address 100. The last example loads data beginning at memory address 100 from the disk in drive A (0 is A, 1 is B, and so on). Sectors 00 through 0F (the first 15 sectors) are loaded.

Move	Moves (or copies) the contents of a range of memory addresses to another specified memory address. The source data remains intact unless it is part of the destination range. `M 2AF 2BC 300` Moves the contents of memory addresses 2AF through 2BC to 300 through 30A.
Name	Establishes a filename for Load and Write operations if a filename was not used when DEBUG was started. `N filename`
Output	Sends a byte to the specified output port. `O 2F8 15` Sends a 0E to the port corresponding to 2F8.

Option	*Description*
Proceed	Executes a loop, a subroutine call, a repeating string, or a software interrupt. You supply the address and number of instructions to execute. Upon completion, control returns to Debug. The loop number default is 1. When PROCEED transfers control to the loaded program, it runs until the loop, repeated string instruction, software interrupt, or subroutine call (at the specified address) is completed, or until the specified number of machine instructions have executed. `P=121F 2` Debug uses the program's CS register if an address (121F in the example) is not specified. The address is always preceded by an equal sign, which prevents it from being interpreted as a loop number. PROCEED cannot be used to trace through ROM.
Quit	Quits the DEBUG program without saving any changes. `Q`

Register	Displays the contents of the registers of your microprocessor, where registers are `AX BX CX DX SP BP SI DI DS ES SS CS IP PC F`
	`R`
	`R AX`
	`R F`
	The first example displays all registers. The second displays the contents of the AX register. You can change it by entering a new value from the keyboard. The last example displays the flag settings, which follow:

Flag	*Set*	*Clear*
Overflow (yes/no)	OV	NV
Direction (decrement/increment)	DN	UP
Interrupt (enable/disable)	EI	DI
Sign (negative/positive)	NG	PL
Zero (yes/no)	ZR	NZ
Auxiliary carry (yes/no)	AC	NA
Parity (even/odd)	PE	PO
Carry (yes/no)	CY	NC

The eight flags are displayed in either the set or clear position as indicated by the set or clear designation. To change a flag, enter the set or clear values to be changed in the reverse (right to left) order. For example, say your display is OV DN EI NG ZR AC PE CY and you want to change OV to NV, DN to UP, and PE to PO. Your entry, which follows the dash, is

```
OV DN EI NG ZR AC PE CY - POUPNV
```

Option	*Description*
Register (cont.)	This sets the flags as follows: `NV UP EI NG ZR AC PO CY`

Search	Lets you find a specific character string within a designated range of memory addresses.
	`S CS:100 300 OA OD`
	`S CS:100 300 "Hello"`
	The first example searches for the sequence 0A 0D in the range 100 through 300. The second searches the range for the hexadecimal equivalent of the ASCII string Hello.

Trace	Executes program instructions at a specified memory address or for a specified value.
	`T`
	`T 10`
	`T=210 10`
	The first example executes the value contained in IP. The second executes 16 instructions beginning at CS:IP. The last example executes 16 instructions beginning at memory address 210.

Unassemble	Unassembles (or converts) the memory contents into assembler statements, displaying memory addresses and values.
	`U`
	`U 200`
	`U 200 208`
	`U 200 L 8`
	The first example unassembles 32 bytes of memory (16 bytes in the 40-column mode). The second example begins unassembly at memory addresses 200. The last two examples perform identical tasks. They unassemble memory addresses beginning at 200 and ending at 208.

Write	Writes all or a portion of the debugged data to disk.
	`W`
	`W 180`
	`W 180 1 100 0F`

Option	*Description*
Write (cont.)	The first example writes the entire debugged file to disk. The second writes the debugged file to disk beginning at memory address 180. The last example writes the debugged file, beginning at memory address 180, to 16 (0F) sectors of the disk in drive B (1) beginning at the 256th (100) disk sector.
XA (Allocate Expanded Memory)	Allocates a specified number of 16K pages to expanded memory. This command returns a hexadecimal number that corresponds to the handle created by the command. If insufficient memory exists, an error message is displayed. `XA 4` Allocates 4 16K pages of expanded memory.
XD (Deallocate Expanded Memory)	Removes a specified logical page from expanded memory. `XD 0002` Removes logical page 0002 (the handle name) from expanded memory.
XM (Map Expanded Memory Pages)	This command maps an expanded memory page specified by XA to a physical page within expanded memory. You must specify the number of the logical page, the number of the physical page to which the logical page is to be mapped, and the handle number (returned by XA). `XM 3 2 0002` Maps logical page 3 having the handle 0002 to physical page 2.
XS (Display Expanded Memory Status)	Displays handles and physical pages that have been allocated in expanded memory. `XS`

SAMPLE SESSIONS WITH DEBUG You can experience some hands-on fun with DEBUG by following the two sample sessions in the Typical Operation section of this module. The first lets you experiment with the Dump, Enter, Write, and Quit options. The second lets you experiment with the Assemble, Register, and Name options in addition to the ones used in the first session.

APPLICATIONS

The DEBUG program is used by programmers to find program errors, to write small assembly language programs in object form, and to perform a host of other programming tasks. If you are not a programmer, you may rarely use DEBUG. However, even nonprogrammers often perform some light program maintenance and modifications with the DEBUG utility. However, be cautious when using DEBUG, because it is easy to modify program contents (which may render a program useless). Be sure you have a backup disk before attempting to use the DEBUG program on a valuable piece of software.

TYPICAL OPERATION

In this activity you use the DEBUG program to experiment with a number of commonly used options. If you are not inclined to be a programmer, don't worry. The procedures provided take you step-by-step through DEBUG so you can sample some of its functions. The second session requires DOS versions 2.00 or later.

DEBUG Session One Go ahead and create a sample file with EDLIN as follows:

1. Type **EDLIN TEST** and press **Return**.
2. Type **i** to insert some text and press **Return**.
3. Type the following text, ending each line with **Return**. Do not type the line numbers and colons.

```
1: This is a test file that is being created with EDLIN.
2: It will be displayed, modified, and saved using DEBUG.
3:
```

4. Press **Ctrl-C** to end text entry.
5. Type **e** and press **Return** to save the file and exit EDLIN.
6. Now that you have a sample file, use DEBUG to display the file by typing **DEBUG TEST** and pressing **Return**.
7. Notice that DEBUG's prompt is a dash. Type **D** and press **Return** to dump (or display) your TEST file in both hexadecimal and decimal notation. Notice a display similar the following screen illustration.

```
A:\>DEBUG TEST
-D
135C:0100  54 68 69 73 20 69 73 20-61 20 74 65 73 74 20 66   This is a test f
135C:0110  69 6C 65 20 74 68 61 74-20 69 73 20 62 65 69 6E   ile that is bein
135C:0120  67 20 63 72 65 61 74 65-64 20 77 69 74 68 20 45   g created with E
135C:0130  44 4C 49 4E 2E 0D 0A 49-74 20 77 69 6C 6C 20 62   DLIN...It will b
135C:0140  65 20 64 69 73 70 6C 61-79 65 64 2C 20 6D 6F 64   e displayed, mod
135C:0150  69 66 69 65 64 2C 20 61-6E 64 20 73 61 76 65 64   ified, and saved
135C:0160  20 75 73 69 6E 67 20 44-45 42 55 47 2E 0D 0A 1A    using DEBUG....
135C:0170  F6 06 02 0E 20 74 35 FF-76 12 FF 76 10 FF 76 0E   .... t5.v..v..v.
-
```

8. To enter characters with DEBUG, you can type e followed by the memory address. Go ahead and type **e100** and press **Return**. Notice that the contents of memory location 100 (the first byte following 0100 on the top line) are displayed, followed by the cursor.

```
-e100
135C:0100  54.
```

9. Type the following values (hexadecimal) and then press **Spacebar** after each. Press **Return** after "36."

   `30 31 32 33 34 35 36`

   The current value is replaced with the one you type; Spacebar moves you to the next memory location. Pressing Return completes the exchange function and returns you to the DEBUG prompt. Your screen should resemble the following illustration when you have finished entering the above values.

```
-e100
135C:0100  54.30   68.31   69.32   73.33   20.34   69.35   73.36
-
```

10. Type **d100** and press **Return** to display the changes just made. Notice the following display:

```
-d100
135C:0100  30 31 32 33 34 35 36 20-61 20 74 65 73 74 20 66   0123456 a test f
135C:0110  69 6C 65 20 74 68 61 74-20 69 73 20 62 65 69 6E   ile that is bein
135C:0120  67 20 63 72 65 61 74 65-64 20 77 69 74 68 20 45   g created with E
135C:0130  44 4C 49 4E 2E 0D 0A 49-74 20 77 69 6C 6C 20 62   DLIN...It will b
135C:0140  65 20 64 69 73 70 6C 61-79 65 64 2C 20 6D 6F 64   e displayed, mod
135C:0150  69 66 69 65 64 2C 20 61-6E 64 20 73 61 76 65 64   ified, and saved
135C:0160  20 75 73 69 6E 67 20 44-45 42 55 47 2E 0D 0A 1A    using DEBUG....
135C:0170  F6 06 02 0E 20 74 35 FF-76 12 FF 76 10 FF 76 0E   .... t5.v..v..v.
-
```

11. Write the changed file to disk by typing **w** and pressing **Return**. Notice that DEBUG displays the message.

```
-w
Writing 00070 bytes
-
```

12. Type **q** and press **Return** to quit.

DEBUG Session Two You must have DOS version 2.00 or later to perform this session. In this session, you start DEBUG without a filename. You then use DEBUG to perform a number of tasks. These include using the:

- Register option to display the microprocessor registers.
- Assemble option to write a small assembly language program that displays your name on the screen.
- Enter option to enter your name into the program.
- Name option to name the program.
- Register option to set the file length.
- Write option to save the file to disk.
- Quit option to exit DEBUG.

Once the program is saved, you can run it to display your name. Go ahead and use the following procedure to explore more DEBUG capabilities.

1. Type **DEBUG** and press **Return**.
2. Type **r** and press **Return**; notice the register display.

```
A:\>DEBUG
-r
AX=0000  BX=0000  CX=0000  DX=0000  SP=FFEE  BP=0000  SI=0000  DI=0000
DS=135C  ES=135C  SS=135C  CS=135C  IP=0100   NV UP EI PL NZ NA PO NC
135C:0100 F646F802       TEST    BYTE PTR [BP-08],02                SS:FFF8=7F
-
```

3. Type **a** for Assemble, press **Return**, and type the following assembler statements, ending each line with **Return**. Press **Return** twice after the last line. Do not type the remarks.

```
What You Type           Remarks
-a
push cs         Specifies code segment (where DOS loads this program).
pop ds          Loads data at the same location.
mov ax, 900     Puts display function (09) into AX, 00 into AL.
mov dx, 112     Moves data beginning at address 112 into register DX.
int 21          Calls DOS interrupt vector 21 (DOS function call).
int 20          Calls DOS interrupt vector 20 (DOS program exit call).
```

Your screen looks like the following:

```
-a
135C:0100 push cs
135C:0101 pop ds
135C:0102 mov ax, 900
135C:0105 mov dx, 112
135C:0108 int 21
135C:010A int 20
135C:010C
-
```

4. Type **e 112 'your name$'**, where *your name* is actually your name; be sure to end your name with a $ and press **Return**. The entire string should be in single quotes similar to the following:

   ```
   e 112 'Barney Barnyard$'
   ```

5. Type **n myprog.com** and press **Return** to name the program.
6. Type **r cx** and press **Return**; notice the following display:

   ```
   -r cx
   CX 0000
   :
   ```

7. Type **100** to specify a 100-byte program length and press **Return.**
8. Type **w** and press **Return** to write the program to disk; notice the "Writing 0100 bytes" message.
9. Type **q** and press **Return** to quit; the DOS prompt is displayed.
10. Type **MYPROG** and press **Return** to run your new assembly language program.
11. This completes the DEBUG practice activity. If you wish, you can delete the new practice files from your disk to preserve disk space.
12. Turn to Module 39 to continue the learning sequence.

Module 19
DIRECTORY COMMANDS (DIR, MKDIR, RMDIR, CHDIR, DIRCMD)

DESCRIPTION

A directory is a list of filenames that is automatically displayed on the screen when you type DIR and press Return from the system prompt. The DIR command is an internal DOS command. In DOS versions beginning with 2.00, multiple disk directories allow directory subdivisions. This feature lets you group common files into separate directories. This is similar to subdividing information into file cabinet drawers and file folders. This is particularly convenient when you use a fixed disk containing hundreds of files. Instead of listing all files in one directory, you can list files in smaller, more manageable subdirectories. The following commands, which are explained later in this section, became available with the introduction of DOS 2.00.

Command	*Purpose*
MKDIR or MD	Make a new directory
CHDIR or CD	Change to another directory
RMDIR or RD	Remove (or delete) a directory from the disk

Each subdirectory is assigned a unique pathname. Therefore, you might create a word processing pathname, a database manager pathname, a spreadsheet pathname, and so on. More about pathnames later in this section.

In addition to pathnames, DOS version 2.00 introduced the ability to assign a volume name to different disks. Module 67 describes the VOLUME command and provides information about the use and purpose of volume names.

FORMS OF THE DIRECTORY COMMAND There are many forms of the DIR command. Each form is described in the following list.

All DOS versions:

DIR	Lists a directory of the disk located in the active (or logged) disk drive (disk A if the A> prompt is displayed, B if the B> prompt is displayed, and so on).
DIR D:	Lists a directory of the specified disk D:.

DIR /P or DIR D:/P	Pauses the directory listing when the screen is full. Press any key to see the next screen load of filenames. Typing DIR ¦MORE achieves a similar result.
DIR /W or DIR D:/W	Displays a wide directory; omits file size, date, and time information.
DIR *filename.ext*	Displays the specified filename; used to verify the presence of a file on the logged or specified disk.
DIR *filename.** or DIR filename.???	Displays a directory of all files having the same filename with different extensions.
DIR *.*ext* or DIR ????????.ext	Displays a directory of all filenames having the specified extension.

DOS versions beginning with 2.00:

DIR \pathname or DIR D:\pathname	Displays a directory of all filenames within the specified subdirectory (pathname).
DIR \pathname\filename	Displays a directory of the specified filename within the specified pathname.
DIR \pathname\pathname	Displays a directory of the second-tier subdirectory. (Subdirectories can have subordinate directories of their own. This is called branching.)
DIR .. or DIR \	Displays a parent directory from a subdirectory.

DOS version 5.00:

DOS 5.00 introduced a number of new DIR parameters which are summarized in the following list. In addition to the new parameters, DOS 5.00 also displays the number of bytes contained in the files in the listed directory. Prior DOS versions only displayed the number of files in the listed directory.

DIR/A:*attribute* — Displays files having certain file attributes, where *attribute* is one of the following:

h	hidden files
-h	nonhidden files
s	system files
-s	nonsystem files
d	directory names
-d	files only (no directory names)
a	files that need archiving (backup)
-a	files that have been archived
r	read-only files
-r	files that are not read-only

DIR /A:r-h — Displays read-only files that are not hidden.

DIR /B	Displays a bare filename listing without size, date, and time information.
DIR /L	Displays file information in lowercase.
DIR /O:*sortorder*	Specifies sort order by name, extension, date, or file size, where *sortorder* is: n alphabetical by name (default value if no sort order is specified) -n descending alphabetical order by name e alphabetical by extension -e descending alphabetical order by extension d date and time order (earliest first) -d date and time order (most recent first) s file size (smallest first) -s file size (largest first) g directories grouped before files (default) -g directories grouped after files
DIR: /O:-d/p	Sorts the directory with the most recently saved files listed first. The /p pauses the directory display.
DIR /O:e-s	Displays files by extension and then by file size.
DIR /S	Displays all files in all subdirectories.

THE SET DIRCMD COMMAND If you are using DOS 5.00, you can place the following line in your AUTOEXEC.BAT file or enter it directly from the DOS prompt to preset DIR command parameters. For example, the command line *SET DIRCMD /o:-gn/p* results in paused directories that are sorted by filename with directory names grouped at the end of the listing.

PAUSING AND RESTARTING A DIRECTORY DISPLAY In addition to the /P parameter with the DIR command, there are two other ways to pause the directory display. First, you can press Ctrl-S or the Pause key, which stops the directory display in its tracks. Press any key to resume the display. If you are using DOS version 2.00 or later, you can pause the display with the MORE filter. This is done by typing DIR ¦MORE. Pausing the display is often necessary when the directory listing exceeds the number of lines on your screen.

SORTING YOUR DIRECTORY ALPHABETICALLY If you are using DOS 5.00, you can use the /n parameter to sort your directory display. A handy tool introduced in DOS version 2.00 and present in all versions of DOS is the SORT filter. If you have DOS 4.01 or earlier, you can use SORT with the directory command to arrange the directory listing in alphabetical order. This makes it easier to locate specific filenames. The command for sorting your directory is

```
DIR ¦SORT
```

If you wish to sort the directory into a file, use DIR ¦SORT > filename. You direct the sorted directory to your printer with DIR ¦SORT > PRN (or LPT1, as appropriate).

SUBDIRECTORIES If you are using DOS version 2.00 or later, imagine your directory structure in the shape of a tree. There is a main directory (the root) and subdirectories (the branches). This relationship is often referred to as parent and children directories. The following illustration shows a typical directory structure:

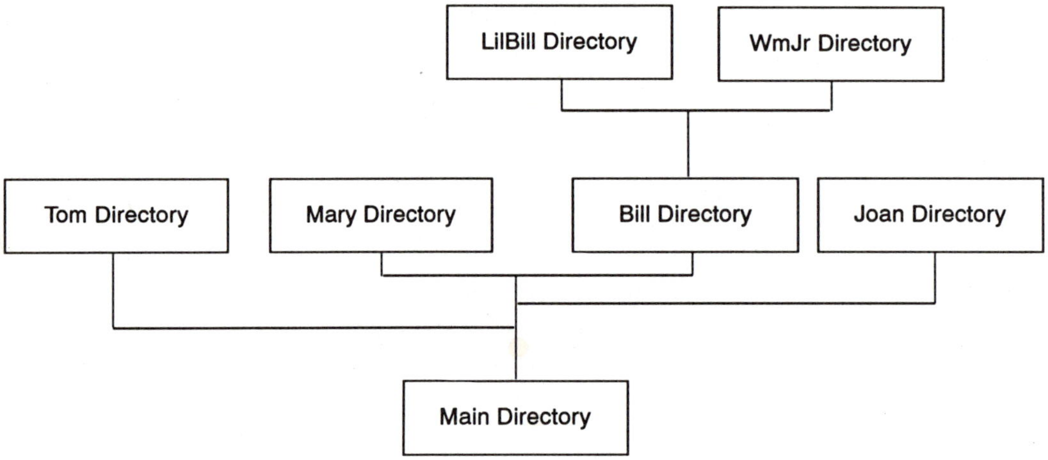

Notice that the Bill directory has two subdirectories. Therefore, Bill is a parent to LilBill and WmJr. Both LilBill and WmJr can have subdirectories, or children, if desired. Once directories are created with the MKDIR (or MD) command, you can move in and out of the directories with the CHDIR (or CD) command. You can remove directories with the RMDIR (or RD) command. These three commands are described in the following paragraphs.

The MKDIR Command The MKDIR (or MD) command is used to make (or create) a new subdirectory that is subordinate to the currently logged directory. To make a subdirectory having the pathname WP (for word processing), log your root directory, type MKDIR WP, and press Return. You may prefer the short form of this command, which is MD.

If you list a directory of the disk containing your new WP subdirectory, the subdirectory listing is displayed:

```
WP     <DIR>     6-07-88   11:25p
```

The CHDIR Command The CHDIR (or CD) command is used to change from one directory to another. If you are in the main directory and wish to move down to the BILL directory, type CD BILL and press Return.

To move to WMJR (one level down), use CD WMJR or CD\BILL\WMJR. To move back up to the parent (one directory level up), type CD .. and press Return. To move to the root directory from any logged subdirectory, use CD\. You can move directly to any directory (or filepath) from another by including the complete pathname in your CD command. For example, the command CD\BILL\WMJR takes you directly to the \BILL\WMJR filepath from any logged location.

The RMDIR Command The RMDIR (or RD) command is used to remove a subdirectory. First you must delete all files within a subdirectory before it can be deleted. If necessary, you can copy the files you want to keep to another directory with the COPY command, and then delete them from the subdirectory to be deleted. To remove an empty subdirectory having the pathname WP, go to the directory level immediately above the one to be removed and type RD WP.

The following two lines are common to a subdirectory display.

```
.            <DIR>      02-26-91    3:50p
..           <DIR>      02-26-91    3:50p
        2 file(s)             0 bytes
                        1457152 bytes free

A:\>
```

The single dot represents the directory being listed, while the double dot indicates the parent directory. With some versions of DOS, you can list the parent directory by typing DIR .. and pressing Return. You can list the local directory by typing DIR . and pressing Return.

Regardless of the currently logged directory, you can view the files in another subdirectory by using a command like DIR \BILL\WMJR.

APPLICATIONS

The directory command is essential in knowing what files exist on a specified disk. In addition to listing filenames, the command tells you how many files are present and, in DOS 2.00 and later, tells you how much disk space remains.

In DOS 5.00, the number of bytes contained in the listed files is also displayed. This feature tells you whether or not the files in a hard disk directory will fit on a floppy disk.

The ability to create subdirectories lets you organize your files into logical groups. The subdirectory capability is especially helpful for large fixed disks capable of storing thousands of files.

TYPICAL OPERATION

In this activity you use the DIR command to view a disk directory in the conventional and wide form. The screen illustrations show characteristics of DOS versions later than 2.00, although the commands also apply to earlier DOS versions. Begin at the DOS prompt.

1. Type **DIR** and press **Return**; notice the following display.

```
A:\>DIR

 Volume in drive A has no label
 Volume Serial Number is 0F66-14F7
 Directory of A:\

COMMAND  COM     46246 12-13-90   4:09a
FORMAT   COM     32285 12-13-90   4:09a
UNDELETE EXE     13666 12-13-90   4:09a
DOSKEY   COM      5693 12-13-90   4:09a
HLPFILES     <DIR>     01-01-91  10:20a
MEM      EXE     22104 12-13-90   4:09a
SYS      COM     13200 12-13-90   4:09a
SMARTDRV SYS      8005 12-13-90   4:09a
HIMEM    SYS     11120 12-13-90   4:09a
DRIVER   SYS      5384 12-13-90   4:09a
ANSI     SYS      8868 12-13-90   4:09a
DISPLAY  SYS     15682 12-13-90   4:09a
CONFIG   SYS       165 02-21-91   9:42a
AUTOEXEC BAT       128 02-25-91   3:57p
       14 file(s)     182546 bytes
                       96256 bytes free

A:\>
```

2. Type **DIR /W** and press **Return**; notice the following display.

```
A:\>DIR /W

 Volume in drive A has no label
 Volume Serial Number is 0F66-14F7
 Directory of A:\

COMMAND.COM     FORMAT.COM      UNDELETE.EXE    DOSKEY.COM      [HLPFILES]
MEM.EXE         SYS.COM         SMARTDRV.SYS    HIMEM.SYS       DRIVER.SYS
ANSI.SYS        DISPLAY.SYS     CONFIG.SYS      AUTOEXEC.BAT
       14 file(s)     182546 bytes
                       96256 bytes free

A:\>
```

NOTE

If you have DOS 2.00 or later, perform the following steps. Otherwise, go to step 11.

3. Type **MKDIR FORFUN** and press **Return**.

4. Type **DIR** and press **Return** and notice that the FORFUN subdirectory is displayed.

```
A:\>DIR

 Volume in drive A has no label
 Volume Serial Number is 0F66-14F7
 Directory of A:\

FORFUN       <DIR>     02-26-91   3:53p
COMMAND  COM     46246 12-13-90   4:09a
FORMAT   COM     32285 12-13-90   4:09a
UNDELETE EXE     13666 12-13-90   4:09a
DOSKEY   COM      5693 12-13-90   4:09a
HLPFILES     <DIR>     01-01-91  10:20a
MEM      EXE     22104 12-13-90   4:09a
SYS      COM     13200 12-13-90   4:09a
SMARTDRV SYS      8005 12-13-90   4:09a
HIMEM    SYS     11120 12-13-90   4:09a
DRIVER   SYS      5384 12-13-90   4:09a
ANSI     SYS      8868 12-13-90   4:09a
DISPLAY  SYS     15682 12-13-90   4:09a
CONFIG   SYS       165 02-21-91   9:42a
AUTOEXEC BAT       128 02-25-91   3:57p
       15 file(s)     182546 bytes
                       95232 bytes free

A:\>
```

5. Type **CD FORFUN** and press **Return** to change directories.
6. Type **DIR** and press **Return**; notice the following display.

```
A:\FORFUN>DIR

 Volume in drive A has no label
 Volume Serial Number is 0F66-14F7
 Directory of A:\FORFUN

.            <DIR>     02-26-91   3:53p
..           <DIR>     02-26-91   3:53p
        2 file(s)          0 bytes
                       95232 bytes free

A:\FORFUN>
```

7. Type **CD ..** and press **Return**; you are now back in the original directory.
8. List a directory of the FORFUN subdirectory by typing **DIR FORFUN** and pressing **Return**. Notice the following display.

```
A:\>DIR FORFUN

 Volume in drive A has no label
 Volume Serial Number is 0F66-14F7
 Directory of A:\FORFUN

.            <DIR>      02-26-91   3:53p
..           <DIR>      02-26-91   3:53p
        2 file(s)            0 bytes
                         95232 bytes free

A:\>
```

9. Type **RD FORFUN** and press **Return**; you have just removed the FORFUN directory from your disk.
10. Verify that the **FORFUN** subdirectory is gone by listing the directory one last time.

NOTE

If you are using DOS 5.00, perform the following step.
Otherwise, proceed to step 12.

11. Type **DIR /o:-gn /p** and press **Return** to display a directory that is sorted by filename first and file directories last. The /p parameter pauses directories that exceed 24 lines. Notice that the number of files and bytes is displayed.
12. Turn to Module 61 to continue the learning sequence.

Module 20
DISKCOMP (1.00+)

DESCRIPTION

The DISKCOMP command is an external DOS command that compares the contents of two floppy disks to ensure they are identical. DISKCOMP is available on all versions of DOS.

The general form of the DISKCOMP command is

```
DISKCOMP A: B:
```

where the disk in drive A: is read first and then compared to the disk in drive B. You can control which disk is read first by using the appropriate disk drive designator A:, B:, C:, etc.

There are a few options available with the DISKCOMP command. You can add a /1 to the end of the command line in the form

```
DISKCOMP A: B:/1
```

to restrict the comparison to one side of a disk. You can add a /8 to the end of the command line in the form:

```
DISKCOMP A: B:/8
```

which allows you to compare only eight sectors per track, even if the disks contain nine sectors per track (as do versions of DOS later than 2.00).

After two disks are compared, the prompt "Compare more diskettes (Y/N)?" is displayed. Typing Y (for "yes") lets you compare another disk; typing N (for "no") redisplays the DOS prompt.

If you compare two dissimilar disks, DISKCOMP displays an error message similar to this:

```
A:\>DISKCOMP A: B:

Insert FIRST diskette in drive A:

Insert SECOND diskette in drive B:

Press any key when ready . . .

Compare error on side 1, track 34

Compare error on side 0, track 35

Compare error on side 1, track 35

Compare error on side 0, track 38


Compare another diskette (Y/N) ?
```

If you compare identical disks, the display resembles the following screen illustration:

```
A:\>DISKCOMP A: B:

Insert FIRST diskette in drive A:

Insert SECOND diskette in drive B:

Press any key when ready . . .

Comparing 40 tracks
9 sectors per track, 2 side(s)

Compare OK


Compare another diskette (Y/N) ?
```

If you use the COPY *.* command instead of DISKCOPY, the disks will not compare "ok." This is because the location of each file changes when files are copied individually.

APPLICATIONS

The most common use of DISKCOMP is to compare one or more copies of a master disk to that master to verify exact replication. This is the quickest way to ensure a good quality copy. If you suspect copy problems, you may wish to use DISKCOMP each time you make a disk copy just to be on the safe side.

TYPICAL OPERATION

In this activity you use the DISKCOPY command to make a copy of DOS and then the DISKCOMP command to verify that the copy is accurate. Begin at the DOS prompt.

NOTE

If you have a fixed disk system, you can use drive A and exchange diskettes as necessary to simulate a two removable disk system.

1. Place a scratch disk in drive B: and close the load lever.
2. Insert your DOS diskette in drive A. Then type **DISKCOPY A: B:** and press **Return**.
3. Type **DISKCOMP A: B:** and press **Return**; if your copy is good, you see the following display.

```
A:\>DISKCOMP A: B:

Insert FIRST diskette in drive A:

Insert SECOND diskette in drive B:

Press any key when ready . . .

Comparing 40 tracks
9 sectors per track, 2 side(s)

Compare OK


Compare another diskette (Y/N) ?
```

4. Type **N** to return to the system prompt.
5. Turn to Module 13 to continue the learning sequence.

Module 21
DISKCOPY (1.00+)

DESCRIPTION

The DISKCOPY command is an external command that is available with all versions of DOS. It makes a verbatim copy of one removable disk (the source disk) on another (the target disk). The involved diskettes must be of the same size and format for DISKCOPY to operate properly. Never specify a fixed disk with the DISKCOPY command. If the target disk is unformatted, DISKCOPY formats it for you during the copy operation.

The form of the DISKCOPY command is

```
DISKCOPY A: B:
```

where A: is the disk drive that contains the source disk (the disk being copied) and B: is the disk drive containing the target disk (the disk to which the copy is transferred).

The DISKCOPY command makes an exact replica of the source disk. If it is single sided or contains data errors, the resulting copy is single sided or contains data errors, also. If you only want to copy the first side of a disk, you can use the /1 parameter in the form:

```
DISKCOPY A: B:/1
```

When copying is complete, the prompt "Copy another (Y/N)?" is displayed. Typing N discontinues the DISKCOPY process and returns to the system prompt. Typing Y lets you repeat the DISKCOPY command, allowing you to make multiple copies of the source disk.

You should know that as files are created and modified, they begin to occupy available disk space in a random fashion. For example, when a file is first created and saved on a new disk, it occupies contiguous (or end-to-end) sectors. As other files are created and edited, they begin to occupy the disk's geography in a random, helter-skelter fashion.

After several reading, editing, and writing sessions, you may detect some degradation in file access time. If it reaches an annoying level, you may wish to copy the files to a new disk. You should use the COPY command to do this, rather than the DISKCOPY command. Why? Because the COPY command collects files one at a time and writes them in contiguous sectors to the target disk. DISKCOPY, on the other hand, simply copies everything in its original configuration, without regard to poor file organization.

NOTE

Here is the recommended way to recollect your scattered files into contiguous disk geography. First, format your target disk and place it in a target drive, such as B. Place your source disk in the source drive, such as A, and type COPY A:*.* B: and press Return.

APPLICATIONS

The DISKCOPY command is most often used to make working copies of new program disks or backup copies of disks containing important data files, programs, or both. The format feature of DISKCOPY saves valuable time. If you wish to make several copies of a disk, using DISKCOPY eliminates the need to use a two-step format/copy procedure.

TYPICAL OPERATION

In this activity you use the DISKCOPY command to make a copy of your DOS disk. Begin at the DOS prompt.

1. Place a new or used disk in drive B and close the load lever.

NOTE

In the following step, the disk in drive B is formatted. This destroys any files that may reside on the disk in drive B. If the disk to be formatted contains files, be sure that they are expendable. The DISKCOPY command erases these files.

2. Type **DISKCOPY A: B:** and press **Return** twice; notice that the red disk drive lights indicate read-write activity.
3. Type **N** in response to the "Copy another (Y/N)?" prompt. Notice that the system prompt is redisplayed.
4. Turn to Module 26 to continue the learning sequence.

Module 22
DOSKEY (5.00+)

DESCRIPTION

The DOSKEY command, introduced with DOS 5.00, is initiated by typing DOSKEY and pressing Return. This command stores all DOS commands typed from the DOS prompt into a *memory buffer*. Any commands in the buffer are recalled by using the Up or Down Arrow key to list each command in the order stored.

You can also load DOSKEY to operate in a variety of ways. Several special parameters are available to let you adjust the way DOSKEY reacts. There are also a number of special keys and text codes that give the DOSKEY program considerable flexibility. You can even create and store DOSKEY macros. A macro is a series of keystrokes (or commands) that are played when an assigned name or keystroke is entered.

DOSKEY PARAMETERS Following is a list and corresponding descriptions of DOSKEY parameters (or "switches").

DOSKEY /INSERT	Puts DOSKEY in the insert mode. This lets you insert text within the body of a displayed command. You can press Ins to temporarily activate the overstrike mode.
DOSKEY /OVERSTRIKE	Puts DOSKEY in the overstrike mode. This strikes over text within the body of a displayed command. You can press Ins to temporarily activate the insert mode.
DOSKEY /REINSTALL	Installs a new copy of DOSKEY, replacing the loaded program and its command buffer.
DOSKEY /BUFSIZE=n	Sets the size of the command buffer to n characters; the default value is 3,000 characters.
DOSKEY /MACROS	Displays stored macros. You can combine this parameter with a DOS pipe to redirect a macro to a batch file. (DOSKEY /MACROS > DOIT.BAT)
DOSKEY /HISTORY	Displays all commands presently in the DOSKEY buffer. You can use /HISTORY to write the stored commands to a batch file as with /MACROS by using the DOS pipe or DOSKEY's $G code, which performs the pipe operation.

DOSKEY *macro=text* — Creates a macro, where *macro* is the name and *text* is the macro command text.

DOSKEY COMMAND KEYS The following list contains a series of DOSKEY command keys and corresponding descriptions.

Key	Description
Up/Down Arrow	Recall DOS commands; use Esc to clear the command line.
F7	Display a history of commands
Alt-F7	Clear the command history
F8	Search the command history
F9	Select a command by the number displayed using F7
Alt-F10	Clears all macro definitions

Special codes used with DOSKEY macro definitions:

Code	Description
$T	Separate commands to allow the use of multiple commands in a macro.
$1-$9	Substitution parameter that operate in the same way as %1-%9 in batch files.
$*	Uses commands you type following the macro text. Here, you may wish to add a DOS parameter or pipe.

PIPING You can use the DOS piping command (>) or $G to route saved DOSKEY commands to a designated file or to the printer. Step 7 of the activity in the Typical Operation section of this module makes use of a DOS pipe.

DOSKEY MACROS The DOSKEY macro feature lets you create a macro which stores a series of commands. Then you can recall the command by playing the macro. When you create a macro, give it the desired name. The name may be that of a DOS command that is used in the macro. The command may include special command parameters that you want issued each time you use that command. For example, you might use:

```
DOSKEY TYPE $1 $G FILE1.TXT
```

This command issues the TYPE command and the supplied filename ($1). The $G is the same as >, and the typed file is saved to FILE1.TXT. If you use multiple commands, you can separate them with $T (or $t). For example:

```
DOSKEY WPDIR=CD\WP $TDIR *.WPF ¦MORE
```

The preceding DOSKEY macro issues two commands. The first (CD\WP) changes directories. The second (DIR *.WPF ¦MORE) displays files in the WP directory, using MORE to pause each screen of information.

APPLICATIONS

Because DOSKEY saves frequently used keystrokes, it provides a fast way to reissue frequently used DOS commands. For example, if you are using a sequence of two or more commands, you can use DOSKEY to automatically recall each command without having to retype the entire command text.

The DOSKEY macro capability is excellent for combining frequently used commands. For example, if you want to see a sorted list of directory names, you might combine DIR with SORT, FIND, and MORE.

The DOSKEY command also provides a history, or audit trail, of your activities. You can always list your commands to see what you have done and how you did it.

TYPICAL OPERATION

In this activity you load the DOSKEY program, issue a series of DOS commands, and then display and replay several of the stored commands. Begin at the DOS prompt.

1. Type the following series of commands from the DOS prompt. End each command by pressing **Return**.

   ```
   DOSKEY /INSERT
   CD\
   DIR /P
   MEM /P
   ```

2. Press **Up Arrow** to see the previous command.
3. Type **F7** to display the list of DOS commands.
4. Type **F9 2** and press **Return** to reissue the stored DIR /P command.
5. Type **DOSKEY DX=CD\$tDIR /P** and press **Return** to store a macro named DX.
6. Type **DX** to play the macro.
7. Type **DOSKEY /MACROS > DR.BAT** to write the contents of the macro to the file DR.BAT.
8. Type **TYPE DR.BAT** and press **Return** to display the contents of the DR.BAT file.
9. Type **DEL DR.BAT** and press **Return** to delete the file.
10. Turn to Module 4 to continue the learning sequence.

Module 23
DOSSHELL (4.01+)

DESCRIPTION

The DOSSHELL program is a menu-driven file utility that performs a number of file management, program execution, and system status tasks. Introduced in DOS version 4.01 and simplified and enhanced in DOS 5.00, this program is intended to simplify user interaction with files and programs by displaying a series of simple menu screens. Once you understand the operating philosophy of DOSSHELL and learn its keystrokes, it becomes a convenient "shell" to DOS that lets you move between file directories, add programs to the DOSSHELL environment, and execute them from within the environment. You can also move in and out of the DOSSHELL environment with a few keystrokes.

This module covers the DOSSHELL program found in both DOS 4.01 and 5.00. The DOSSHELL found in DOS 5.00 is described first. If you have DOS 4.01, skip to the 4.01 DOSSHELL description.

DOS VERSION 5.00

STARTING DOSSHELL To start the DOSSHELL, you must have the following files on your DOS 5.00 disk.

DOSSHELL.COM
DOSSHELL.EXE
DOSSHELL.GRB
DOSSHELL.HLP
DOSSHELL.INI
DOSSHELL.VID
DOSSWAP.EXE

Start DOSSHELL by typing DOSSHELL and pressing Return. A screen similar to the following one is displayed.

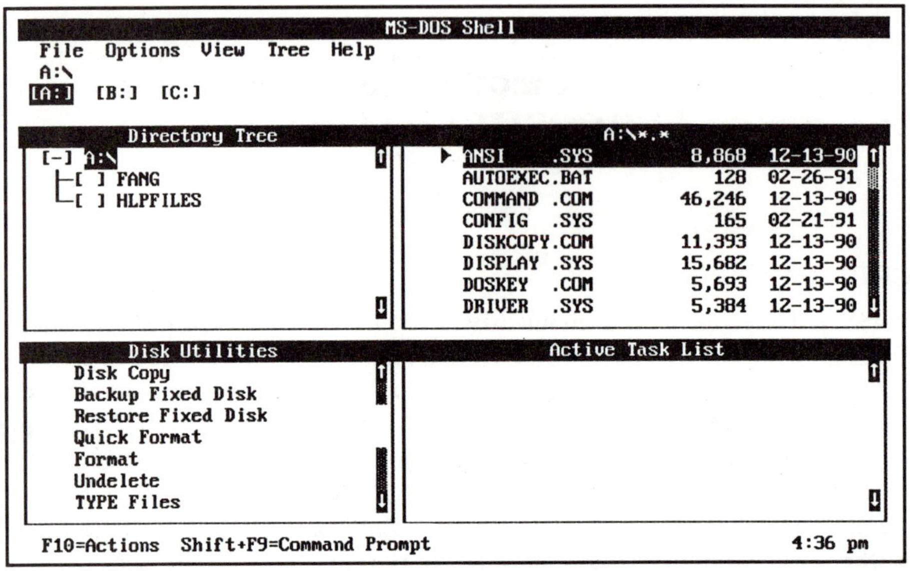

USING THE MENUS You can press F10 or the Alt key to highlight the File menu. Then move to the desired menu using the cursor keys or by typing the first letter of the name, such as V for View, to pull down the menu box. Finally, type the highlighted letter or point to the menu line using the cursor keys. If you have a mouse, you can pull down menus and make selections by pointing and clicking. Be sure to install your mouse before starting DOSSHELL.

Notice that a Help menu is also available. This menu provides information about how DOSSHELL works. You may want to browse the help information, although operation is fairly intuitive once you understand a few basics. These basics are provided in this module. If you have a mouse, you may wish to use it, as operations are quicker when one is used.

QUICK TOUR Before looking at all the menu selections, a quick tour will help you understand some of the benefits offered by DOSSHELL. The tour uses your keyboard. If you have a mouse, you may want to use it for selecting menus and commands. Begin at the DOS prompt.

1. Type **DOSSHELL** and press **Return**. The DOSSHELL windows are displayed like the ones shown in the preceding illustration.
2. Press **Alt-O** to see the Options menu. Type **D** to display the Screen Mode dialogue box. If you have an EGA or VGA display, pick *Graphics 25 lines*. Otherwise, leave the display set to *Text 25 lines*. Press **Tab** to move to "OK" and press **Return**.
3. Use the Tab key to move to the file list (C:*.*) window and use the cursor keys to highlight AUTOEXEC.BAT.

4. Tab to the Disk Utilities window and use the cursor keys to highlight [Main]. Press **Return** to open Main. A dialogue box appears, asking you for a file to edit. AUTOEXEC.BAT is displayed. Press **Return** to run the EDIT program and load the AUTOEXEC.BAT file.

   NOTE

   If the bottom left window displays MAIN instead of DISK UTILITIES, select Disk Utilities from the list and press Return.

5. Type **Alt-F X** to exit EDIT and return to DOSSHELL.
6. Type **Alt-O E** to enable the Task Switcher. This lets you run two or more programs at the same time and switch between them.
7. With Editor still highlighted, press **Return** twice to restart the EDIT program and reload AUTOEXEC.BAT.
8. Press **Ctrl-Esc** to switch back to DOSSHELL without exiting EDIT. Notice that "Editor" is displayed in the Active Task List window.
9. Tab to the Directory Tree window and highlight DOS (the directory name).
10. Tab to the file list (C:\DOS*.*) window, highlight QBASIC.EXE, press **Return**, and then press **Esc** to start the QuickBASIC program and display a blank edit window.
11. Press **Ctrl-Esc** to switch back to DOSSHELL. Notice that QBASIC.EXE and Editor are both listed in the Active Task List window. Now you can switch back and forth between these programs by picking them from the list and pressing Return.
12. Tab to the Active Task List, highlight Editor, and press **Return**.
13. Press **Alt F X** to exit the EDIT program. Notice that Editor is removed from the Active Task List; QBASIC.EXE still remains.
14. With QBASIC.EXE highlighted, press **Return** to return to the QuickBASIC program.
15. Type **Alt F X** and press any key to return to DOSSHELL. Notice that all active tasks are now closed.
16. Type **Alt F X** to exit DOSSHELL.

The preceding activity shows you one of the powerful features of DOSSHELL — the ability to switch between active tasks. The following paragraphs provide additional information about the menu selections available in DOSSHELL.

DOSSHELL MENUS Following is a description of the selections available in the DOSSHELL menus.

File — The File menu varies selections depending on the active window. If a file is selected, the selections include ones that work with the selected files. If an item in the Main menu is selected, File menu selections include operations that let you add, delete, or reorder utilities within the Main menu. File selection operations are listed first.

File-related selections:

Open — Run the selected file and any companion file if associated.

Run — Run the selected program file.

Print — Print the selected file to the connected printer.

Associate — Associate a file with a program; this causes the associated file to be used by the program when Run or Opened.

Search — Locate a file on the selected disk.

View File Contents (F9) — View the contents of the selected file. Press F9 to switch between an ASCII and Hex display. Esc to exit display.

Move (F7) — Move a file from its current location to a specified disk and/or directory.

Copy (F8) — Copy a file to a specified destination.

Delete (Del) — Delete the selected file; a confirmation prompt is displayed.

Rename — Change the name of a file or a directory. You cannot change directory names using conventional DOS commands.

Change Attributes — Change or assign new file attributes including hidden, system, archive, and read-only.

Create Directory — Select a parent directory in the directory list; use Create Directory to add a subdirectory.

Select/Deselect All — Select or deselect all files currently displayed in the file list.

Exit (Alt-F4) — Exit DOSSHELL returning to the DOS prompt.

File menu selections when a Main menu is selected:

New — Add a new selection (or group) to the Main menu list or add a program to one of the existing groups. Supply title, commands, start-up directory, shortcut keys, password, window title, information, a prompt, and the ability to use a selected file from the file list.

Open (Enter) — Start the selected application and any associated file or display the selections of the highlighted group.

Copy — Copy a selected program to a specified group. The steps are to select a program, pick Copy, pick the destination group, and press F2.

Delete (Del) — Delete a selected program or group from the Main menu list.

Properties — Modify the properties created with New, i.e., title, command string, start-up directory, etc.

Reorder — Move a program or group to another location in the displayed group or program list.

Run — Display a dialogue box for a command entry. For example, you could type DIR A: and press Return.

Exit (Alt-F4) — Exit DOSSHELL.

Options — The Options menu selections let you adjust the way DOSSHELL operates and displays information about files and directories.

Confirmation — Set confirmation keystroke (Return or mouse click) for delete and replace operations. Also accepts or rejects a mouse click as a confirming action.

File Display Options — Set the way files are displayed, i.e., order and basis of filename sorts and whether or not hidden and system files are displayed.

Select Across Directories — Use files located in multiple directories when file operations are performed.

Show Information — Display file and directory statistics including name, size, attribute, number of files, and disk space.

Enable Task Swapper — Open Active Task List window; run applications and use Ctrl-Esc to return to DOSSHELL to leave your application running. Run other applications and use Ctrl-Esc to switch between active applications. Open and quit a running program to remove it from the Task List.

Display — Select a different text or graphics display mode.

Colors — Change the color or black and white reversal to your liking.

View — The View menu selections are used to control the way information is displayed on the DOSSHELL work surface. The purpose of each selection is described in the following list.

Single File List — Limit display to two windows: a Directory Tree and corresponding file list.

Dual File List — Display two directory and file windows at the same time so you can view the files in two directories.

All Files — Display all files on the selected disk in a single file window. Use the File Display Options of the Options menu to set the sorting order.

Program/Files List — Display Directory, files, and Main or *Program List* windows. This is the default View mode.

Program List — Display the Main or Program List window; suppresses the display of the Directory and file windows.

Repaint Screen (Shift-F5) — Used to refresh the display following the creation of new directories and files.

Tree — The Tree menu controls the way directories are displayed in the Directory window. You can use the indicated shortcut key by pointing to the directory and pressing +, *, Ctrl-* or –.

Expand One Level (+) — Display one subdirectory level for the selected directory.

Expand Branch (*) — Display all subdirectories for the selected directory.

Expand All (Ctrl-*) — Display all directories and subdirectories.

Collapse Branch (–) — Suppress subdirectory display for the selected directory.

Help — The Help menu is used to display information about special keys, commands, and procedures used by DOSSHELL. Rather than explaining the use of each Help selection, you can browse them on your own.

The preceding example showed you how to use the DOSSHELL to switch between tasks. The Typical Operation section of this module guides you through the addition of a program to the Disk Utilities group of the Main window.

DOS VERSION 4.01

STARTING DOSSHELL To start the DOSSHELL, you must have the following programs in the directory listing of your DOS 4.01 disk.

DOSSHELL.BAT
SHELL.CLR
SHELL.HLP
SHELL.MEU
SHELLB.COM
SHELLC.EXE

Type DOSSHELL and press Return to display the first DOSSHELL screen. This screen resembles the following illustration.

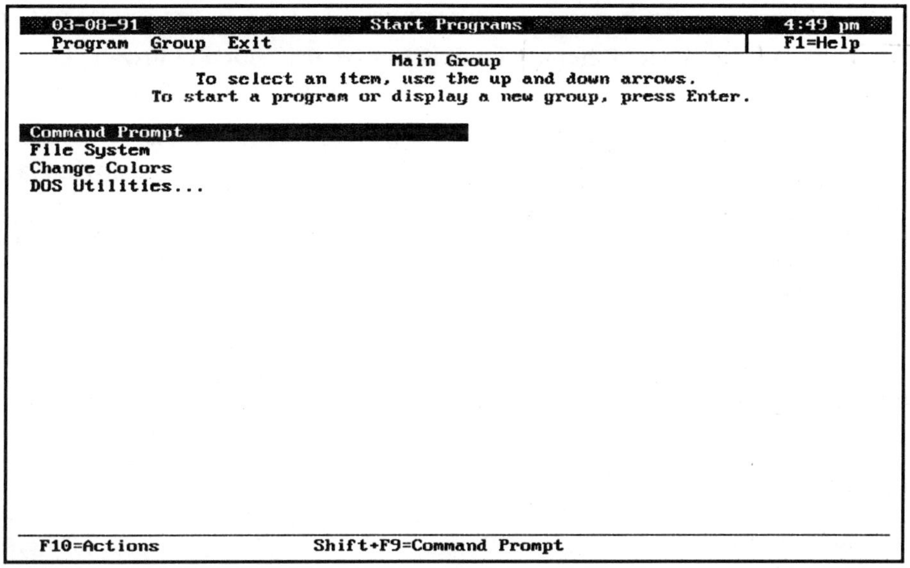

DOSSHELL KEYS When in the DOSSHELL, you can use a mouse or cursor keys to move between selections. The DOSSHELL has a large amount of on-line help information. You can browse this information by pressing F1 and then F11 to see an index of all the descriptive help information. You should begin by reviewing the keys used to move between DOSSHELL options. The term *point* means to select a menu option with either your cursor keys or a mouse. For now, a few commonly used keys are listed for your information.

Key	*Description*
Esc	Cancel the previous command
Up/Down Arrows	Pick an entry in a vertical list
Left/Right Arrows	Pick an entry in a horizontal list
Tab/Shift-Tab	Jump between entries in the File Manager
F1	Display help about the current operation
F11	Display an index of file information
F9	Displays keys that perform special functions
F10	Move from pick list to action bar at the top of the menu
Spacebar	Select a file in the File Manager

DOSSHELL OVERVIEW Before exploring commonly used DOSSHELL commands, knowing the structure of the shell should help you better understand its purpose. Once you have an idea of the various capabilities, then procedures to use DOS utilities, add and execute applications programs, and run the File System are presented.

There are two main parts to the DOSSHELL environment. These are the Start Programs and the File System menus. Each is briefly described below. Then they are explored in more detail, giving you a series of step-by-step procedures in their use.

Start Programs This is the first DOSSHELL menu, which was illustrated previously. Note that you can exit the DOS shell by pressing F3. Notice what is called the "Main Group" of options.

Command Prompt
File System
Change Colors
DOS Utilities . . .

Command Prompt is selected by pointing to it and pressing Return. This takes you to the DOS prompt. Type EXIT from the DOS prompt to reenter the DOSSHELL and to redisplay the Start Programs screen. To quit the DOSSHELL entirely, move to the action bar by pressing F10, then press F3 or type X and press F3.

File System selection displays the File System screen, which is the second main part of the DOSSHELL environment. This screen resembles the following illustration.

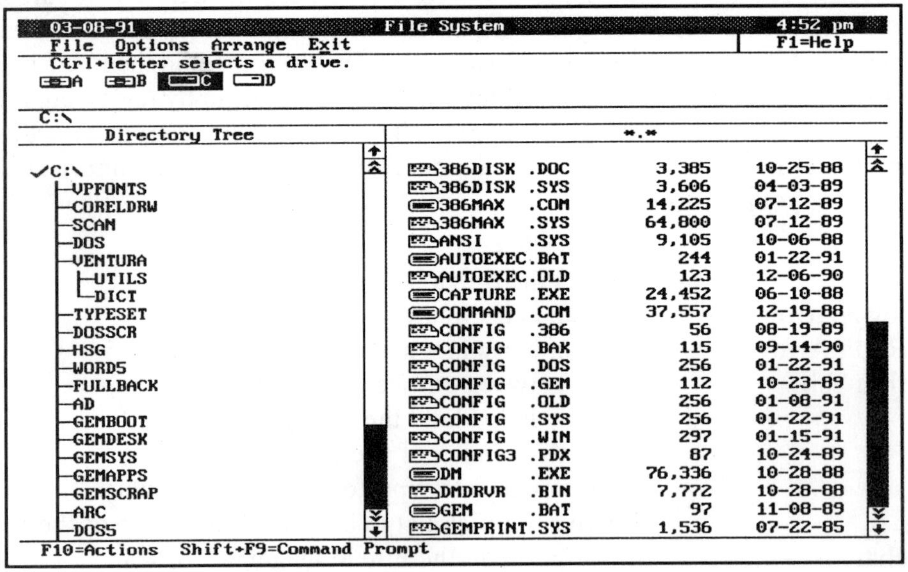

The File System lets you perform a host of operations on file directories and files. This system is described in more detail later in this module.

Change Colors selection lets you change the colors displayed by DOSSHELL screens. This is achieved by pressing the Left or Right Arrow key to display optional colors. Press Return to accept the displayed color combination you like.

DOS Utilities . . . This selection displays a small group of DOS programs. You may wish to add other DOS programs that you use to this group.

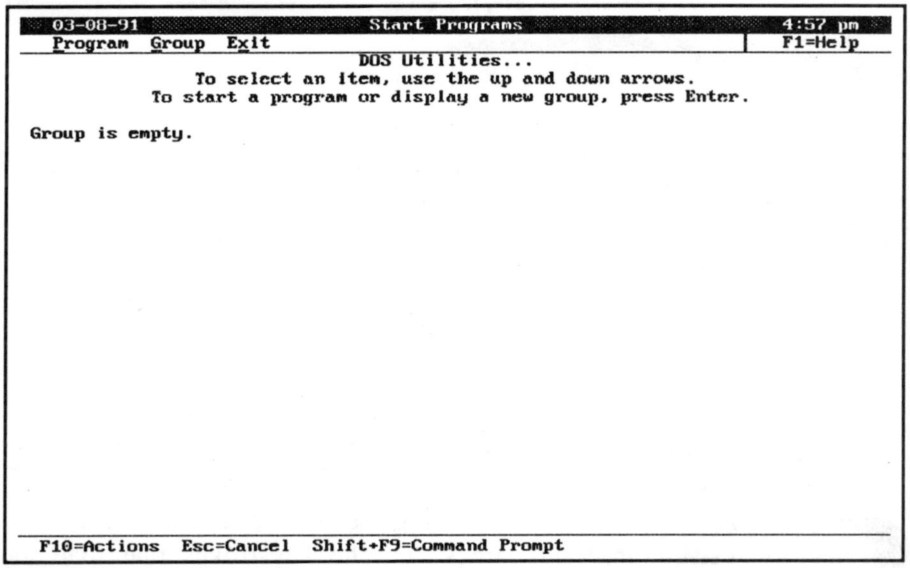

The DOS Utilities group is typical of a group of programs that can be added to the shell, changed, or deleted from it. This is where the power of the DOSSHELL becomes evident. You can select and execute programs from a displayed list rather than having to remember filenames or special commands and key sequences. However, you must first learn how to add groups and programs to the shell and then change and delete them. The activities in the Typical Operation section of this module guide you through these processes.

The action bar is the horizontal strip at the top of the screen. Here, you see a series of options. These vary between the Start Programs and File System screens. In the File System screen, you access the action bar by pointing to a selection, such as Command Prompt, and pressing F10. You can move between the action bar options using the Left or Right Arrow keys. Notice that the Start Programs action bar displays Program, Group, and Exit. These commands have the following uses.

Program — Lets you start, add, change, delete, or copy files and program, as appropriate.

Group — Lets you add, change, delete, or reorder a group of programs.

Exit — Lets you exit or resume use of the DOSSHELL environment.

Program Options With the Start Programs/DOS Utilities screen displayed, pressing F10 and then Return displays a pull-down menu.

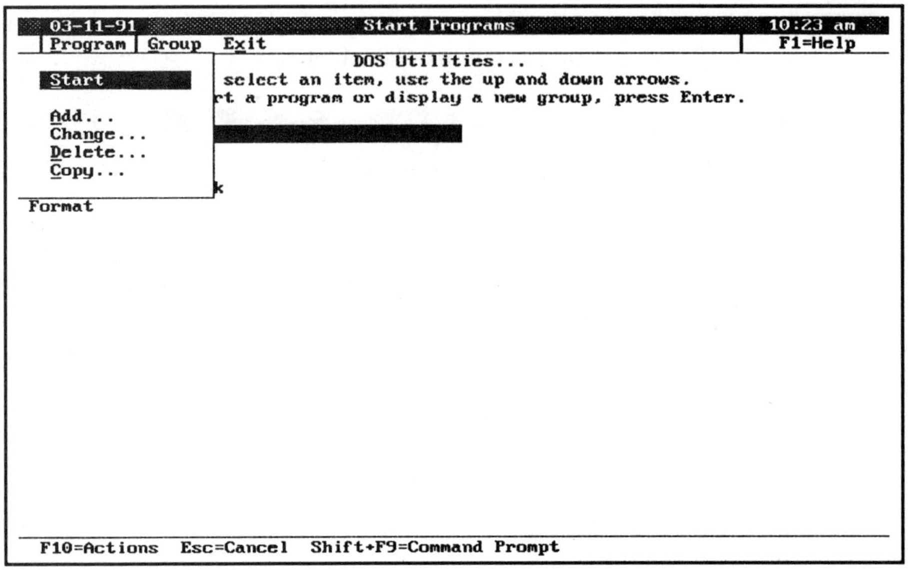

Notice the Program menu Add and Change selections. These display submenus that let you assign program names and the keystrokes that load and run programs, as if you were entering them directly from the DOS prompt. You can also create and call batch (.BAT) files from DOSSHELL, although this is usually unnecessary if you use the proper commands from within the Add/Change Programs submenus. However, if you wish to call a batch file, use "CALL *filename*" within the Add Program Commands line.

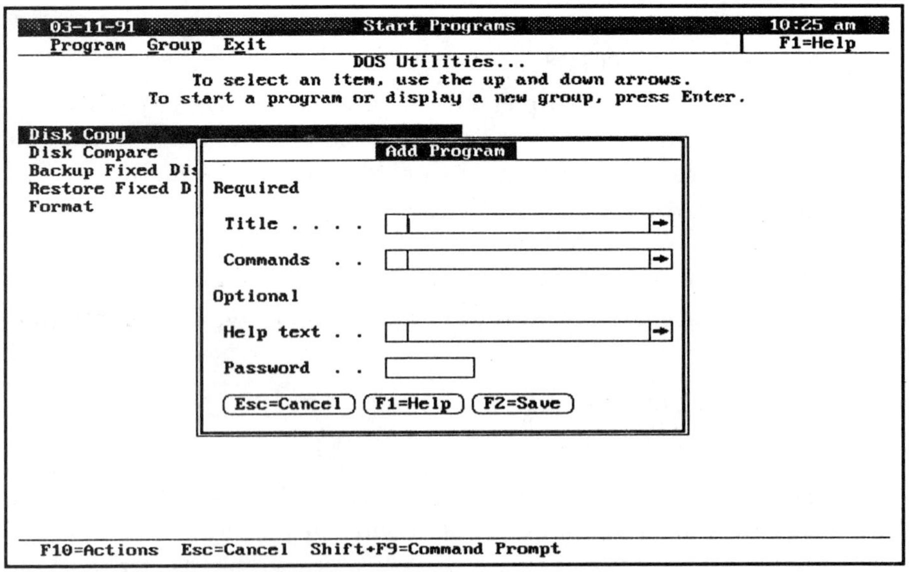

Pointing to Add and pressing Return (or typing A) displays an Add Program dialogue box. The entry boxes within this dialogue box have the following purposes.

Title — Type the title you want displayed within the group. You may use a program name or a generic legend, like "WordPerfect" or "Word Processing."

Commands — Type the commands that you ordinarily type from the DOS prompt to start a program. For example, you may type the following series. C:\¦CD\WS¦WS. Note that the vertical bars are like pressing Return and are inserted by pressing the F4 key.

Help text — Type text you want used as help information when you point to the title and press F1.

Password — Type an optional password if you wish to restrict access to a particular program.

There are a number of optional command parameters that let you display keyboard entry prompts, optional instructions, and much more. These are summarized in the following table. To see a few of these in operation, perform the Typical Operation located at the end of this module. There, several examples of DOSSHELL operations are provided to show you how to add new programs to the Start Programs screen.

Table 22-1 Program Add/Change Commands Options

Option	*Description*
[ ]	Brackets are used to display an optional command parameters box, which lets you input additional parts of a command, such as path and/or filename, from the keyboard. `Commands . . EDLIN [ ]`

[/P"text"]	Displays text as a prompt; accepts keyboard entry.
	`Commands . .`
	`C:CD\DOSEDLIN[/P:"\Path\Filename"]`

[/T"text"]	Displays text as a title at the top of the command parameters box. Up to 40 characters are permitted. The following example combines the /T and /P parameters.
	`Commands . .`
	`TYPE[/T"View a File"/P"\Path\Filename"] ¦MORE`

[/I"text"]	Displays text as an instruction within the command parameters box; the following example combines /I and /P.
	`Commands . .`
	`TYPE[/I"Type the complete filename to view"/P"Name"] ¦MORE`

Table 22-1 Program Add/Change Commands Options (Cont.)

Option	*Description*
¦PAUSE¦	Pauses execution until a key is pressed.

ECHO text]¦PAUSE¦	Displays text as prompt and "Press any key to continue . . ." on following line until a key is pressed.
	`Commands . .`
	`ECHO Insert diskette in A:¦PAUSE¦DIR A: ¦SORT ¦MORE`

[/D"text"]	Enters text as the default value in the entry field; changed at run time by typing different text.
	`Commands . .`
	`DIR [/P"Pathname"/D"C:\"] ¦SORT ¦FIND "<DIR>" ¦MORE PAUSE`
	Notice the SORT, FIND, and MORE filters are used. Also, notice the use of the PAUSE parameter.

[/R]	Clears a default value within the entry field if the first typed character is not a conventional edit key, such as a cursor key, End, Ins, etc.
[/F"filename"]	Checks for the presence of the filename.
[/L"n"]	Limits length of a command parameter entry to n characters.
[/M"e"]	Only permits the entry of existing filenames.
%n	Records the value entered at run time into %n, which is placed outside the brackets in this instance. For example, if n is 1, the value of the last filename entered is substituted for %1.

[%n]	Records and reuses a command parameter entry. The value of n is a number from 1 to 10. The following command line displays the file you enter in the command parameter box; next it displays a DIR listing of the file, recalling the filename with %1. The DIR listing shows size, date, and time information. The display is paused with PAUSE.
	`Command . .`
	`TYPE [%1/T"Check File"/P"Filename"]DIR %1PAUSE`

[/C"%n"]	Saves the %n value used in the preceding task; otherwise, %n is null (has no value).
[/D"%n"]	Displays the default value (up to 40 characters) in the entry field at run time. This is the value saved with the %n option. The value is changed at run time by typing a new value.

THE FILE SYSTEM The File System is started by pointing to File System and pressing Return. The following File System screen is displayed.

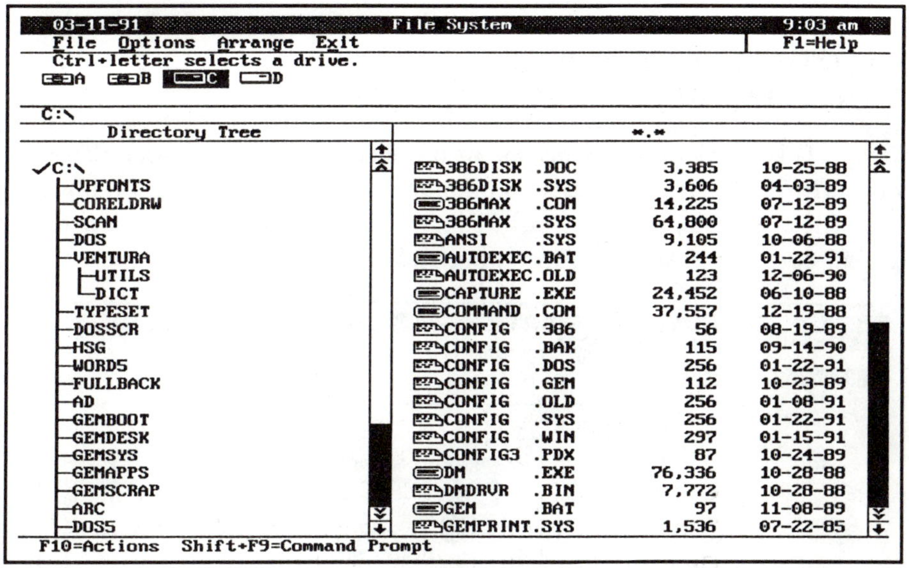

The File System performs a number of convenient file management operations. You can display a single directory or multiple directories and perform a host of operations on files and directories. In general, you can move between File System options with Tab and Shift-Tab. Move vertically and horizontally within lists using the cursor keys. Files are selected individually with the Spacebar. Here is a summary of these keys.

Key	*Description*
Tab, Shift-Tab	Move between File System options.
Esc	Cancel operation.
Cursor keys	Point to directory, file, or option.
PgUp/PgDn	Page Directory Tree or filename list up or down.
F10	Move to the action bar.
Shift-F9	Display the DOS command prompt.
Spacebar	Select/deselect an individual file within a file list.
Return	Execute a selected program (selected by pointing to an executable program file, pressing the Spacebar, and then pressing Return).

Disk Drive/Directory Selection Before you can effectively operate on files, you must log the appropriate disk drive and directory. This is achieved by tabbing to the disk drive icon and pressing the Ctrl key in combination with the drive letter (A, B, C, D, etc.). You can also use the cursor keys and press Return for drive selection. Next,

CAN you use the shell on floppy disc? yes

select the directory by tabbing to the Directory Tree, pointing to the directory choice, and pressing Return.

File System Menus The following series of illustrations depict the File System menus, which show most of the File System capabilities. Clarifying descriptions are provided where helpful.

File Menu This menu operates on one or more selected files. Notice that this menu lets you perform a number of DOS commands that operate on individual files or groups of files. In contrast, the Start Programs/DOS Utilities selection is used for more global operations, such as formatting and backup.

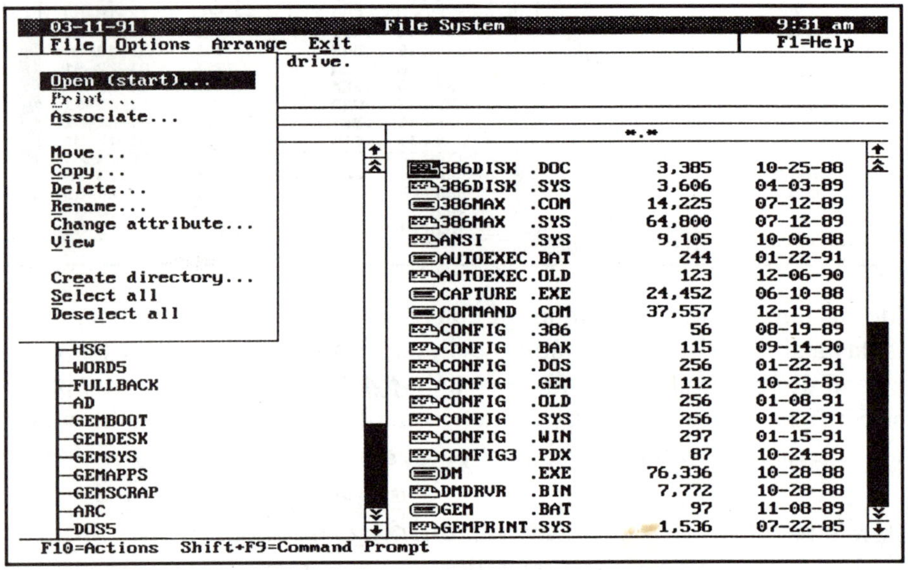

Notice the Associate selection. This lets you enter a filename or extension type to associate with an executable program. If you enter a specific filename, the program starts using the associated filename automatically. If you associate a file extension type, the program will automatically use the specified extension. If you start a program by pointing to it in the file list and pressing Return, you are given the opportunity to enter an associated filename from the keyboard. Pressing Return bypasses the use of an associated file.

Options Menu This menu lets you pull down three easy-to-use submenus. All of the Options submenus are depicted so you can determine their capabilities.

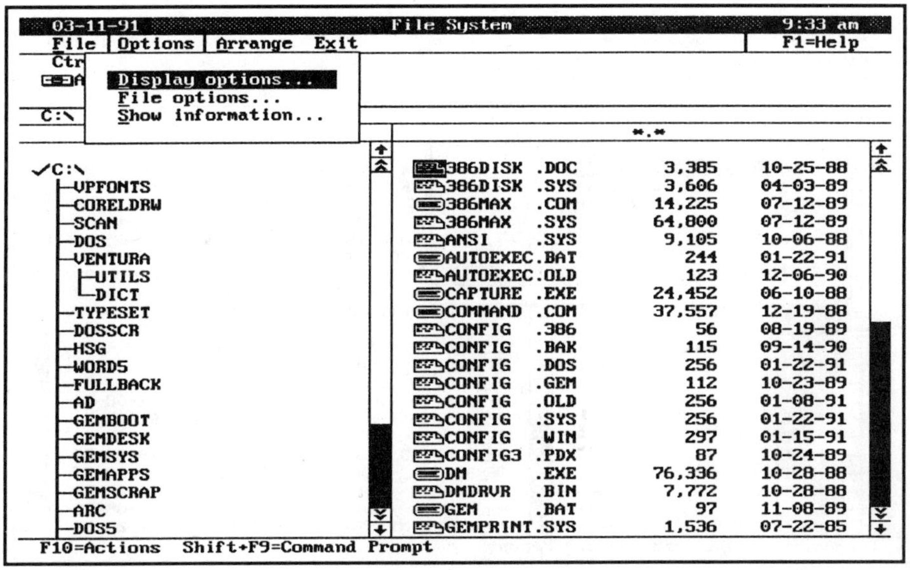
03-11-91 File System 9:33 am
File Options Arrange Exit F1=Help
Display options...
File options...
Show information...
C:\
.
C:\
VPFONTS
CORELDRW
SCAN
DOS
VENTURA
UTILS
DICT
TYPESET
DOSSCR
HSG
WORD5
FULLBACK
AD
GEMBOOT
GEMDESK
GEMSYS
GEMAPPS
GEMSCRAP
ARC
DOS5
386DISK .DOC 3,385 10-25-88
386DISK .SYS 3,606 04-03-89
386MAX .COM 14,225 07-12-89
386MAX .SYS 64,800 07-12-89
ANSI .SYS 9,105 10-06-88
AUTOEXEC.BAT 244 01-22-91
AUTOEXEC.OLD 123 12-06-90
CAPTURE .EXE 24,452 06-10-88
COMMAND .COM 37,557 12-19-88
CONFIG .386 56 08-19-89
CONFIG .BAK 115 09-14-90
CONFIG .DOS 256 01-22-91
CONFIG .GEM 112 10-23-89
CONFIG .OLD 256 01-08-91
CONFIG .SYS 256 01-22-91
CONFIG .WIN 297 01-15-91
CONFIG3 .PDX 87 10-24-89
DM .EXE 76,336 10-28-88
DMDRVR .BIN 7,772 10-28-88
GEM .BAT 97 11-08-89
GEMPRINT.SYS 1,536 07-22-85
F10=Actions Shift+F9=Command Prompt

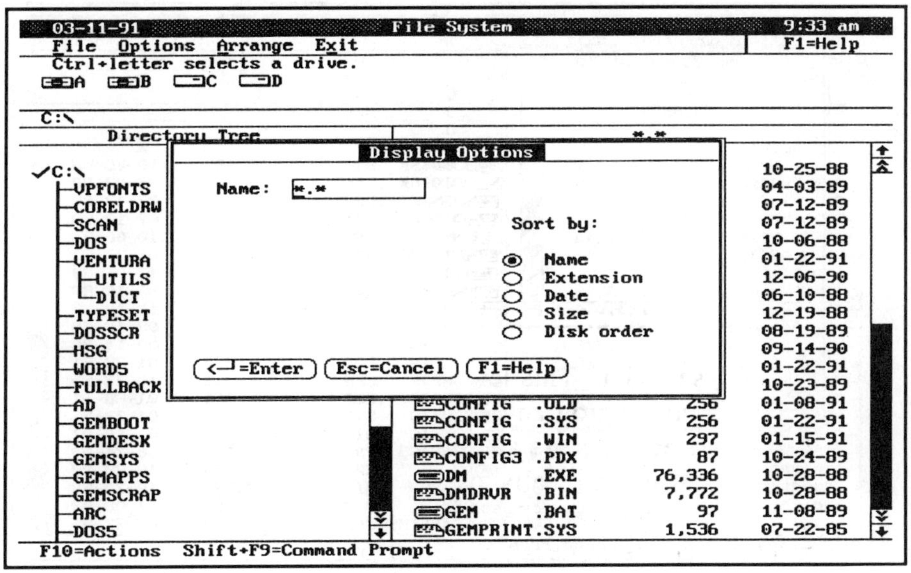
03-11-91 File System 9:33 am
File Options Arrange Exit F1=Help
Ctrl+letter selects a drive.
A B C D
C:\
Directory Tree
Display Options
Name: *.*
Sort by:
Name
Extension
Date
Size
Disk order
<┘=Enter Esc=Cancel F1=Help
C:\
VPFONTS
CORELDRW
SCAN
DOS
VENTURA
UTILS
DICT
TYPESET
DOSSCR
HSG
WORD5
FULLBACK
AD
GEMBOOT
GEMDESK
GEMSYS
GEMAPPS
GEMSCRAP
ARC
DOS5
CONFIG .SYS 256 01-22-91
CONFIG .WIN 297 01-15-91
CONFIG3 .PDX 87 10-24-89
DM .EXE 76,336 10-28-88
DMDRVR .BIN 7,772 10-28-88
GEM .BAT 97 11-08-89
GEMPRINT.SYS 1,536 07-22-85
F10=Actions Shift+F9=Command Prompt

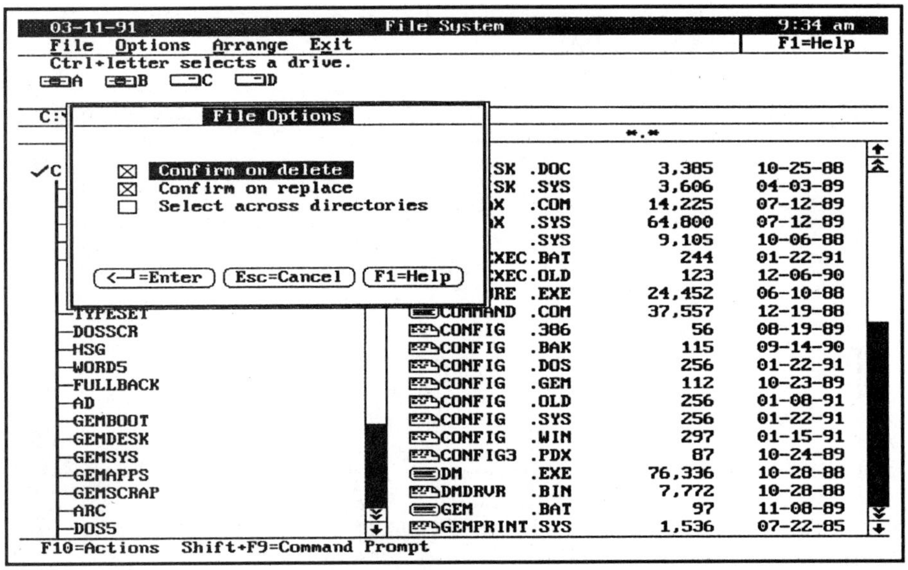
03-11-91 File System 9:34 am
File Options Arrange Exit F1=Help
Ctrl+letter selects a drive.
A B C D
File Options
Confirm on delete
Confirm on replace
Select across directories
<─┘=Enter Esc=Cancel F1=Help
.
SK .DOC 3,385 10-25-88
SK .SYS 3,606 04-03-89
X .COM 14,225 07-12-89
X .SYS 64,800 07-12-89
.SYS 9,105 10-06-88
XEC.BAT 244 01-22-91
XEC.OLD 123 12-06-90
RE .EXE 24,452 06-10-88
COMMAND .COM 37,557 12-19-88
CONFIG .386 56 08-19-89
CONFIG .BAK 115 09-14-90
CONFIG .DOS 256 01-22-91
CONFIG .GEM 112 10-23-89
CONFIG .OLD 256 01-08-91
CONFIG .SYS 256 01-22-91
CONFIG .WIN 297 01-15-91
CONFIG3 .PDX 87 10-24-89
DM .EXE 76,336 10-28-88
DMDRVR .BIN 7,772 10-28-88
GEM .BAT 97 11-08-89
GEMPRINT.SYS 1,536 07-22-85
TYPESET
DOSSCR
HSG
WORD5
FULLBACK
AD
GEMBOOT
GEMDESK
GEMSYS
GEMAPPS
GEMSCRAP
ARC
DOS5
F10=Actions Shift+F9=Command Prompt

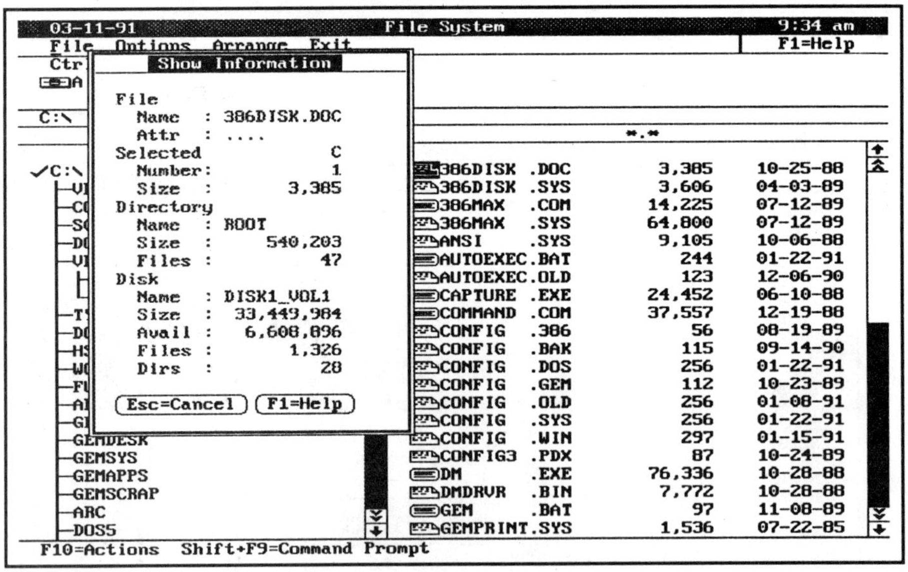
03-11-91 File System 9:34 am
F1=Help
Show Information
File
Name : 386DISK.DOC
Attr : ....
Selected C
Number: 1
Size : 3,385
Directory
Name : ROOT
Size : 540,203
Files : 47
Disk
Name : DISK1_VOL1
Size : 33,449,984
Avail : 6,608,896
Files : 1,326
Dirs : 28
Esc=Cancel F1=Help
.
386DISK .DOC 3,385 10-25-88
386DISK .SYS 3,606 04-03-89
386MAX .COM 14,225 07-12-89
386MAX .SYS 64,800 07-12-89
ANSI .SYS 9,105 10-06-88
AUTOEXEC.BAT 244 01-22-91
AUTOEXEC.OLD 123 12-06-90
CAPTURE .EXE 24,452 06-10-88
COMMAND .COM 37,557 12-19-88
CONFIG .386 56 08-19-89
CONFIG .BAK 115 09-14-90
CONFIG .DOS 256 01-22-91
CONFIG .GEM 112 10-23-89
CONFIG .OLD 256 01-08-91
CONFIG .SYS 256 01-22-91
CONFIG .WIN 297 01-15-91
CONFIG3 .PDX 87 10-24-89
DM .EXE 76,336 10-28-88
DMDRVR .BIN 7,772 10-28-88
GEM .BAT 97 11-08-89
GEMPRINT.SYS 1,536 07-22-85
GEMSYS
GEMAPPS
GEMSCRAP
ARC
DOS5
F10=Actions Shift+F9=Command Prompt

Arrange Menu The Arrange menu lets you display one or two menu lists or a list of system files. Look at the Arrange menu options.

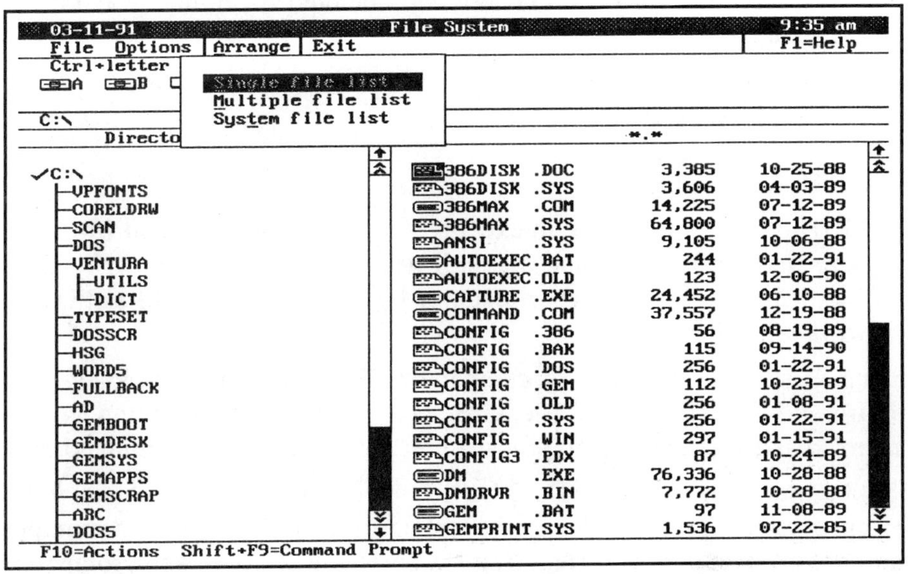

Use "Multiple file list" to display a second drive and/or file directory at the bottom half of the screen.

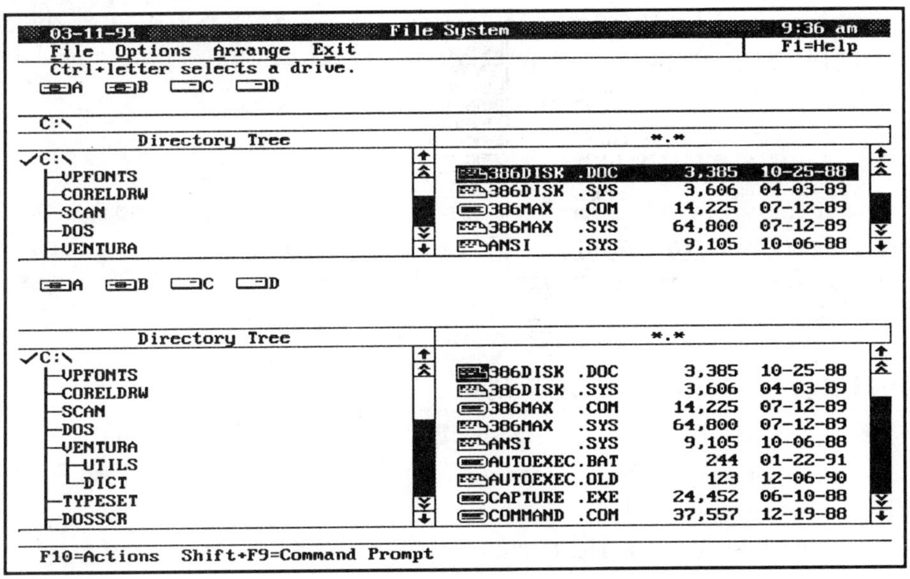

If you have a mouse driver different from the default driver used by DOS 4.01, your DOSSHELL.BAT file SHELLC line should resemble the following lines. Notice that the supplied reference to a different mouse is deleted to eliminate conflicts with another mouse driver.

```
SHELLC /TRAN/COLOR/DOS/MENU/MUL/SND/MEU:SHELL.MEU/CLR:SHELL.CLR/PROMPT
/MAINT/EXIT/SWAP/DATE
```

APPLICATIONS

The DOSSHELL utility provides an excellent operating environment from which to run programs and perform file and disk utilities. Because files are easily organized and listed alphabetically, by creation date, or by file size, it simplifies the way you find and work with files.

Organizing groups and associating companion files is another extremely powerful feature offered by the DOSSHELL environment. Grouping and storing associations saves many keystrokes that are otherwise entered from the DOS command prompt.

In DOS 4.01, the Start Programs DOS Utility selection and the File menu within the File System section eliminates the need to return to the DOS command prompt to run DOS commands. However, if you must, it is easy to select Command Prompt and type a standard DOS command. Then type EXIT and press Return to move back into the DOSSHELL environment.

The DOSSHELL found in DOS version 5.0 is more intuitive than its predecessor in DOS 4.01. A powerful feature supplied by this version of DOSSHELL is the ability to run multiple programs and then quickly switch between those programs using the task switcher.

TYPICAL OPERATION

There are two activities in this section — one for DOS 5.0 and a second for DOS 4.01. The activities guide you through the addition of programs and groups to the DOSSHELL. Use the activity that corresponds to your version of DOS. Begin at the DOS prompt.

ACTIVITY FOR USERS OF DOS 5.00:

1. Start DOSSHELL by typing **DOSSHELL** and pressing **Return**.
2. Tab to the Main window, cursor down to Disk Utilities, and press **Return** to display the utilities list.
3. Press **Alt F N** and press **Return** to display the Add Program dialogue box.
4. Type the information shown in the following two dialogue box illustrations; use the cursor keys to move between the entry fields. Insert "CTRL+T" by moving

to the field and pressing **Ctrl-T**. Pressing **Return** in the Application Shortcut Key field moves to the next screen.

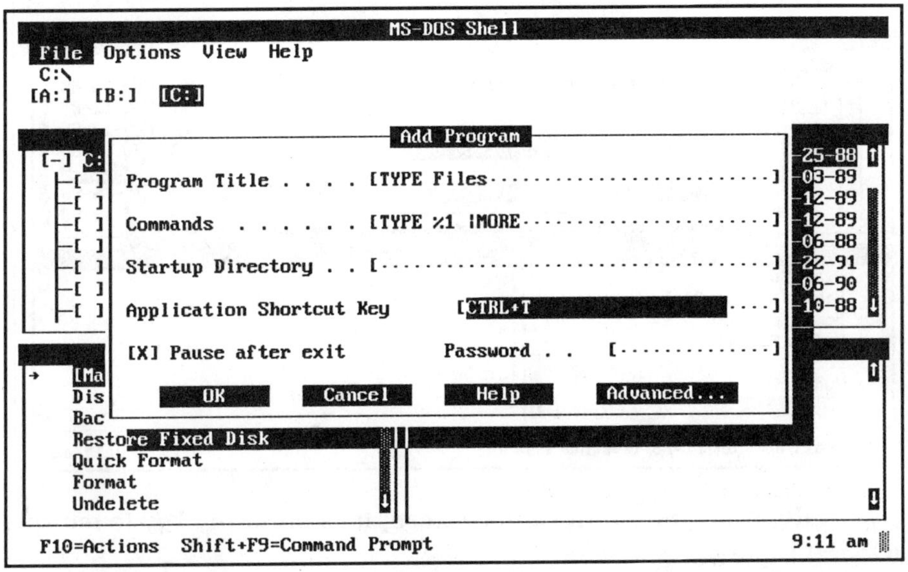

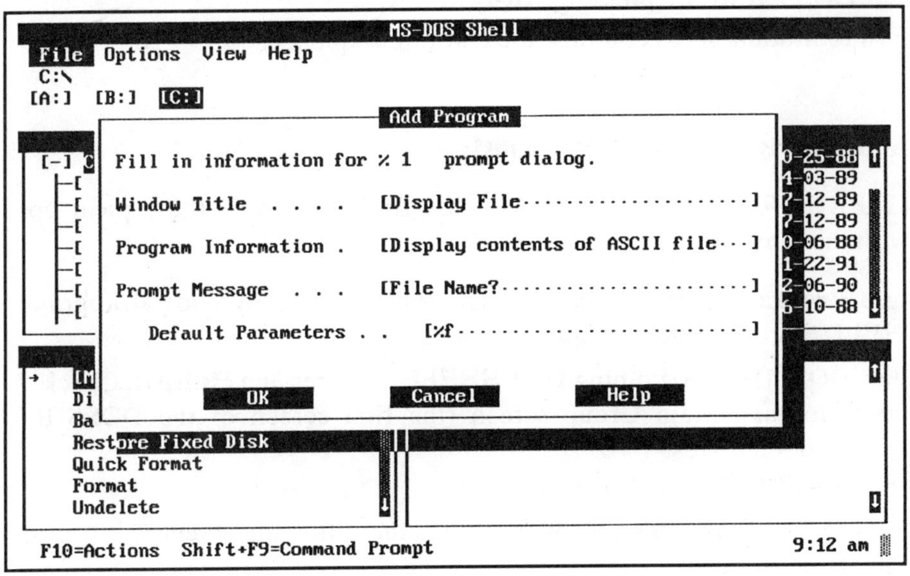

5. Press **Return** to select OK. Then tab to the Directory Tree window and pick C:\.
6. Tab to the file list window and highlight AUTOEXEC.BAT.
7. Tab to the Disk Utilities menu, highlight TYPE files, and press **Return** to pop up the new dialogue box.

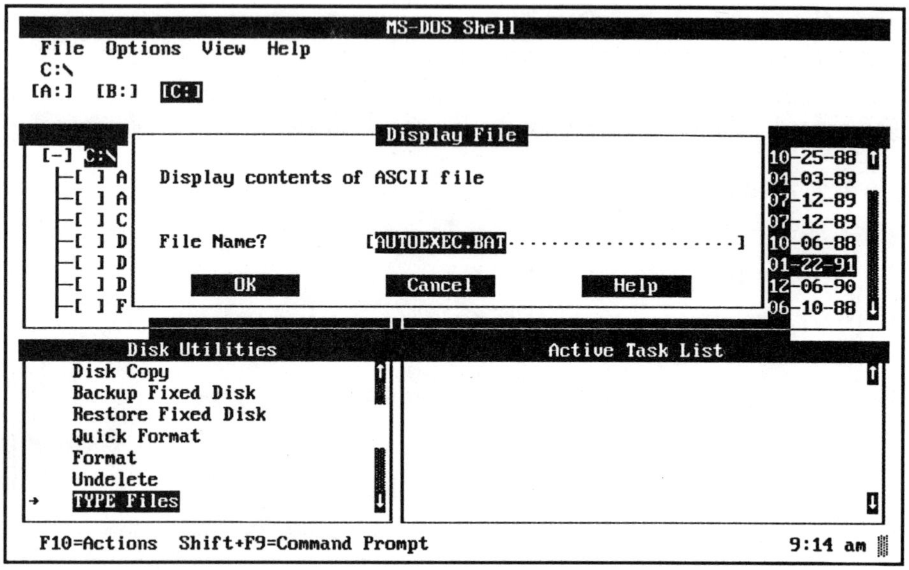

8. Press **Return** to type the file to the screen; then press any key to redisplay the DOSSHELL.
9. Exit DOSSHELL by pressing **Alt-F X**.
10. Turn to Module 22 to continue the learning sequence.

ACTIVITY FOR USERS OF DOS 4.01:

START PROGRAMS ACTIVITIES The first portion of the typical operation deals with the Start Programs screen.

Adding a Program to the DOSSHELL The first activity adds a program to the DOSSHELL Start Programs screen.

1. Start DOSSHELL by typing **DOSSHELL** and pressing **Return.** Check that the Start Programs/Main Group screen (the first screen of the DOSSHELL) is displayed; then press **F10**.
2. Check that "Program" is selected and press **Return**.
3. Point to "Add" and press **Return**; notice the following screen:

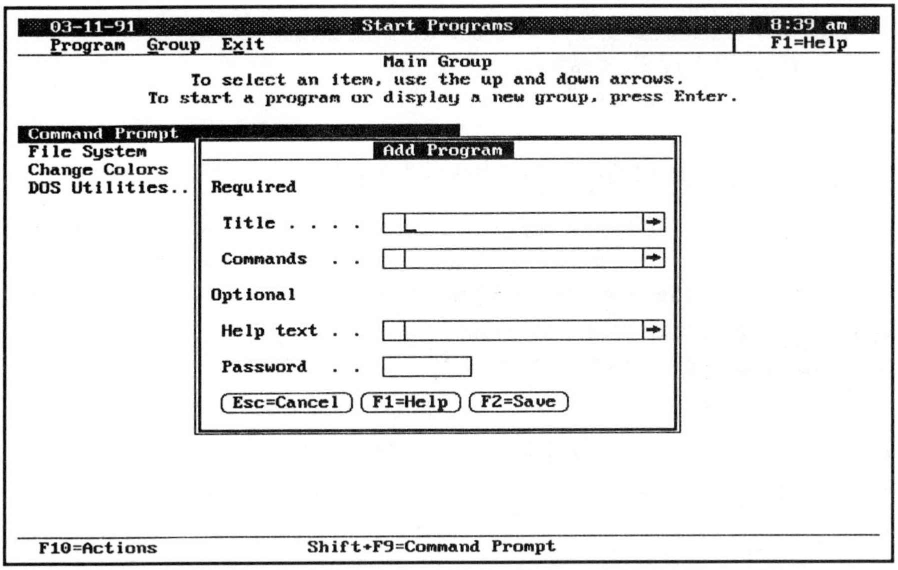

4. Type the following information on the indicated line. End each line by pressing **Return**. Press **F4** to enter the ¦ symbol, which issues a hard return in the command line.

NOTE

On the following Commands and Help text lines, substitute a command string and text that matches the word processing program you normally use. If necessary, use \DOS as the file directory and EDLIN TEMP as the program/filename.

Title:	**Word Processing**
Commands:	**C:¦CD\WS6¦WS**
Help text:	**Run WordStar 6**

5. Press **F2** to save; notice that "Word Processing" has been added to the Main Group.
6. Run the Word Processing program by pointing to it and pressing **Return**.
7. Exit the Word Processing program; notice the Start Programs screen is redisplayed.

NOTE

Skip step 8 if you want to keep the "Word Processing" selection in the Start Programs menu.

8. Delete "Word Processing" from the Main Group as follows:
   a. Point to "Word Processing."
   b. Press **F10** and press **Return**.
   c. Point to "Delete" and press **Return**; notice the Delete Item screen.
   d. Press **Return** again to complete the deletion process.

Adding a Group to the DOSSHELL A group is a series of related programs, such as program tools, data files, and so on. The following activity adds a group and then adds two programs to the Database Management group. You may wish to substitute your own file paths and program names in place of those used in the sample procedure. Begin at the Start Programs/Main Group screen.

1. Press **F10**, select "Group" on the action bar, and press **Return**.
2. Point to "Add" and press **Return**; notice the "Add Group" dialogue box.
3. Type the following information on the indicated line and press **Return** after each.

   Title: **WDatabase Management**
   Filename: **DBASE**
   Help text: **Run database programs**

4. Press **F2** to save; notice "Database Management..." is added to the Main Group.

Add programs to the group as follows:

5. Point to "Database Management..." and press **Return**. Notice that the group is presently empty.
6. Press **F10**, **Return**, point to "Add," and press **Return** to display the "Add Program" dialogue box.
7. Type the following information on the indicated line and press **Return** after each. (Press F4 to enter the ¦ symbol.)

   Title: **dBASE III Plus**
   Commands: **C:¦CD\DB¦DBASE**
   Help text: **Run dBASE III Plus**

8. Press **F2** to save; notice "dBASE III Plus" is added to the Database Management group.

From the Database Management group screen, perform the following steps to add a second program. The Commands line of the "Add Program" menu includes a prompt for keyboard entry.

9. Press **F10**, **Return**, point to "Add," and press **Return**.

10. Type the following information on the indicated line and press **Return** after each.

    Title: **Clipper Compiler**

    Commands: **C:¦CD\CLIPPER¦CLIPPER [/P"CLIPPER COMMAND"/P"Filename"]**

    Help text: **Run Clipper; provide filename from keyboard**

11. Press **F2** to save; notice "Clipper Compiler" is added to the Database Management group.
12. This completes the Add Group, Add Program procedure. You may use the Delete selection of the Group and Program selections to remove groups and programs.
13. Redisplay the Main Group by pressing **Esc**.

USING THE FILE SYSTEM Perform the following steps to view a file within the File System. Begin by selecting File System from the Start Programs/Main Group screen. Notice that the File System screen is displayed.

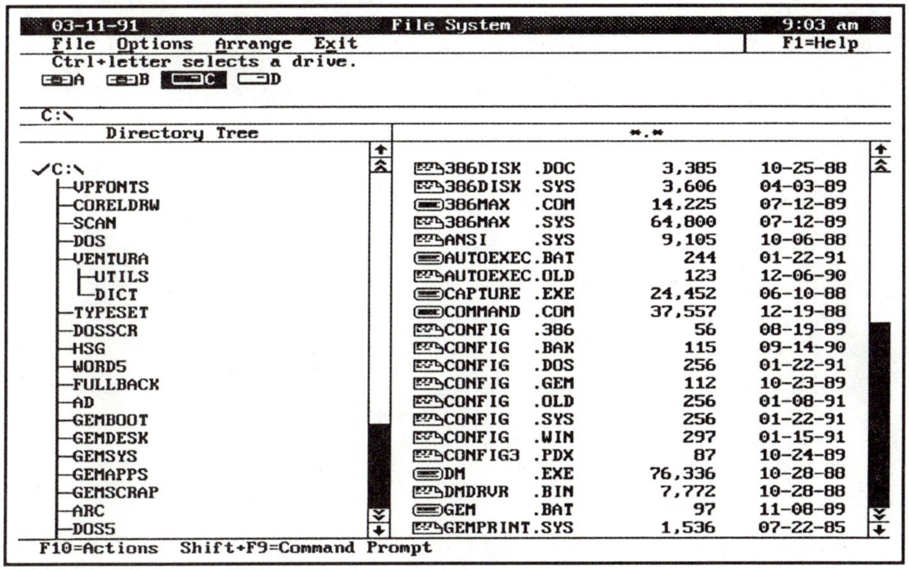

1. Press **Tab**, point to drive C, and press **Return**; then use **Tab** to highlight the Directory Tree and point to the root directory (a check mark next to C:\).
2. Press **Tab** until a filename is highlighted.
3. Point to either CONFIG.SYS or AUTOEXEC.BAT and press **Spacebar**. Notice that the file icon is highlighted.
4. Press **F10** and then press **Return** to pull down the File menu.

5. Point to View and press **Return**. Notice that the contents of the selected file is displayed.
6. Press **F9** and check for a hexadecimal display; press **F9** again to redisplay in ASCII format.
7. Press **Esc** to cancel; the File View screen is closed.
8. Experiment with other DOSSHELL File System selections. For example, use the Options menu to list your files by date.

NOTE

You should find that use of the File System is fairly intuitive once you understand which keys are used to move between options.

9. Exit the DOSSHELL by pressing **F3** twice.
10. Turn to Module 22 to continue the learning sequence.

Module 24
EDIT (5.00+)

DESCRIPTION

The EDIT program, which is a convenient full-screen editor, was introduced as a standard feature with the release of DOS 5.00. The EDIT program makes use of the editor found in the QBASIC (*QuickBASIC* interpreter) program. EDIT does not operate without the presence of the QBASIC.EXE program file.

A full-screen editor differs from a line editor. A full-screen editor lets you display multiple lines and move within displayed text both vertically and horizontally. In contrast, a line editor, such as EDLIN, requires that you move to and edit one line at a time.

STARTING EDIT The EDIT program is started by typing EDIT and pressing Return. In addition to being able to specify a filename at startup, there are several parameters you can use to set the way the program displays text. These parameters rely on the type of display that your computer uses. Typical command lines are shown in the following list.

EDIT *filename*	Start EDIT and load the specified filename.
EDIT /B	Puts EDIT in the black and white mode; ideal for laptops that have CGA cards and a black and white display. A variation of this command is EDIT *filename* /B.
EDIT /G	Causes the screen of a computer equipped with a CGA monitor to be refreshed as fast as possible. If you see snow when this option is used, avoid its use.
EDIT /H	Displays the maximum number of lines supported by your graphics card.
EDIT /NOHI	Lets you use a monitor that does not support high intensity output. Do not use with Compaq laptops.

In addition to being able to load a program from the DOS prompt, you can also use the File Open command to load files once the program is active.

EDIT PROGRAM STRUCTURE The EDIT program has four pull-down menus which are accessed by pressing the Alt key. Once the Alt key is pressed, you can use the Left or Right Arrow key to pull down File, Edit, Search, or Options, or you can type the first letter of the menu name, F, E, S, or O. You can also press Alt-F or Alt-E to pull down a menu without using the Arrow keys. Once a menu is pulled down, you can highlight the selection using the Up and Down Arrow keys or by typing the highlighted letter that corresponds to the desired item. Use Esc to back out of menu operations.

A description of each menu is presented in the following list.

Help — You can press F1 to display help about the current operation. Help is *context sensitive*. That is, the help information pertains to the operation in process.

File — This menu performs all operations required to open and save files or to exit the EDIT program.

- New — Create a new document; clears the current document. A dialogue box gives you the opportunity to save or cancel work on any currently displayed document.
- Open — Open a document; prompts you for a filename and displays a list of filenames in the current directory. You may type a filename and press Return. You may also press Tab, point to the filename, highlight it using an Arrow key, and press Return to open the file. You may also Tab to the Dirs/Drives box. Use wildcards (*.*, *.BAT, or ????????.???) to list specific filenames.
- Save — Save the current file using the existing filename.
- Save As — Save the current file under a new filename.
- Print — Print either the complete document or a selected passage of text. The passage is selected by highlighting it using Shift-Arrow.
- Exit — Exit the editing session. If you have modified the current file, you are given a chance to save it before quitting.

Edit — This selection lets you cut, copy, paste, or clear selected text.

- Cut (Shift-Del) — Removes selected text from the screen and puts it on the "clipboard," which is a memory buffer. Pressing Shift-Del is a shortcut way to cut selected text. Text is selected (or highlighted) using the Shift-Arrow keys.
- Copy (Ctrl-Ins) — Places the selected text on the clipboard without cutting it from the screen. Use Shift-Ins to paste it at the desired location.

Paste (Shift-Ins)	Inserts text from the clipboard to the present cursor location.
Del (Del)	Deletes selected text without putting it on the clipboard.

Search — Use this menu to locate a specified text string within the current document.

Find (Ctrl-QF)	Finds a specified string. You may specify whole words only and upper/lowercase matching.
Repeat Last Find (Ctrl-L or F3)	Finds the next match in the current document.
Change (Ctrl-QA)	Finds a specified string and replaces it with another. You can verify the change before replacement. This option lets you skip the replacement and advance to the next occurrence of the search string.

Display — This menu lets you set up display colors, turn the scroll bar on or off, change the tab stop settings, and set the file path for the EDIT help file.

Display	Picks foreground and background colors from a list, turn the scroll bars on or off, and set tab stops.
Help Path	Picks the file path in which the EDIT.HLP file is located.

SPECIAL KEYS A number of special editing keys are available for use in the EDIT window. If you are familiar with the QuickBASIC editor, WordStar, or Borland International editors, you already know them. These special keys are summarized in the following list.

Description	*Key Sequence*
help	F1
help menu	Shift-F1
cursor right	Ctrl-D or Right Arrow
cursor left	Ctrl-S or Left Arrow
cursor up	Ctrl-E or Up Arrow
cursor down	Ctrl-X or Down Arrow
end of line	Ctrl-QD or End
beginning of line	Ctrl-QS or Home
scroll up	Ctrl-C or PgDn
scroll down	Ctrl-R or PgUp
word right	Ctrl-F or Ctrl-Right Arrow
word left	Ctrl-A or Ctrl-Left Arrow
scroll up	Ctrl-Z or Ctrl-Down Arrow
scroll down	Ctrl-W or Ctrl-Up Arrow

top of document	Ctrl-QR or Ctrl-Home
bottom of document	Ctrl-QC or Ctrl-End
mark text (block)	Shift-Arrow
mark word	Shift-Ctrl-Arrow
delete character	Ctrl-G or Del
delete word	Ctrl-T
delete line	Ctrl-Y
delete to line end	Ctrl-QY
delete marked block	Del
cut block	Shift-Del
paste block	Shift-Ins
clear block	Del
find string	Ctrl-QF
find/replace string	Ctrl-QA
find again	Ctrl-L or F3
insert/overstrike	Ctrl-V or Ins
insert blank line	Ctrl-N (cursor at left margin)

APPLICATIONS

The EDIT program is convenient for reviewing, editing, and creating text files. It is particularly useful for reviewing and modifying batch files, including your AUTOEXEC.BAT and CONFIG.SYS files. Finally, you may wish to use EDIT to create, save, and print program source code, memorandums, or any other file using ASCII-based characters.

TYPICAL OPERATION

In this activity you create a screen-size file using HELP and a piping command. Next, you start the EDIT program, load the file, and perform editing operations. Begin at the DOS prompt.

1. Type **HELP DIR > TEMP.TXT** and press **Return** to direct the help output to a file named TEMP.TXT.
2. Type **EDIT** and press **Return**. Then press **Esc** to display the EDIT program's text window.
3. Type **Alt-F O** to open a file. Press **Tab**, highlight TEMP.TXT by pressing **Down Arrow**, and press **Return** to open the selected file.

```
  File  Edit  Search  Options                                          Help
                                  TEMP.TXT
Displays a list of files in a directory.

DIR [pathname] [/P] [/W] [/O[:sortorder]] [/A[:attributes]] [/S] [/B] [/L]

  pathname     The directory and/or files to list.
  /P           Pause after each screenful of information.
  /W           Use wide list format.
  /S           Display files in the specified directory and all subdirectories.
  /B           Use bare format (filenames only).
  /L           Use lower case.
  /O           List files in sorted order.
  sortorder     N  name                    S  size
                E  extension               D  date and time
                G  group subdirectories    -  prefix to reverse order
  /A           Display files with specified attributes.
  attributes    D  subdirectories          R  read-only files
                H  hidden files            A  files ready for archive
                S  system files            -  prefix meaning "not"

Switches may be preset in DIRCMD environment variable.  Override
preset options by prefixing any switch with -, e.g., /-W.

MS-DOS Editor  <F1=Help> Press ALT to activate menus          CN 00001:001
```

4. Press **Ctrl-QF**, type **Switches**, and press **Return** to find the word Switches near the bottom of the document.
5. Mark the last two lines of the displayed text as a block by pressing **Shift-Down Arrow** twice. (Use the arrow keys on the numeric keypad if you are using a 101 keyboard.)
6. Press **Shift-Del** to cut the marked block.
7. Move to the line beginning with "pathname" (00005:001 at the lower right-hand corner of the screen; this represents line 5 column 1).
8. Press **Shift-Ins** to insert the cut block. Your screen now resembles the following illustration.

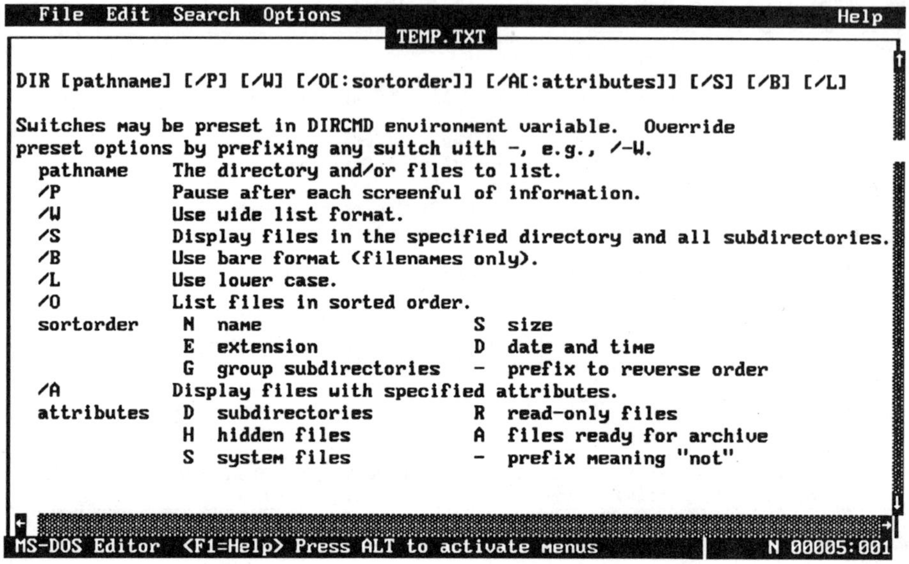

```
 File  Edit  Search  Options                                      Help
                               TEMP.TXT

DIR [pathname] [/P] [/W] [/O[:sortorder]] [/A[:attributes]] [/S] [/B] [/L]

Switches may be preset in DIRCMD environment variable.  Override
preset options by prefixing any switch with -, e.g., /-W.
  pathname    The directory and/or files to list.
  /P          Pause after each screenful of information.
  /W          Use wide list format.
  /S          Display files in the specified directory and all subdirectories.
  /B          Use bare format (filenames only).
  /L          Use lower case.
  /O          List files in sorted order.
  sortorder    N  name                    S  size
               E  extension               D  date and time
               G  group subdirectories    -  prefix to reverse order
  /A          Display files with specified attributes.
  attributes   D  subdirectories          R  read-only files
               H  hidden files            A  files ready for archive
               S  system files            -  prefix meaning "not"

MS-DOS Editor  <F1=Help> Press ALT to activate menus          N 00005:001
```

9. Move to the beginning of line 7 (00007:001) and press **Return** to insert a blank line.
10. Experiment with other editing features before ending this activity. Be sure to press **Alt-S** and then **F1** to see how help information is displayed.
11. Finish the activity by pressing **Alt-F X**, tab to No, and press **Return**. Then delete the TEMP.TXT file using **DEL TEMP.TXT** and pressing **Return**.
12. Turn to Module 25 to continue the learning sequence.

Module 25
EDLIN (1.00+)

DESCRIPTION

EDLIN is a line editor program that is available on all versions of DOS. A line editor is used to create and save text and program files. It also lets you modify file contents through insertion and deletion commands.

A line editor uses line numbers to display and edit text. This is different from what are called *full-screen* editors. Full-screen editors, which describes most word processing programs, let you move the cursor anywhere on a displayed screen of text. Although line editing may sound crude in comparison to full-screen editing, you will find EDLIN quite fast for creating files and performing minor touch-up work. Just a few keystrokes let you create and modify text files.

When an existing text file is edited and saved, EDLIN automatically converts the original file to a backup file (with a .BAK extension) for safekeeping. Then, when you view your directory, you see that the edited file exists with its original filename and extension and with the filename and a .BAK extension.

Now that you know what EDLIN does, you can learn how to use EDLIN by experimenting with the commands described in the following pages of this module. Although EDLIN commands may seem awkward at first, you should begin to appreciate the way EDLIN behaves with just a few minutes of practice.

To create a new text file (or "document") with EDLIN, just type EDLIN *filename* and press Return. A screen similar to the following is displayed:

```
A:\>EDLIN MYTEXT
New file
*
```

The asterisk (*) is EDLIN's prompt, similar to DOS' A> or C> prompt. You can quit EDLIN by typing Q (for "quit"), typing Y, and pressing Return; the DOS prompt is redisplayed.

EDLIN COMMANDS Because the EDLIN prompt does not tell you any more than the DOS prompt, it is necessary to know EDLIN commands before using it. A list of EDLIN commands follows in Table 25-1. With use, they should become just as familiar as DOS commands. Either uppercase or lowercase is acceptable.

NOTE

All EDLIN commands are followed by pressing the Return key. EDLIN's *pointer* is a conceptual place within a document. For example, if you want to edit text in line 5, you can "move the pointer" to line 5 by typing 5 and pressing Return. If you want to check the position of the pointer, you can type . (a period) and press Return.

Table 25-1 EDLIN Commands and Examples

Command	*Meaning*
	NOTE The asterisk (*) is shown in the examples within this table to designate EDLIN's prompt; it is not typed as part of the commands.
Return	Executes the typed EDLIN command or moves the pointer to the next line in the document. If you edit a line and change your mind, press Ctrl-C to cancel the changes and return to the EDLIN prompt. Table 25-2 is a list of EDLIN editing keys.
#	Moves the pointer one line below the last line of the document. Example: *#i Inserts a new line at the bottom of the file.

. (period)	Displays the current line (the last line edited).
	Example:
	*.
	    1: This is text for line number 1.
	    1: _

number 1 to 65529	Typing a line number moves the pointer to that line. The cursor is at the beginning of the line ready for you to make changes. The change process is described later.
	Examples:
	*3
	    3: This is the text on line number 3.
	    3: _
	*+2 Moves pointer two lines down.
	*-10 Moves pointer 10 lines up.

Table 25-1 EDLIN Commands and Examples (Cont.)

Command	*Meaning*
A	Append (or add) a specified number of lines to the bottom of the current file (which is loaded in your computer's memory). This command is used with the W (write) command. When memory becomes full, you can write the first portion of your file to disk with the Write command. Then use Append to add more lines from disk to the end of that part of the file in memory. The message "End of input file" is displayed if the last line of the input file is read into memory. Example: *100A — Adds 100 lines to the end of your file.
C	Copies specified lines to another location in the file, beginning at the designated line. An optional count can be used to make multiple copies. Following lines are automatically renumbered. If you want 3 copies, the count is 3. Copied lines can't overlap, i.e., you can't copy lines 4 through 6 to lines 4, 5, or 6. Format: (beginning line),(ending line),(target line),(no. of copies)c Examples: *3,10,15C — Copy lines 3 through 10 to line 15. *2,5,9,2C — Copy lines 2 through 5 to line 9 twice (2 copies).
D	Deletes specified lines from the file. Format: (beginning line),(ending line)d Examples: *4,6D — Deletes lines 4 through 6 from the file. *,10D — Deletes lines beginning with the current line number through line 10. *6D or 6,D — Deletes line 6 from the file. *D — Deletes the current line from the file.
E	End editing and save the file to disk. Example: *E — Ends editing session and saves the file to disk. If the file already existed, the previous version is converted to a backup file with the .BAK extension.
I	Inserts a line in the document beginning at the current pointer location. Pressing Return inserts another new line. Following lines are automatically renumbered. Pressing Ctrl-C or Ctrl-Break ends the insert operation and redisplays the EDLIN prompt. Examples: *6I — Inserts a line in front of line 6. *#I — Inserts a line at the bottom of the file. *I — Inserts a line in front of the current line.

Table 25-1 EDLIN Commands and Examples (Cont.)

Command	Meaning	
L	Lists lines on the screen; the current line is marked by * following the displayed line number. You can list ranges of lines by specifying one or more line numbers.	
	Format: (beginning line),(ending line)L	
	Examples:	
	*3,12L	Lists lines 3 through 12.
	*,12L	Lists 11 lines beginning with line 12.
	*8,L or *8L	Lists 23 lines beginning with line 8.
	*L	Lists 23 lines of text including 11 lines before the current line, the current line, and 11 lines following the current line.
M	Moves specified lines from one location in the file to another.	
	Format: (beginning line),(ending line),(target line)m	
	Examples:	
	*3,5,9M	Moves lines 3 through 5 to line 9; lines are automatically renumbered.
	*,+5,25M	Moves the current line plus 5 more lines to line 25.
	*,-3,9M	Moves the 3 lines preceding the current line and the current line to line 9.
	*5M	Moves the current line ahead of line 5.
P	Lists specified lines of text (or a "page") on the screen. You can use this command to move through a document. Unlike the List command, the Page command changes the current line number.	
	Format: (beginning line),(ending line)p	
	Examples:	
	*5,25P	Displays lines 5 through 25.
	*P	Displays 23 lines; the last line displayed becomes the current line.
Q	Quit EDLIN without saving the file.	
	Example:	
	*Q	EDLIN asks, "Abort edit (Y/N)?" Typing Y abandons the file and displays the DOS prompt.
R	Replaces the first text string (or *find string*) with the second (or *replace string*) within a designated range of lines.	
	NOTE You can use Ctrl-Z in place of F6 in the Replace command line. The question mark is optional and is used when you want EDLIN to give you a Yes or No replacement option each time the search string is found. Omitting the Replace string deletes the search string. Uppercase and lowercase characters must be matched.	

Table 25-1 EDLIN Commands and Examples (Cont.)

Command	Meaning
R (Cont.)	Format: (beginning line),(ending line)?r(find string)(F6)(replace string) Examples: *1,25?RSmith F6 Jones — Replaces Smith with Jones within lines 1 through 25. Displays O.K.? prompt before each replacement. *1,25RDobbs Ctrl-Z Evans — Replaces every occurrence of Dobbs with Evans within lines 1 through 25. *RDobbs F6 Jones — Replaces every Dobbs with Jones throughout the entire file. *1,25Rvery F6 — Deletes every occurrence of the word "very." This is the same as replacing it with nothing.
S	Searches for a specified text string within a designated range of lines. Format: (beginning line),(ending line)?s(search string) Examples: *10,30?STotal — Finds "Total." The ? causes the text line containing the search string to be displayed. The search is made within lines 10 through 30. *10,30S — Finds the last search string used; searches within lines 10 through 30. *STotal — Finds "Total" beginning with the line following the current line and ending with the last line in the file. *S — Finds the last search string used following the current line.
T	Reads (or transfers) a named file into the current file ahead of a designated line. Format: line T D:*filename.ext* Examples: *6T B:LOVE.LTR — Reads (transfers) the file named LOVE.LTR on the disk in drive B: to the current file beginning at line 6. *T MYFILE — Reads (transfers) MYFILE from the default disk beginning at the current line.
W	Writes a specified number of lines from the current file to disk, beginning with line number 1. Used when memory becomes full. After writing lines to disk, you can resume editing. You may wish to append additional lines to the bottom of the file using the Append command. Format: number of lines w Example: *500W — Writes 500 lines to disk, beginning with the first line in memory.

Table 25-2 EDLIN Editing Keys

Command	*Use*
Ctrl-C	Returns to the EDLIN prompt without changing the current line.
F1	Displays the next character on the current line each time F1 is pressed.
F3	Displays all text on the current line.
F5	Cancels changes to the current line without changing the original text.
F6	Used with the replace command to identify the replace string.
Ins	Inserts a blank space to the right of the cursor.
Del	Deletes the character at the cursor.

EDLIN PRACTICE SESSION The only way to see whether you like EDLIN is to try it out. The Typical Operation section of this module lets you experiment with some of EDLIN's commands.

APPLICATIONS

Because EDLIN occupies a minimum amount of disk space, is fast, and is easy to use, many people use EDLIN to write and edit program source files and documents. The disk space issue is particularly important if you are creating large files on a microcomputer with floppy disks. Many word processors occupy nearly all the available space on early technology removable disks. EDLIN uses less than 5,000 bytes (or characters) of disk space, making it one of the smallest editors available.

TYPICAL OPERATION

In this activity you use the EDLIN program to create and edit a practice file. Begin at the DOS prompt.

1. Type **EDLIN MYFILE** and press **Return**. Notice the following display.

```
A:\>EDLIN MYFILE
New file
*
```

2. Type **i** (for insert) and press **Return** to begin entering text. Notice that the cursor moves to line 1.

```
A:\>EDLIN MYFILE
New file
*i
        1:*
```

The asterisk following 1 designates that line 1 is the current line.

3. Type the following file, pressing **Return** at the end of each line until you reach line 6.

```
A:\>EDLIN MYFILE
New file
*i
        1:*This is a new document named myfile.
        2:*Edlin is being used to create it.
        3:*Notice how a new line number is displayed each time I press
        4:*the Return key.
        5:*Now that I've created this document, I can save it.
        6:*
```

4. Press **Ctrl-C** to redisplay the EDLIN prompt.
5. Type **e** and press **Return** to exit EDLIN and save the file.
6. Start EDLIN again by typing **EDLIN MYFILE** and pressing **Return**. Notice the following screen.

```
A:\>EDLIN MYFILE
End of input file
*
```

7. Type **L** and press **Return** to list the file.

```
A:\>EDLIN MYFILE
End of input file
*L
        1:*This is a new document named myfile.
        2: Edlin is being used to create it.
        3: Notice how a new line number is displayed each time I press
        4: the Return key.
        5: Now that I've created this document, I can save it.
*
```

8. Change the word "Return" on line 4 to "Enter." To go to the line, type **4** and press **Return**; notice the following display:

```
*4
        4:*the Return key.
        4:*
```

9. Press **F1** four times to move the cursor to the space following "the."

10. Type **Enter**.
11. Press the **Del** key once.
12. Press **F3** to display the rest of the line; then press **Return**. Your document should now resemble the following illustration.

```
*4
        4:*the Return key.
        4:*the Enter key.
*
```

13. Type **L** and press **Return** to list the document; notice the display. The asterisk indicates that line 4 is the active line.

```
*L
        1: This is a new document named myfile.
        2: Edlin is being used to create it.
        3: Notice how a new line number is displayed each time I press
        4:*the Enter key.
        5: Now that I've created this document, I can save it.
*
```

14. Insert a line ahead of line 5 as follows:
    a. Type **5i** and press **Return**.
    b. Type **This is new line number 5.**.
    c. Press **Return** at the end of the line.
    d. Press **Ctrl-C** to return to the EDLIN prompt.
    e. Check to see if your screen resembles the following illustration:

```
*5i
        5:*This is new line number 5.
        6:*^C

*
```

15. Type **L** and press **Return** to list the file; notice that it resembles the following screen:
16. Replace the word "Edlin" with "EDLIN" as follows:
    a. Type **1,5rEdlin**, press **Ctrl-Z** (or **F6**), type **EDLIN**, and press **Return**.
    b. Notice the display.

```
*1,5rEdlin^ZEDLIN
        2: EDLIN is being used to create it.
*
```

17. Copy lines 1 through 4 to line 7 (lines 1 - 4 to lines 7 - 10) as follows:
    a. Type **1,4,7c** and press **Return**.
    b. Type **L** and press **Return** to list the file; notice the following screen.

```
*1,4,7c
*L
         1: This is a new document named myfile.
         2: EDLIN is being used to create it.
         3: Notice how a new line number is displayed each time I press
         4: the Enter key.
         5: This is new line number 5.
         6: Now that I've created this document, I can save it.
         7:*This is a new document named myfile.
         8: EDLIN is being used to create it.
         9: Notice how a new line number is displayed each time I press
        10: the Enter key.
*
```

18. Move lines 1 through 4 to line 6 as follows:
    a. Type **1,4,6m** and press **Return**.
    b. Type **L** and press **Return** to list the change. Notice the results of the move.

```
*1,4,6m
*L
         1: This is new line number 5.
         2:*This is a new document named myfile.
         3: EDLIN is being used to create it.
         4: Notice how a new line number is displayed each time I press
         5: the Enter key.
         6: Now that I've created this document, I can save it.
         7: This is a new document named myfile.
         8: EDLIN is being used to create it.
         9: Notice how a new line number is displayed each time I press
        10: the Enter key.
*
```

19. Type **e** and press **Return** to end editing and save the file.
20. This concludes the practice EDLIN session. To conserve disk space, delete the files MYFILE and MYFILE.BAK by typing **DEL MYFILE.*** and pressing **Return**.
21. Turn to Module 46 to continue the learning sequence.

Module 26
ERASE (or DELETE) (1.00+)

DESCRIPTION

The DEL (or ERASE) command removes files from a diskette and reallocates the disk space that the file previously occupied. DEL is an internal command available on all versions of DOS. The shortest form of the command is DEL; therefore, DEL is used as the command form in this module. However, there are some DOS users who have adopted the alternative form, ERASE.

The general form of the command is:

```
DEL filename
```

Regardless of the logged drive or filepath, you can delete a file from any disk by placing the disk drive designator, such as B:, at the beginning of the filename. If you have DOS version 2.00 or later, you can use the directory pathname in the command, such as DEL C:\DATA\TEMP.DTA.

Be cautious when deleting a file. Once deleted, a file is gone forever, unless you have a file recovery utility. Even then, if additional disk operations occur, the recovery utility may be rendered useless.

You can delete multiple files by using the wild card in your DEL command line. For example, if you want to delete all .OBJ files on the disk in drive B, you can use DEL B:*.OBJ. This command deletes every filename that has the extension .OBJ. You also can delete every file on a disk with DEL *.*. However, DOS alerts you to the fact that you are on the brink of possible disaster by displaying "Are you sure (Y/N)?" Typing Y (for "Yes") followed by Return does the deed. Typing N cancels the deletion and redisplays the DOS prompt without deleting any files.

DOS Version 4.01 introduced the /P parameter, which displays each filename prior to deletion and prompts you for an erasure decision. For example, if you have several files that you wish to delete having the extension .BAK, you can use the command form DEL *.BAK /P.

Each file is displayed in the following fashion.

```
A:\>DEL *.BAK /P

A:\EXTLIST.BAK,    Delete (Y/N)?Y
A:\LETTER1.BAK,    Delete (Y/N)?Y
A:\NOTES.BAK,    Delete (Y/N)?Y

A:\>
```

APPLICATIONS

The DEL command is used normally to delete individual, unwanted files from a disk. Many programs automatically create backup files that occupy valuable disk space. The EDLIN program, MicroPro's WordStar word processing program, and Ashton-Tate's dBASE series are examples of such programs. The backup files have the extension .BAK. This makes it easy to delete your old backup files with the command DEL *.BAK. If you have DOS version 4.01, you may opt to use the command form DEL *.BAK /P.

TYPICAL OPERATION

In this activity you use the DEL command to erase an unneeded file. Begin at the DOS prompt.

1. Create a temporary file using the COPY command as follows:
   a. Type **COPY CON: TESTFILE** and press **Return.**
   b. Type This **is a test file..**
   c. Press **Ctrl-Z**; then press **Return** to write the file to disk.
2. Type **DIR TESTFILE** then press **Return** and notice the following display.

```
A:\>DIR TESTFILE

 Volume in drive A has no label
 Volume Serial Number is 0F66-14F7
 Directory of A:\

TESTFILE            20 02-27-91   9:09a
        1 file(s)          20 bytes
                        94208 bytes free

A:\>
```

3. Type **DEL TESTFILE** and press **Return** to delete the file from your disk.
4. Verify that the file is gone by typing **DIR TESTFILE**; notice the following display.

```
A:\>DIR TESTFILE

 Volume in drive A has no label
 Volume Serial Number is 0F66-14F7
 Directory of A:\

File not found

A:\>
```

5. Turn to Module 63 to continue the learning sequence.

Module 27
EXE2BIN (1.00+)

DESCRIPTION

The EXE2BIN command, which is available on all DOS versions, converts compiled program files, usually having the extension .EXE, to binary command files, which use the extension .COM. This is where the name EXE2BIN was derived. The utility is used to convert an .EXE file to a BINary file.

The form of the EXE2BIN command is

```
EXE2BIN file1.exe file1.com
```

If the .EXE extension is not used with the source filename, the extension .EXE is assumed. If the .COM extension is not used with the target filename, the extension .BIN is assigned to the target filename, where BIN stands for "binary." You may then rename the file with the REN command to change the .BIN extension to .COM. The Typical Operation section of the LINK command module uses EXE2BIN to convert a file.

The EXE2BIN command converts program files with the extension .EXE to a "memory image." Once converted, the program is smaller and loads faster. The resulting program must be smaller than 64K.

APPLICATIONS

If you are a programmer and have compiled and linked a program, you can convert that program to a "COM file" using EXE2BIN. Otherwise, you will not have an application for the EXE2BIN utility.

TYPICAL OPERATION

Because this is an advanced DOS command requiring you to first write a program source file and then compile and link it into an object file, the typical operation activity is not appropriate for the general audience of this book. However, if you are a programmer, you can use EXE2BIN to convert your compiled program files into COM files using the form of the EXE2BIN command shown in the Description section of this module. You can also review the LINK command module to see how EXE2BIN interacts with other commands. This concludes the learning sequence.

Module 28
FASTOPEN (3.30+)

DESCRIPTION

The FASTOPEN command is an external command that was introduced in DOS version 3.30. The FASTOPEN command gives fast access to a specified number of recently used pathnames and filenames by storing their names and locations in memory. The most recent file used goes to the front of the FASTOPEN search queue, moving previously queued files one level down.

This eliminates the need and corresponding time required to search a series of filepaths for frequently used files. On large disks with complex directory structures, the search time can cause unwanted delays.

The general form of the FASTOPEN command is:

```
FASTOPEN D:=(n,m) /X
```

where: D: is the drive designation. Multiple drives may be specified.

n is the number of directories or filenames you want stored in memory. The value *n* may range from 10 to 999. If *n* is not specified, a default value of 34 is used.

m specifies the number of continuous space buffers for the files on the selected drive, D:. This value ranges from 1 to 999. The default value is also 34.

/X parameter, introduced with DOS version 4.01, uses expanded memory. This gives you more space in low memory for your applications programs. If you use the /X parameter, be sure that the appropriate device driver (XMAEM.SYS or XMA2EMS.SYS) is first placed in your CONFIG.SYS file. Next, you can start FASTOPEN using a command line that resembles one of the following examples within your CONFIG.SYS file.

```
INSTALL=FASTOPEN.EXE C:=(100,200) /X
```

or

```
INSTALL=FASTOPEN C: = 100
```

Drives defined with the ASSIGN, JOIN, or SUBST commands are ineligible for use with the FASTOPEN command.

The command FASTOPEN C:=(20,) lets you maintain a total of 20 file and directory entries in the queue. The continuous space buffer storage feature is not used.

Exceeding the use of 20 files "pushes" the last entry out of the queue. Therefore, be sure that the value of *n* is sufficiently large to hold all of the directory levels and filenames you wish to use. Some other command examples are given for your review.

```
FASTOPEN C:=(,200)
```

Only the continuous space buffers for drive C: are placed in low memory. The file and directory storage component is not enabled.

```
FASTOPEN C:=(50:100) D:=(25,50)
```

This example places 50 file and directory entry buffers and 100 continuous space buffers for drive C and 25 file and directory entry buffers and 50 continuous space buffers for drive D in low memory.

The FASTOPEN command is used once per system turn on. If you wish to change the parameters, it is necessary to reboot your system and reenter the command.

DOS Version 4.01 speeds up the FASTOPEN operation. It retrieves recently opened files faster than in DOS 3.3 by storing the file information in memory.

APPLICATIONS

You may wish to use the FASTOPEN command if you have a large fixed disk and spend a lot of time opening and closing files located in several different filepaths. The FASTOPEN command is normally placed in an AUTOEXEC.BAT. This gives you automatic access to its capability, eliminating the need to enter the command each time you think you may need it.

TYPICAL OPERATION

In this activity you use FASTOPEN to give you quick access to 50 files. Begin at the DOS prompt.

NOTE

In the following step, use either A: or C: in place of D: to use a disk drive available on your system.

1. Type **FASTOPEN D:=(50,)** and press **Return**. Notice the message.

```
FASTOPEN installed
```

   You now have fast access to a total of 50 directories and files.

2. Turn to Module 34 to continue the learning sequence.

Module 29
FDISK (2.00+)

DESCRIPTION

The FDISK command is an external DOS command that prepares a fixed (or hard) disk for use. This command is available with DOS versions 2.00 and later. It is used to organize your fixed disk into partitions, which allocates disk space to separate usable areas.

Each partition is assigned a logical drive letter, like C, D, and E when more than one partition is used on a single disk device. Because the maximum amount of disk space addressed by DOS versions released prior to 4.01 was 32 megabytes, it was necessary to be familiar with partitioning strategies offered by the FDISK command in order to organize disk drives having storage capacities in excess of the 32-megabyte barrier. Smaller disks are normally given a single DOS partition.

The FDISK command is used after your fixed disk has received a *low-level* format. The low-level format process is described briefly in Module 32. You may have to perform a low-level format yourself if you purchase a new fixed disk and controller card directly from the manufacturer or a distributor. If you purchase your computer from a reputable dealer, the fixed disk should be partitioned and formatted for you.

FIXED DISK GEOGRAPHY AND PARTITIONING Fixed disks are divided into what are called cylinders. If you have a 10-, 20-, or even 40-megabyte fixed disk (where a megabyte is a million characters), your disk probably contains 305 cylinders beginning with cylinder number 000 and ending with cylinder number 304. A typical cylinder has a 34,816-character capacity. The cylinder number varies with capacity and number of heads used by your fixed disk.

The maximum size of a fixed disk partition is 32 megabytes. Each partition may have its own operating system. If DOS is the only operating system you wish to use, then you can assign the entire fixed disk to DOS. However, if your disk is larger than 32 megabytes, you must use a primary and extended DOS partitions.

Using a single operating system is most common, as most people use software that is compatible with DOS. A procedure for formatting, transferring DOS, and copying external files to a fixed disk is described. In addition, a description of partitioning also is provided.

PREPARING YOUR FIXED DISK FOR DOS To prepare a fixed disk for use with DOS version 3.30 or earlier, perform the following procedure. The FDISK program supplied with DOS version 4.01 and 5.00 is much easier to use, as it is menu driven and supplies additional information about your disk. The DOS 5.00 menu system is shown following this procedure.

CAUTION

Performing this procedure erases all stored data. Therefore, if your fixed disk is already formatted, you may wish to read the procedure instead of actually using it. Your disk must also have received a low-level format.

1. Place your DOS system diskette in drive A and turn on your computer.
2. Respond to the date and time prompts.
3. Type FDISK and press Return; notice a screen similar to the following:

```
IBM Personal Computer
Fixed Disk Setup Program Version 3.30
(C)Copyright IBM Corp. 1983,1987

FDISK Options

Current Fixed Disk Drive: 1

Choose one of the following:

    1. Create DOS partition
    2. Change Active Partition
    3. Delete DOS partition
    4. Display Partition Information



Enter choice: [1]



Press ESC to return to DOS
```

4. Type 1 and press Return; you should see

```
Create DOS Partition

Current Fixed Disk Drive: 1


    1. Create Primary DOS partition
    2. Create Extended DOS partition



Enter choice: [1]



Press ESC to return to FDISK Options
```

5. Press Return to accept 1. Check the following display.

```
Create Primary DOS Partition

Current Fixed Disk Drive: 1



Do you wish to use the maximum size
for a DOS partition and make the DOS
partition active (Y/N) . . . . . . ? [Y]




Press ESC to return to FDISK Options
```

6. Type Y to allocate 32 megabytes for DOS. This also makes DOS the default operating system when you turn your computer on or reset with Ctrl-Alt-Del. The cylinder numbers are displayed on your screen as they are allocated.
7. When the process is finished, check to see that your DOS diskette is in drive A and press any key in response to the "Press any key..." prompt.
8. Press any key, such as Spacebar, and the DOS prompt is redisplayed.

NOTE

In the following steps, the fixed disk is formatted, the system transferred, and all DOS files copied to it. It is assumed that the fixed disk is drive C.

9. Type FORMAT C:/S/V and press Return; the following prompt is displayed.

```
A:\>FORMAT C:/S/V
Enter current Volume Label for drive C:
Press any key to begin formatting drive C:
```

10. Press a key to begin the formatting process. Notice that the "Formatting..." message is displayed. Later versions of DOS display the head and cylinder numbers. After several minutes, a "System transferred" message is displayed, and you are prompted to enter a 1- to 11-character disk volume name.
11. Type a volume name and press Return, or just press Return if you do not want a volume name. Your fixed disk is now formatted and contains DOS. The system prompt is redisplayed.

12. Type C: and press Return; then type MD DOS and press Return to create a DOS subdirectory.
13. Type CD\DOS to log the DOS subdirectory.
14. Type COPY A:*.* and press Return. Each external DOS command is copied to the DOS subdirectory of drive C. As they are copied, notice that their filenames are simultaneously displayed.
15. If you have a DOS Supplemental Programs disk, put it in drive A and repeat step 14 to transfer these files to your fixed disk.
16. Remove the disk from drive A and press and release Ctrl-Alt-Del to restart your computer. Notice that your system boots from the fixed disk. (Drive A must be empty to boot from the fixed disk.)

Creating Extended DOS Partition If you wish to create an extended partition, you must type N and press Return in response to the prompt shown in step 5 of the preceding procedure.

The example in step 5 shows a total of 305 cylinders, which is the total capacity of the fixed disk. Entering a number, such as 150, sets aside 150 cylinders for DOS in the Extended partition. To access this partition, it is necessary to use Option 2 of the FDISK option menu.

If you have already allocated the entire disk to DOS, you see a screen similar to the following one. Notice the message "No space to create a DOS partition."

```
Create Extended DOS Partition

Current Fixed Disk Drive: 1

Partition Status   Type   Start  End Size
 C: 1        A    PRI DOS     0  609  610









No space to create a DOS partition

Press ESC to return to FDISK Options
```

Changing an Active Partition (Option 2) You can change partitions using Option 2 of the first FDISK menu. Typing 2 and pressing Return displays a screen similar to the following one. Notice that this screen indicates a primary and an extended partition.

```
Change Active Partition

Current Fixed Disk Drive: 1

Partition Status   Type   Start  End  Size
 C: 1         A    PRI DOS     0  609  610




Total disk space is 306 cylinders

Enter the number of the partition you
want to make active...............: [ ]

Press ESC to return to FDISK Options
```

The A status indicates the active disk partition. To change the active partition to 2, type 2 and press Return. Use Esc to back your way out of the FDISK utility.

Deleting a Partition (Option 3) You can delete either the primary or extended partition using Option 3 of the first FDISK menu. Typing 3 and pressing Return displays the following information.

```
Delete DOS Partition

Current Fixed Disk Drive: 1

Choose one of the following:

    1.  Delete Primary DOS partition
    2.  Delete Extended DOS partition



Enter choice: [ ]



Press ESC to return to FDISK Options
```

Typing 1 and pressing Return displays the following screen.

```
Delete Primary DOS Partition

Current Fixed Disk Drive: 1

Partition Status   Type   Start   End Size
 C: 1         A    PRI DOS     0  609  610





Warning! Data in the Primary DOS
partition will be lost. Do you wish
to continue......................? [N]


Press ESC to return to FDISK Options
```

Pressing Esc or Return redisplays the first FDISK menu, canceling the delete operation. Typing Y and pressing Return deletes the partition.

```
Display Partition Information

Current Fixed Disk Drive: 1

Partition Status   Type   Start   End Size
 C: 1         A    PRI DOS     0  609  610


Total disk space is  610 cylinders.





Press ESC to return to FDISK Options
```

The preceding display represents what you see with a single partition. The Delete and Change Partition examples contain screens that are typical of a fixed disk that contains two partitions.

Once you have partitioned your fixed disk, you must format each partition. You can use either the FORMAT/S or SELECT command, as appropriate.

CAUTION

Never use FORMAT or SELECT on a disk containing wanted information or files, as these commands erase all data.

If you plan to use default values, FORMAT will do nicely. However, if you wish to use a special country and keyboard setup, use SELECT. The SELECT command, available with DOS 3.1 through 4.01, lets you specify country and keyboard codes for a number of languages. In addition, the selected country code controls the way that date, time, currency, and decimal notation is displayed. It also affects sorting operations. For more information about the effect of the SELECT command, see Module 54. SELECT was discontinued in version 5.00.

THE DOS 5.00 FDISK MENU The FDISK program released in DOS 5.00 is similar to prior versions except for a few additional bits of status information. The FDISK Options menu, the Create DOS Partition or Logical DOS Drive menu, and the Display partition information menu are shown for your review in the following screen illustrations.

```
                           MS-DOS Version 5.00
                          Fixed Disk Setup Program
                  (C)Copyright Microsoft Corp. 1983 - 1990

                              FDISK Options

Current fixed disk drive: 1

Choose one of the following:

1. Create DOS partition or Logical DOS Drive
2. Set active partition
3. Delete partition or Logical DOS Drive
4. Display partition information


Enter choice: [1]




Press Esc to exit FDISK
```

Selection 1 displays the following menu.

```
                    Create DOS Partition or Logical DOS Drive

Current fixed disk drive: 1

Choose one of the following:

1. Create Primary DOS Partition
2. Create Extended DOS Partition
3. Create Logical DOS Drive(s) in the Extended DOS Partition



Enter choice: [1]




Press Esc to return to FDISK Options
```

Notice how selection 4 from the FDISK Options menu displays additional status information.

```
                        Display Partition Information

Current fixed disk drive: 1

Partition  Status   Type    Volume Label  Mbytes   System   Usage
 C: 1         A    PRI DOS   DISK1_VOL1     32     FAT12      70%
    2              Non-DOS                  14                30%


Total disk space is    46 Mbytes (1 Mbyte = 1048576 bytes)






Press Esc to continue
```

As you can see, the DOS 5.00 menus are quite similar to those used in earlier DOS versions. For example, their structure and use is quite similar to the DOS 3.3 menu series shown previously.

APPLICATIONS

The FDISK command is vital if you have a system with a fixed disk. The ability to share the fixed disk with different operating systems or to have multiple partitions is often convenient if not necessary. If you have a 40-, 70-, or 120-megabyte disk, you must use partitions to take advantage of the entire disk if you have a PC-XT or AT compatible microcomputer.

If you own programs that operate on non-DOS operating systems, such as Xenix, UNIX, or CP/M-86, you must install that operating system on a partition other than the one allocated for DOS. This is accomplished using format utilities supplied with the other operating systems. When multiple partitions are used, you will use FDISK to switch between them, to change their size, and possibly to delete partitions used for programs that you no longer want to use.

TYPICAL OPERATION

NOTE

Perform the following procedure only if you have a fixed disk system. Otherwise, turn to Module 8 to continue the learning sequence.

In this activity you use the FDISK command to display the status of your fixed disk. Begin at the DOS prompt.

1. With the A> prompt displayed, type **FDISK** and press **Return**. Notice a display similar to the following.

```
                         MS-DOS Version 5.00
                       Fixed Disk Setup Program
                (C)Copyright Microsoft Corp. 1983 - 1990

                             FDISK Options

Current fixed disk drive: 1

Choose one of the following:

1. Create DOS partition or Logical DOS Drive
2. Set active partition
3. Delete partition or Logical DOS Drive
4. Display partition information


Enter choice: [1]




Press Esc to exit FDISK
```

2. Type **4** and press **Return**; notice a display similar to the following:

```
                    Display Partition Information

Current fixed disk drive: 1

Partition  Status   Type    Volume Label  Mbytes   System   Usage
 C: 1         A    PRI DOS   DISK1_VOL1      32    FAT12      70%
    2              Non-DOS                   14               30%


Total disk space is   46 Mbytes (1 Mbyte = 1048576 bytes)






Press Esc to continue
```

3. Press **Esc** twice to redisplay the DOS prompt.
4. Turn to Module 8 to continue the learning sequence.

Module 30
FILENAMES (1.00+)

DESCRIPTION

It is important to understand DOS file naming conventions and their use. This module describes filenames and some special filename "tools" called *wild cards* and *literals*.

WHAT IS A FILENAME? Every program and data file is given a name to differentiate it from other programs and data files. A program is one or more computer instructions collected into a file. A data file is normally a collection of characters (or data) that make up a document, like a letter, or a database, like a collection of accounting transactions or customer records.

You should use descriptive filenames. For example, if you create and save a letter to Mom, you might give it the filename MOM.LTR. A letter to Dad could be called DAD.LTR. A word processing program file might have the filename WP.COM. Examine these filenames a little closer.

First, notice that each filename is meaningful. This is important if you want to know what is in a file by looking at its name. Obscure filenames are of little use when viewing a disk directory (or filename list).

Also notice that the filenames have two parts separated by a period. In our filename examples, the first part was used to differentiate Mom's letter from Dad's. The second part of the filename, called an extension, specifies the file type. These files are letters, so (for convenience) we assigned the extension .LTR. When we look at a list of filenames, we can tell which ones are letters by looking at extensions; we can tell who the letters are to by reading the first part of the filenames. The extension COM designates a command file type. Command files and files having the extension EXE are executable program files. You can run files having the extension COM or EXE by typing the first part of the filename. For example, in the WP.COM example, typing WP and pressing Return causes the WP program to run. It is not necessary to type the filename extension. If you have program files having extensions like OVR, WKS, DBF, HLP, or PRN, use some other extension to avoid possible confusion.

FILENAME RULES There are a few simple rules associated with filenames. These are:

1. Filenames are one to eight characters in length with an optional one- to three-character filename extension.
2. Filenames can include any of the following characters.

   A - Z (or a - z)
   0 - 9
   $ & # @ ! % ' ' ( ) - { } _ / \

   Other characters are not allowed, such as : , ; ¦ +, as they have special meanings.
3. Reserved device names, described in Table 3-3 in Module 3, are not allowed.
4. A period is used to separate the first part of a filename from the extension.
5. When a filename includes an extension, include the extension when used in conjunction with a DOS command (like COPY, TYPE, or ERASE).

WILD CARDS AND LITERALS Now that you understand filename rules, you should understand the use of two convenient tools: *wild cards* and *literals*.

Wild Cards In the card game poker, a wild card may be any card that the player chooses. For example, if deuces are "wild," a player can make three kings by using two kings and a deuce. In DOS, an asterisk (*) character is "wild." The asterisk stands for one or more characters in a filename or extension, beginning with the asterisk position. If only an asterisk is used, it represents the entire filename. A few examples are in order. If you wish to list a directory of all files having the extension COM, you can type the command DIR *.COM and press Return.

Every filename with the extension COM is listed. If you want to list a directory of every file beginning with the letter W, you can use the command DIR W*.*. Every filename beginning with W and having any extension is listed. Therefore, the wild card lets you select a set of files based upon some common filename characteristic.

Literals The question mark (?) is used within filenames (and extensions) to represent any character. For example, the expression D???????.??? represents all filenames of eight characters beginning with the character D. If you want to list a directory of filenames having four or less characters, you can use the command form DIR ????.???. You can also combine literals and wild cards to accomplish the same result by using the command form DIR ????.*.

To display the filenames DISKCOMP.COM and DISKCOPY.COM, you can use DIR DISKCO??.*.

USING DISK DRIVE DESIGNATORS WITH FILENAMES Now that you know about filenames, you should also know that you can add the disk drive designator A: through G:, depending on the number of logical disk drives used by your system. For example, if you want to list a directory of all files on disk drive B beginning with the character D, use DIR B:D*.*.

Notice that the disk drive designator always includes a colon (:). Leaving the disk drive designator off of a filename causes DOS to "look" on the logged disk drive. That is, if the DOS prompt is A>, disk drive A is logged. If the B> prompt is displayed, disk drive B is logged. Keep in mind that all DOS commands are directed to the logged disk drive unless a different disk drive designator is typed in the command. (Also see ASSIGN.)

You can change logged disk drives by simply typing the drive designator and pressing Return. To change from A to B, type B: and press Return. The B> prompt is displayed.

USING PATHNAME DESIGNATORS WITH FILENAMES Pathnames became available with the introduction of version 2.00 of DOS. Pathnames let you subdivide a disk into separate directories (often called *subdirectories* or *file paths*). Every subdirectory has a pathname. This gives you the ability to collect similar kinds of information into separate directories, as you would collect files into a file cabinet and into file folders within the file cabinet. You can compare a pathname to the label on a file cabinet drawer or file folder. Module 19, which describes the DIR command, includes information about the creation, naming, and removal of subdirectories.

Pathnames use the same naming conventions as filenames. This is true with respect to:

- legitimate characters
- length of the pathname
- optional extension name and length

However, attempting to use the same pathname and filename within a common directory is not permitted by DOS.

For clarification, examine a complete filename. Include the disk drive, pathname, and filename designations. A file named MYDATA.DTA on drive C in the filepath \MASTER\SLAVE has the complete name C:\MASTER\SLAVE\MYDATA.DTA.

APPLICATIONS

A filename is an essential part of a file. As mentioned in the Description section of this module, meaningful filenames should be used if you are to know the use or contents of a displayed filename.

The wild card and literal characters give you expanded control in the way filenames are displayed, copied, or renamed. You can use wild cards and literals to restrict your operations to certain groups of filenames having common characteristics. For example, wild cards are often used to display a filename directory or to copy, delete, and rename groups of files. Literals also are used for the same purpose, although to a lesser extent.

TYPICAL OPERATION

In this activity you use filenames, wild cards, and literals with the DIR command. Begin at the DOS prompt.

1. Display a directory of all files beginning with the character D by typing **DIR D*.*** and pressing **Return**. Notice a display similar to the following:

```
A:\>DIR D*.*

 Volume in drive A has no label
 Volume Serial Number is 0F66-14F7
 Directory of A:\

DOSKEY   COM      5693 12-13-90   4:09a
DRIVER   SYS      5384 12-13-90   4:09a
DISPLAY  SYS     15682 12-13-90   4:09a
        3 file(s)      26759 bytes
                       91136 bytes free

A:\>
```

2. Display a directory of all files having the extension EXE by typing **DIR *.EXE** and pressing **Return**. Notice a display similar to the following:

```
A:\>DIR *.EXE

 Volume in drive A has no label
 Volume Serial Number is 0F66-14F7
 Directory of A:\

UNDELETE EXE     13666 12-13-90   4:09a
MEM      EXE     22104 12-13-90   4:09a
        2 file(s)      35770 bytes
                       91136 bytes free

A:\>
```

3. Display a directory of all files having four characters or less in the first part of the filename by typing **DIR ????.*** and pressing **Return**. Notice a display similar to the following:

```
A:\>DIR ????.*

 Volume in drive A has no label
 Volume Serial Number is 0F66-14F7
 Directory of A:\

MEM      EXE     22104 12-13-90   4:09a
SYS      COM     13200 12-13-90   4:09a
ANSI     SYS      8868 12-13-90   4:09a
        3 file(s)      44172 bytes
                       91136 bytes free

A:\>
```

4. Turn to Module 19 to continue the learning sequence.

Module 31
FIND (2.00+)

DESCRIPTION

Beginning with DOS version 2.00, several external commands, called filters, were introduced. These filter commands are used to intercept, rearrange, and output selected data. Three filter commands are: SORT, FIND, and MORE. This module deals with the FIND command. However, examples include combining this command with other DOS commands and filters.

The FIND filter is used to search a file for one or more designated characters (called a *text string*). Depending upon the form of the FIND command, each line having (or not having) the text string is sent to an output device, such as the display screen, a file, or the printer. The text string is always typed within quotes ("text string"). There are three parameters available with the FIND command:

/V Display lines not having the designated text string.

/C Counts and displays the number of lines containing the text string.

/N Displays the relative line number in front of each line containing the text string.

/i Ignores uppercase or lowercase during the search (available in DOS 5.00).

A few examples of how the FIND filter is used are shown below. Like SORT, piping commands are also available for use with the FIND command.

FIND "PN-1256" PARTFILE — Finds "PN-1256" in the file named PARTFILE and displays the information on the screen.

FIND "Bob" TEX CAL — Finds "Bob" in the files TEX and CAL and displays the information on the screen.

FIND "Bob" TEX /V — Displays the lines in the TEX file that do not contain the text string "Bob."

FIND "PART NO." PARTS.DOC /i — Displays "Part No.", "PART NO.", and "part no." in the PARTS.DOC file; the /i switch ignores upper or lowercase (available in DOS 5.00).

DIR ¦ FIND "TXT" — Displays a directory of filenames having a "TXT" extension.

DIR ¦ FIND "<DIR>" >FILE1 — Places a directory of pathnames having a "<DIR>" in the directory listing in the file FILE1.

DIR ¦ FIND "<DIR>" /N — Counts and displays the number of pathnames in a directory listing.

DIR ¦ SORT ¦ FIND "<DIR>" — Displays a sorted list of pathnames, where pathnames have <DIR> listed in the directory.

APPLICATIONS

Filter commands have many uses. The FIND filter is often used with the DIR command to find specific files or file types within a directory. As shown in one of the FIND examples, you can combine SORT with it to provide a sorted list of specified file types, such as pathnames having "<DIR>" entries.

TYPICAL OPERATION

In this activity you use the FIND filter command to find, sort, and display a specified group of filenames. Then you use EDLIN to create a small file and use the FIND filter command to locate specified character strings. Begin at the DOS prompt.

1. Type **DIR ¦FIND "EXE"** and press **Return**; notice that only those files containing EXE in the name or extension are listed.
2. Type **EDLIN TEST.TXT** and press **Return** to open a new file.
3. Type **i** and press **Return** and type the following five lines of text; press **Return** following each line. Press **Ctrl-C** on line 6.

```
A:\>EDLIN TEST.TXT
New file
*i
        1:*Johnson, Bob
        2:*Taylor, Francis
        3:*Jones, Julia
        4:*Tanner, Fred
        5:*Joseph, Liz
        6:*^C

*
```

4. Type **e** and press **Return** to exit and save the file.
5. Type **FIND /N "Jo" TEST.TXT** and press **Return**; your display should resemble the following illustration.

```
A:\>FIND /N "Jo" TEST.TXT

---------- TEST.TXT
[1]Johnson, Bob
[3]Jones, Julia
[5]Joseph, Liz

A:\>
```

Notice that those lines containing the find string "Jo" are displayed. Also notice that the "/N" filter numbers the displayed lines.

6. Type **FIND /N /V "Jo" TEST.TXT** and press **Return**; your display should resemble the following illustration.

```
A:\>FIND /N /V "Jo" TEST.TXT

---------- TEST.TXT
[2]Taylor, Francis
[4]Tanner, Fred

A:\>
```

Notice that the "/V" parameter shows lines that do not contain the FIND text string.

7. Use the DEL command to delete the TEST.TXT practice file from your disk.
8. Turn to Module 41 to continue the learning sequence.

Module 32
FORMAT (1.00+)

DESCRIPTION

The FORMAT command is an external DOS command that is available on all versions of DOS. This command prepares a new disk for use by organizing the disk into magnetic tracks and sectors. The number of sectors per track varies with the DOS version you use. DOS versions prior to 2.00 use eight sectors per track, 40 tracks per side. Version 2.00 and later use nine sectors per track. DOS version 3.00 introduced a high-capacity formatting capability for the IBM PC-AT, which uses a high-capacity disk drive.

With the advent of laptop computers came the smaller 3.5-inch high-capacity diskettes. Two popular formats exist to provide either 720 kilobyte or 1.44 megabyte capacities. Because of the plethora of disk types and capacities, new parameters were added to the FORMAT command in DOS version 4.01. Then, DOS 5.00 introduced a *safe* FORMAT command and the ability to UNFORMAT unintentially formatted disks. These parameters and others are included in this module. Module 64 describes the UNFORMAT command in addition to the MIRROR command, which is used with UNFORMAT.

COMPATIBILITY When DOS 2.00 or later is in use, files on the earlier eight-sector disks can be read and written. However, if your computer is using DOS 1.10 or 1.25, disks formatted with DOS 2.00 or later cannot be read.

With the introduction of DOS version 3.00's high-capacity disk format utility, the high-capacity drive (drive A) on the IBM PC-AT achieved 1.2 million bytes of storage. Like DOS 2.00 and later, the high-capacity disk can use data files and many programs on earlier DOS versions. However, earlier versions of DOS and standard disk drives cannot use DOS 3.00 high-capacity disks. On early AT-compatible machines, if you write a file to a 360KB diskette using the 1.2MB drive, you may render the diskette unusable for later use in a 360KB drive. This is because the track width of 1.2MB drive is much narrower than that of 360KB drives. Even the file allocation table may be damaged, which keeps you from reading a directory when the diskette is later placed in a 360KB drive.

FORMAT COMMAND FORMS There are a number of FORMAT command forms. These are described in the following list.

CAUTION

Be aware that the FORMAT command erases all files from the disk being formatted. Many computer users have accidentally formatted the wrong disk. If you have programs or document files you wish to keep, do not format the disk! (DOS 5.00 lets you UNFORMAT disks, but even with this version of DOS, there are no guarantees that all data will be restored.)

All DOS Versions:

FORMAT	Format the disk in the default drive.
FORMAT B:	Format the disk in drive B.
FORMAT /S	Format the disk in the default drive and transfer the DOS to it. (This places system files including COMMAND.COM, BIO.COM, and DOS.COM on the target disk.) If you plan to use the disk for data only, avoid using /S. The DOS files occupy valuable space.
FORMAT B:/S	Format the disk in drive B and transfer the DOS to it.
FORMAT /1	Format the disk as single sided.
FORMAT /B	Format the disk and reserve space for DOS files BIO.COM and DOS.COM. However, the DOS is not transferred until the SYS command is used (Module 59). The /B option creates a 320KB, eight-sector diskette rather than a 360KB, nine-sector diskette.
FORMAT B:/1/S	Format the disk in drive B as single sided and transfer the DOS to it.

DOS versions 2.00 and later:

FORMAT /8	Format the disk with eight sectors (for compatibility with DOS versions prior to 2.00).
FORMAT /V	Display a prompt that asks for a 1- to 11-character disk volume name. (The /V parameter cannot be used with the /8 parameter.)
FORMAT /S/V	Format the disk, prompt for a volume name, and transfer the DOS to it.
FORMAT /3	Some DOS versions used with laptop computers or those with 3 1/2-inch disk drives use this form of the FORMAT command.

DOS version 3.00:

Command	Description
FORMAT /4	Format a 360K or 180K capacity disk in a high-capacity (1.2-megabyte) drive. This command is typically used with drive A on the IBM PC-AT.

DOS version 3.30:

Command	Description
FORMAT /N:9 /T:80	Computers that use the 1.44MB 3 1/2-inch double-sided diskettes can use and format 720KB diskettes. Use this command to format a 720KB diskette in a 1.44MB drive. The /N:9 parameter specifies nine sectors per track. (A 1.44MB diskette has 18 sectors per track (/N:18).) The /T:80 specifies eighty tracks.

DOS version 5.00

Command	Description
FORMAT /U	Specifies unconditional format, which destroys all data on the target disk to prevent subsequent unformatting with the UNFORMAT command.
FORMAT /Q	Quick format takes less than 10 seconds; this command removes the file allocation table and root directory; it does not scan the disk for bad areas. The /Q switch cannot be used if you change the capacity of the disk, i.e., format a 1.44MB diskette as 720K.
FORMAT /V:*labelname*	Lets you assign a volume label. Otherwise, you are prompted to enter one at the end of the formatting operation. Volume labels are up to 11 characters long.
FORMAT /F:*size*	Specify the size of the disk being formatted. Sizes are entered as follows.

Disk Size		*Use*
5.25	160K	160, 160K, 160KB
	180K	180, 180K, 180KB
	320K	320, 320K, 320KB
	360K	360, 360K, 360KB
3.5	720K	720, 720K, 720KB
	1.44M	1440, 1440K, 1440KB, 1.44, 1.44M, 1.44MB
	2.88M	2880, 2880K, 2880KB, 2.88, 2.88M, 2.88MB

FORMAT COMMAND DIALOGUE When the FORMAT command is used, there is a built-in dialogue to help along the way. Following is a typical dialogue procedure, beginning with the FORMAT command:

```
C:\>A:

A:\>FORMAT B:
Insert new diskette for drive B:
and press ENTER when ready...

Checking existing disk format
Saving UNFORMAT information
Verifying 1.44M
Format complete

Volume label (11 characters, ENTER for none)?

   1457664 bytes total disk space
   1457664 bytes available on disk

       512 bytes in each allocation unit
      2847 allocation units available on disk

Volume Serial Number is 1048-15F5

Format another (Y/N)?
```

DOS 3.10 added the display of cylinders and tracks during the formatting process. This display provides information about the location of defective tracks on your media.

With the release of DOS version 3.20, you must type the drive designator when formatting the default drive. This makes you think about formatting your default drive. Accidental formatting loses all data.

The DOS 4.01 FORMAT command displays the percentage formatted, letting you know how much of the diskette has been formatted. This version also displays the number of bytes in each allocation unit and the number of allocation units on the formatted disk. This is similar to the information displayed by the CHKDSK command. The DOS 4.01 FORMAT command also displays a volume serial number. Prior DOS versions are not serialized.

FIXED DISK FORMATTING You can use the FORMAT command to format a fixed (hard) disk. A factory-fresh fixed disk must undergo a low-level format before the FORMAT command is used. Low-level formatting, which organizes tracks and sectors, is accomplished using special utilities from the manufacturer or the DOS DEBUG command. After the low-level process is completed, the DOS FDISK command is used to partition a fixed disk.

A common low-level format process for many computers is summarized in the following procedural steps. The precise procedure depends upon the number of disk drive heads and cylinders and the interleave factor recommended by the manufacturer of the drive and controller.

1. Insert the DOS diskette containing the DEBUG.COM file into drive A.
2. Type DEBUG and press Return; notice that a hyphen is displayed. This is DEBUG's way of prompting you for a command.
3. Type G=C800:5 and press Return to start the low-level process.
4. Respond to the prompts using values recommended by the disk drive and controller manufacturers.
5. Upon completion of the low-level format, use the DOS FDISK setup utility to specify the number of fixed disk partitions.

Because fixed disks are so large, formatting takes several minutes. Be sure to read Module 29 before formatting a fixed disk.

Some disk manufacturers provide disk manager utilities, which let you perform the entire low-level, partitioning, and high-level format operations using an easy-to-use menu.

VOLUME NAMES The /V parameter, which is available on DOS versions 2.00 and later, is handy for assigning a 1- to 11-character name to a disk. Like filenames and pathnames, volume names should be meaningful. When FORMAT /V is used, the prompt:

```
Volume label (11 characters, ENTER for none)?
```

is displayed. In response, type a volume name of your choice and press Return (or Enter as it is sometimes called). The formatted disk is now tagged with the name you have chosen. The volume name is displayed when a directory is listed or when the VOL command is used. The VOL command is described in detail in Module 67. The LABEL command (Module 38), introduced with DOS version 3.00, lets you create, change, or delete volume names. Prior to version 3.00, the FORMAT /V parameter was required to create a volume name.

APPLICATIONS

The FORMAT command is essential in preparing new disks for use with your computer. It is also good for reformatting old disks, making them reusable. The /S parameter allows you to transfer the DOS to the target disk. This transfers all internal commands such as COPY, DEL, DIR, REN, and TYPE, and makes the disk "bootable," which means it can be used to start your computer.

TYPICAL OPERATION

In this activity you use the FORMAT command with the /S option to prepare a new disk in drive B. If you have only one floppy disk drive, format the disk in drive A, but specify disk B anyway. Begin at the DOS prompt.

1. Type **FORMAT B:/S** and press **Return**. Notice the following display.

```
A:\>FORMAT B:/S
Insert new diskette for drive B:
and press ENTER when ready...
```

2. Insert the disk to be formatted and press any key to start the disk formatting process; notice a "Formatting..." display. It may include the Head and Cylinder location if you have DOS version 3.10 through 3.3.
3. Wait until the following message is displayed.

```
Checking existing disk format
Saving UNFORMAT information
Verifying 1.44M
Format complete
System transferred

Volume label (11 characters, ENTER for none)?

   1457664 bytes total disk space
    117760 bytes used by system
   1339904 bytes available on disk

       512 bytes in each allocation unit
      2617 allocation units available on disk

Volume Serial Number is 2422-15F7

Format another (Y/N)?
```

4. Type **N** to redisplay the system prompt.
5. Turn to Module 59 to continue the learning sequence.

Module 33
GRAFTABL (3.10+)

DESCRIPTION

The GRAFTABL command, introduced with DOS 3.10, is an external command. This command was introduced to provide the ability to use a Color Graphics Adapter in the graphics mode with additional characters found in a national language code page.

More specifically, GRAFTABL gives users access to ASCII characters 128 through 255. Several of these characters are used to support different national languages. You can display these characters if you are using the graphics mode and have a computer system with a color graphics adapter. When GRAFTABL is used, the memory used by DOS increases.

GRAFTABL is one of several commands that interacts with code page switching. Code page switching, introduced in DOS version 3.30, is used to support different display and keyboard characters and configurations used by different national languages. (See Module 12 for more information about code page switching.)

Three forms of the GRAFTABL command are:

```
GRAFTABL nnn
GRAFTABL /STATUS
GRAFTABL ?
```

where *nnn* is code page number including:

437—United States (default value)
860—Portugal
863—Canada (French)
865—Denmark or Norway
850—Multilingual (added in DOS version 4.01)

/STATUS is used to display the number of the active code page. The message takes the form "Active Code Page: 865." You may also use /STA as a short form for this parameter.

? is used to display the number of the active code page and a list of code page options.

The command GRAFTABL 865 loads a character set for use with the national languages of Denmark and Norway, which are similar.

You may use GRAFTABL as necessary to switch to different character sets.

APPLICATIONS

The ability to display special characters in support of different languages is convenient to users in many countries. If you or your colleagues use a variety of languages in your work, GRAFTABL and a color graphics adapter are recommended.

TYPICAL OPERATION

No activity is provided for the GRAFTABL command, as it requires that your system be configured for use with one or more code pages. However, you may wish to review Module 12, which describes Code Page Switching. Turn to Module 44 to continue the learning sequence.

Module 34
GRAPHICS (2.00+)

DESCRIPTION

The GRAPHICS program is available on DOS versions 2.00 and later. This program is loaded prior to printing displayed graphics. To take effect, a graphics printer, such as an IBM Proprinter or Epson FX-85 or 185 and a color/graphics monitor adapter is required. When you press Shift-PrtSc, graphic images, like those used to produce a pie or bar chart, are reproduced on your printer.

DOS version 4.01 added support of EGA-, VGA-, and LCD-type monitor adapters and IBM PS/2 Display Adapters. It also added support for a number of new printers, 19 shades of gray or 8 colors. Following is a list of the devices supported by DOS 4.01.

- IBM Printers:GRAPHICS
  - 5152 Graphics Printer Model 2
  - 4201 Proprinter
  - 4201 Proprinter II
  - 4202 Proprinter XL, 8.5-inch paper width
  - 4207 Proprinter X24
  - 4208 Proprinter XL24, 8.5-inch paper width
  - 3812 Pageprinter
  - 5201 Quietwriter II
  - 5202 Quietwriter III
- GRAPHICSWIDE
  - 5201 Quietwriter II, 13.5-inch paper width
  - 4202 Proprinter XL, 13.5-inch paper width
  - 4208 Proprinter XL24, 13.5-inch paper width
- COLOR1
  - 5182 Color Printer with monochrome adapter and black ribbon
- COLOR4
  - 5182 Color Printer with red, green, blue (RGB) ribbon
- COLOR8
  - 5182 Color Printer with yellow, magenta, cyan (YMC) ribbon
- THERMAL
  - 5140 PC Convertible Printer

To activate the GRAPHICS command on versions of DOS prior to 4.01, simply type GRAPHICS and press Return. If your computer is in the 320 x 200 color graphics mode, up to four shades of gray can be printed with the screen image upright on the page (portrait mode). In the 640 x 200 color graphics mode, the screen is printed on its side (landscape mode), with the top of the displayed image located at the left side of the paper.

Versions 4.01 and 5.00 offer the following GRAPHICS parameters.

type	Specifies the printer being used. The default type is GRAPHICS, which is for all wide-platen printers.
profile	Specifies a file that contains printer information. Omission of a filename defaults to GRAPHICS.PRO. This file should be kept in the same directory as the GRAPHICS.COM file.
/R	Prevents black on white reversal, which is the default output mode. Black on white puts black lines on white paper, saving ribbon and reducing print time.
/B	Causes the background color to print when using a color printer. Used with COLOR4 and COLOR8 printer types. Omitting /B suppresses background printing.
/LCD	Reproduces the image of an LCD display. (An alternate to /PB:LCD.)
/PB:id	Uses the "Print Box" size corresponding to the id value. Either "PRINTBOX" or "PB" may be used in the command. If the GRAPHICS command is used without a printbox parameter, the last id value used is retained. Printbox id's are: STD The standard printbox, which is the default value. LCD The LCD printbox; normally used with the IBM PC Convertible.

A few command examples follow:

GRAPHICS /R	Prints on a GRAPHICS-type printer using white on black.
GRAPHICS GRAPHICS C:\UTIL\GRAPHICS.PRO	Prints white text and lines as black; uses the GRAPHICS.PRO profile file located in the \UTIL subdirectory.

An alternate to the preceding command line is:

GRAPHICS , C:\UTIL\GRAPHICS.PRO	The comma lets you omit the default type value, GRAPHICS.
GRAPHICS COLOR4 /R /B	Prints on a COLOR4 type printer; colors are printed to resemble displayed foreground and background values as closely as possible.

THE GRAPHICS PROFILE Each printer has specific characteristics, which are defined within the GRAPHICS.PRO file. This file contains sections for each printer type. Within these are subsections for video display modes. You can alter the contents of the GRAPHICS.PRO file by copying it with a new name and then editing it. If you wish to view this file, use the TYPE command by typing TYPE GRAPHICS.PRO and pressing Return. Use Ctrl-S to pause the display so you can read its contents.

Most application users should have little need to modify this file. Therefore, displaying the file is more to satisfy your curiosity than to encourage you to make changes. Notice that comments are preceded by semicolons. These describe the function of each section. You can see setup, graphics, and printbox parameters that correspond to each display mode.

APPLICATIONS

Although graphics printing takes considerably longer than text printing, the GRAPHICS utility is nevertheless a valuable DOS program if you use graphs and charts. Most graphics programs, like Lotus 1-2-3, SuperCalc3 and 4, Microsoft Chart, AutoCAD, and Generic CAD have printer drivers of their own that control graphics printing. If you create and display graphics using BASICA, Pascal, or some other language, you may wish to "dump" your screen to a graphics printer using the Shift-PrtSc sequence. If you are only printing text, you need not use any parameters with the GRAPHICS command.

If you wish to print a display that has black text on a white background, use the /R parameter with a black and white printer. You can also use the /R command for printing color charts to print all colors except for the background.

Using the LCD printbox for printing a 640 x 200 display on a PC Convertible Printer requires legal-size paper (8.5 x 14.5 inches). The printed image occupies 10.5 x 3.5 inches.

TYPICAL OPERATION

Once the GRAPHICS command is typed, the GRAPHICS program operates behind the scenes when displayed graphics are dumped to your printer. In addition, another program is required to create and display meaningful graphics. Therefore, no typical operation procedure is used to demonstrate its use. Turn to Module 24 to continue the learning sequence.

Module 35
HELP, /? (5.00+)

DESCRIPTION

The HELP command was introduced in DOS 5.00. This command displays information about a supplied DOS command.

You can display the information in two ways. First, you can display the information using the form:

```
HELP command
```

A screen full of descriptive information is displayed about the named command. You can also type the command and add /? to achieve the same result. For example, the command

```
CHKDSK /?
```

displays a screen full of information about the CHKDSK command.

APPLICATIONS

The HELP (or /?) command is convenient for displaying information about seldom used commands. You may know the basic command, but not remember all of the available parameters. For example, you want to use the XCOPY command to copy all files created since yesterday. You can't remember the appropriate parameter. Type XCOPY /? and look at the resulting screen. The command form is displayed in addition to a list of parameters and definitions. This display reveals

```
/D:date   Copies files modified on or after the specified date.
```

This is the parameter you want to use.

TYPICAL OPERATION

In this activity you display help information about two commands. Begin at the DOS prompt.

1. Type **HELP XCOPY** and press **Return**. Check your display.
2. Type **CHKDSK /?** and press **Return**. Check your display.
3. Turn to Module 32 to continue the learning sequence.

Module 36
JOIN (3.10+)

DESCRIPTION

The JOIN command is an external command that was introduced in DOS version 3.10. Like ASSIGN and SUBST, it interacts with disk drives and pathnames. The JOIN command is used to create a temporary subdirectory, and join a designated disk drive and all of its subdirectories to the new subdirectory. The root directory is not a valid directory.

The command JOIN A: C:\TEMP creates a subdirectory named C:\TEMP. You can move to this subdirectory with CD \TEMP. In the new subdirectory, commands are redirected to the "joined" drive, which is A in this illustration. If you use the DIR command, a list of the files on the diskette in drive A is displayed as if they were in the TEMP subdirectory.

You can use existing disk subdirectories only if they are empty. Attempting to use a subdirectory having files results in a "Directory not empty" message. Once a JOIN relationship is established, typing JOIN alone displays the relationships. In our example, you see A: = > C:\TEMP. To disconnect a JOIN relationship, use JOIN A: /D.

Here are a few precautions that you should know about:

1. One drive is restricted to one relationship at a time.
2. Avoid joining directories or drives that are involved in ASSIGN or SUBST relationships.
3. JOIN does not allow the use of network drives.
4. Never use BACKUP, DISKCOMP, DISKCOPY, FORMAT, or RESTORE when JOIN is active.
5. The specified path cannot be the current directory.

APPLICATIONS

The JOIN command lets you work with a subdirectory which directs all commands to the joined drive and all of its directories. This lets you operate with a single drive without having to remember which disk drive contains particular files. For example, if your computer has two floppy drives and one hard drive, you can use subdirectory names with the JOIN command that indicate the file types stored on each diskette. For example, if program files are on drive A and data files on B, you can use commands like JOIN A: C:\PROG and JOIN B: C:\DATA. Typing JOIN displays

```
A => C: ¦PROG
B => C: ¦DATA
```

TYPICAL OPERATION

In this activity you use the JOIN command to join the files on drive A: to a subdirectory named C:\TEMP. This activity assumes you are using a fixed disk system, with drive C:\ as the logged disk drive.

1. Insert a floppy disk in drive A: that contains DOS files.
2. Type **JOIN A: C:\TEMP** and press **Return**.
3. Type **DIR C:\TEMP** and press **Return**; notice that the files in drive A are listed.
4. Type **JOIN A:/D** and press **Return** to discontinue the JOIN relationship.
5. Type **CD** and press **Return**. Then remove the TEMP directory by typing **RD TEMP** and pressing **Return**.
6. Turn to Module 12 to continue the learning sequence.

Module 37
KEYB (3.00+)

DESCRIPTION

The KEYB command was originally introduced in DOS version 3.00 to support a variety of keyboard configurations conforming to different language requirements. This gives DOS the ability to replace the default U.S. keyboard layout. The KEYB command was enhanced in DOS version 3.30 and again in DOS version 4.01. The KEYB command is typically placed in an AUTOEXEC.BAT file and loaded upon system turn on.

KEYB should always be loaded before loading application programs that redefine the keys. This is particularly important for programs like Superkey that perform key emulation.

If you are using DOS version 4.01, you can load the KEYB command into your CONFIG.SYS file using the INSTALL command. An example of this is given below.

The general form of the KEYB command form is:

```
KEYB xx,yyy,d:filename
```

where: *xx* is the keyboard code for the desired country.

yyy is the code page number and is used to call a code page that has been prepared in the CONFIG.SYS command.

d:filename is the name of the keyboard definition file, which has a unique KEYB filename. If a filename is not specified, the KEYBOARD.SYS file is used. The root directory is searched for the keyboard definition file.

Using KEYB by itself displays the currently installed keyboard ID and code page.

DOS version 4.01 added a new parameter, /ID:zzz, to the KEYB command. This parameter specifies a keyboard layout that corresponds to the keyboard identification code zzz.

If you use the INSTALL command available in DOS 4.01 and 5.00 to run the KEYB program, the INSTALL command should conform to the following example. This line is part of your system's CONFIG.SYS file, located on the root directory.

```
INSTALL=KEYB.COM FR,437,C:\DOS\KEYBOARD.SYS /ID:189
```

This example installs the keyboard for use in France.

A list of code page and keyboard values are contained in the following table. The keyboard identification codes, zzz, are only operative with DOS version 4.01 and later.

DOS Versions 3.00				*DOS Versions 3.30*			
Country	xx	yyy	zzz	Country	xx	yyy	zzz
United States	US	001	103	Arabic	None	785	
Canada (Eng)	US	001	168,166	Australia	US	061	103
France	FR	033	120,189	Belgium	BE	032	120
Spain	SP	034	172	Canada (Fr)	CF	002	058
Italy	IT	039	141,142	Denmark	DK	045	159
United Kingdom	UK	044	168,166	Finland	SU	358	153
Germany	GR	049	129	Hebrew	None	972	
				Latin America	LA	003	171
				Netherlands	NL	031	143
				Norway	NO	047	155
				Portugal	351	PO	163
				Sweden	046	SV	153
				Switzerland (Fr)	041	SF	150
				Switzerland (Gr)	041	SG	000

The command KEYB SP,034 /ID:172 is used to configure your system for use in Spanish. Omit /ID:172 if you are using a DOS version older than 4.01.

The keyboard code used with the KEYB command selects a table within the KEYBOARD.SYS file. The tables within KEYBOARD.SYS load an ASCII character set that corresponds to a prepared code page.

The SELECT command, described in Module 54, is frequently used to configure a working system disk. Among other things, this command creates an AUTOEXEC. BAT file which includes a KEYB command line. The keyboard and code page numbers correspond to the values used with the SELECT command.

You can reenter the KEYB command using new parameters to switch to a different code page. The parameters (or code page number) must match a code page that has been prepared with the MODE command. See the Code Page Prepare paragraph in Module 42 for an example. You should be aware that the version 3.30 KEYB command is not compatible with earlier versions of DOS.

Some keyboard and code page combinations are incompatible. Use of incompatible code page-keyboard combinations provides unpredictable results. The following table lists legitimate code page and keyboard combinations.

Code Page	*437*	*850*	*860*	*863*	*865*
Keyboard	FR GR IT SV SU UK US	BE CF DK LA NL NO PO SF SG SF SP SV UK US	PO	CF	NO DK

APPLICATIONS

The KEYB command is normally used as a line within an AUTOEXEC.BAT file, in conjunction with other code page switching commands. The proper combination prepares your computer for use with the language of your choice. If you are using several different languages, you can type the desired KEYB command at the DOS prompt to change your keyboard setup. However, the corresponding code page must have been prepared with the MODE command. To ensure proper printing and display, the appropriate device drivers must exist within your CONFIG.SYS file.

TYPICAL OPERATION

Because the KEYB command is used in conjunction with other commands, an activity is not presented here. If you wish to examine the KEYB command form, look at the Typical Operation section within Module 54 which describes the SELECT command. A KEYB command is constructed in that activity. Turn to Module 33 to continue the learning sequence.

Module 38
LABEL (3.00+)

DESCRIPTION

LABEL is an external DOS command that creates, changes, or deletes volume labels on a disk. LABEL was introduced with DOS version 3.00 and a label deletion prompt was added with DOS version 3.10.

To create a new volume (disk) label where none exists, type:

```
LABEL A:label name
```

where *label name* can be any name of your choosing up to 11 characters long. In this example, A is assumed as the logged disk drive. The following prompt is displayed to help you.

```
A:\>label
Volume in drive A has no label
Volume Serial Number is 0F66-14F7
Volume label (11 characters, ENTER for none)?
```

You can change a label name by typing:

```
LABEL A:
```

The following prompt is displayed:

```
A:\>LABEL
Volume in drive A is DATAFILE
Volume Serial Number is 0F66-14F7
Volume label (11 characters, ENTER for none)?
```

You can type the new name and press Return. For example, you may use something like DISK #001. Pressing Return without typing a new volume label deletes the existing volume label. DOS 3.00 deleted the volume label without pause. However, DOS 3.10 added one more precautionary prompt that reads, "Delete current volume label (Y/N)?" This gives you a final chance to change your mind. Typing Y and pressing Return deletes the label name. Typing N and pressing Return keeps it.

APPLICATIONS

Prior to DOS 3.00, once a volume label was assigned, it could not be changed without reformatting the disk with the /V parameter (see Module 32). The LABEL command lets you create, change, and delete label names, making it easy to maintain your disk organization systems.

TYPICAL OPERATION

In this activity you use LABEL to create and then delete a volume label on a scratch disk in drive B. Begin at the DOS prompt.

1. Insert a scratch disk in drive B.
2. Type **LABEL B:NEWNAME** and press **Return**.
3. Check the new volume label name by typing **VOL B:** and pressing **Return**. Notice the display:

```
A:\>VOL B:

 Volume in drive B is NEWNAME
 Volume Serial Number is 3168-16D4

A:\>
```

4. Delete the volume label by typing **LABEL B:** and pressing **Return**. Notice the prompt:

```
A:\>LABEL B:
Volume in drive B is NEWNAME
Volume Serial Number is 3168-16D4
Volume label (11 characters, ENTER for none)?
```

5. Press **Return** and notice the following prompt:

```
A:\>LABEL B:
Volume in drive B is NEWNAME
Volume Serial Number is 3168-16D4
Volume label (11 characters, ENTER for none)?

Delete current volume label (Y/N)?
```

6. Type **Y** and press **Return** to delete the volume label.
7. Turn to Module 30 to continue the learning sequence.

Module 39
LINK (1.00+)

DESCRIPTION

The LINK command is an external command available with all versions of DOS. This command normally is used only by programmers to:

- Combine (or link together) individual program modules that are in compiled (object) form.
- Incorporate program library modules that are referenced by the program being linked.
- Produce a display of the status and error messages encountered during the linking process.
- Produce a relocatable program load module.

After you have written a program and compiled it into an object file (with the extension .OBJ), it is ready to be linked. Depending upon the compiler (or assembler) you use, there may be one or more library files. These have the extension .LIB and are specified by name during the linking process.

The LINK program uses as much memory as needed. If it runs out of memory, it creates a temporary file called VM.TMP (virtual memory.temporary), which lets your disk serve as an extension of memory. Once linking is complete, this file is automatically erased.

If you have an object file called MYPROG.OBJ, you can link it by typing the command

```
LINK
```

or

```
LINK MYPROG
```

or

```
LINK MYPROG,RUNFILE,MAPFILE,LIBFILE
```

Using the second form, a display similar to the following appears:

```
A:> LINK MYPROG

   Microsoft Object Linker V2.00
(C) Copyright 1982 by Microsoft Inc.

Run File [MYPROG.EXE]:
List File [NUL.MAP]:
Libraries [.LIB]:
```

You can enter filenames after each colon on the run file, list file, and libraries lines, or accept the defaults in brackets by pressing Return. The run file always has the extension .EXE. The list file is created only if you enter a filename. You can link multiple object (.OBJ) and library (.LIB) files by typing a plus sign (+) between the filenames. Placing two commas in place of the run and list files accepts default values. The following command line includes multiple object files, a run file, and two library files. The double comma accepts the default map file value.

```
LINK PROG1+PROG2+PROG3,PROG.EXE,,C1.LIB+C2.LIB
```

If you are using one or more libraries, you can specify library filenames on the libraries line. Like run files, use a plus sign between library filenames if more than one is used. If no libraries are used, press Return.

Seven additional parameters for the LINK command also exist. These parameters are placed at the end of the LINK command line. They are:

/D and /H	Control where the programs load in memory.
/L	Place line numbers in the list file.
/M	List all global symbols found in the object modules at the end of the list file.
/O	Link object modules created by version one of the Pascal or Fortran compilers when using the 2.30 linker. The O stands for "old." Added in DOS version 3.10.
/P	Pause for a disk change before producing the run file.
/S:n	Override the size of the stack produced by the Macro Assembler or compiler; n is a number between 0 and 65536.
/X	Adjust the total number of segments that an .EXE file can contain. Varies from 0 to 1024, where the default is 256. Controls the number of segments from all object files and libraries that an .EXE file can contain. Added in DOS version 3.10.

If you have a Macro Assembler package, you can follow the activity in the Typical Operation session of this module. There a source file is created, compiled with the Macro Assembler, linked with LINK, and converted to a .COM file with EXE2BIN. EXE2BIN is described in Module 27. Even if you do not have a Macro Assembler, you may wish to review the compiling and linking steps as a matter of interest.

APPLICATIONS

Although the LINK command is used extensively by professional programmers, you may find that you never have a need for it unless you get into programming. If you are a typical microcomputer user, your interest is probably with computer applications programs rather than programming. However, it may be of interest to know what the LINK program does if you plan to broaden your knowledge of what goes on "behind the scenes" of microcomputing.

TYPICAL OPERATION

In this activity you use the LINK command to link a program that is assembled with the Macro Assembler. If you do not have the Macro Assembler, you may wish to follow the steps involved in creating a source file, assembling it, linking it, and then converting the resulting .EXE file into a .COM file with the EXE2BIN command. Begin at the DOS prompt.

1. Create a source file with EDLIN as follows:
   a. Type **EDLIN MYPROG.ASM** and press **Return**.
   b. Type **i** for insert and press **Return**.
   c. Type the following source file, ending each line with **Return**.

```
A:\>EDLIN MYPROG.ASM
New file
*i
        1:*          title     display name on screen
        2:*code      segment            para public 'code'
        3:*          assume cs:code, ds:code
        4:*          org       100h
        5:*example             proc
        6:*start:              push     cs
        7:*          pop       ds                         ; set DS equal to CS
        8:*          mov       dx , offset my_name        ; DS:DX prints to string to
        9:*          mov       ax , 900h                  ; print page d-19 print string
       10:*          int       21h                        ; DOS function call
       11:*          int       20h                        ; exit program back to DOS
       12:*
       13:*my_name             db      'Your Name Here$'
       14:*example             endp
       15:*
       16:*code      ends
       17:*          end       start
```

   d. Press **Ctrl-C** on line 18 to return to the EDLIN prompt.
   e. Type **e** and press **Return** to save the file and quit EDLIN.

NOTE

The following step requires the Macro Assembler.

2. Type **MASM MYPROG,MYPROG,MYPROG** and press **Return** to assemble the source file. Notice the following display:

```
A:> MASM MYPROG,MYPROG,MYPROG

The Microsoft MACRO Assembler
Version 1.06, Copyright (C) Microsoft Inc. 1982,82

Cross reference [NUL.CRF]:

Warning Severe
Errors  Errors
0       0
A:>
```

3. Type **LINK MYPROG** and press **Return** to link the assembled program. Notice the following display:

```
A:> LINK MYPROG

Microsoft Object Linker V2.00
(C) Copyright 1982 by Microsoft Inc.

Run File [MYPROG.EXE]:
List File [NUL.MAP]:
Libraries [.LIB]:
Warning: No STACK segment

There was 1 error detected

A:>
```

4. Type **EXE2BIN MYPROG MYPROG.COM** and press **Return** to convert the .EXE file into a .COM file.
5. Type **MYPROG** and press **Return** to run your new program; notice that your name is displayed and the DOS prompt reappears.
6. This completes this practice activity. If you wish to recover the disk space occupied by the practice files just created, you may wish to delete them using DEL MYPROG.*.
7. Turn to Module 27 to continue the learning sequence.

Module 40
MEM (4.01)

DESCRIPTION

The MEM command is an external command introduced in DOS version 4.01. MEM is used to display system memory information. The MEM command is entered alone or with a parameter.

MEM	Displays total system memory values, including expanded and extended memory values.
MEM /PROGRAM	Displays programs presently loaded in memory with used and unused memory. You may use /P if you are using DOS 5.00.
MEM /DEBUG	Displays a list of programs, device drivers, install drivers, and used/unused memory. You may use /D if you are using DOS 5.00.
MEM /CLASSIFY	Displays programs and corresponding memory usage. You may use /C. This command form was introduced in DOS 5.00.

Each of these command forms is illustrated in the following paragraphs.

Typing MEM and pressing Return displays information similar to the following (typical of DOS 5.00):

```
C:\>MEM

    655360 bytes total conventional memory
    655360 bytes available to MS-DOS
    605344 largest executable program size

   3145728 bytes total contiguous extended memory
         0 bytes available contiguous extended memory
   3080192 bytes available XMS memory
           MS-DOS resident in High Memory Area

C:\>
```

If your system is not equipped with extended or expanded memory, those lines are suppressed. The MEM command displays extended memory only if your system is equipped with memory above 1 megabyte. Expanded memory is displayed only if an expanded memory device driver (like XMA2EMS.SYS) is in use.

Using the MEM command with the /PROGRAM parameters displays information similar to the following screen illustration.

```
  Address    Name       Size    Type
  -------    --------   ------  ------
  000000                000400  Interrupt Vector
  000400                000100  ROM Communication Area
  000500                000200  DOS Communication Area

  000700     IO         000A80  System Data

  001180     MSDOS      0014F0  System Data

  002670     IO         001920  System Data
               HIMEM    0004A0   DEVICE=
                        000820   FILES=
                        000100   FCBS=
                        000200   BUFFERS=
                        0001C0   LASTDRIVE=
                        000740   STACKS=
  003FA0     MSDOS      000040  System Program

  003FF0     COMMAND    000940  Program
  004940     MSDOS      000040  -- Free --
  004990     COMMAND    000100  Environment
  003FA0     MSDOS      000040  System Program

  003FF0     COMMAND    000940  Program
  004940     MSDOS      000040  -- Free --
  004990     COMMAND    000100  Environment
  004AA0     MSMOUSE    000070  Environment
  004B20     MSMOUSE    001AE0  Program
  006610     GRAB       000070  Environment
  006690     GRAB       005C30  Program
  00C2D0     MEM        000070  Environment
  00C350     MEM        0135A0  Program
  01F900     MSDOS      0806F0  -- Free --

    655360 bytes total conventional memory
    655360 bytes available to MS-DOS
    605344 largest executable program size

   3145728 bytes total contiguous extended memory
         0 bytes available contiguous extended memory
   3080192 bytes available XMS memory
           MS-DOS resident in High Memory Area

C:\>
```

Using MEM /DEBUG results in a display that resembles the following screen illustration.

```
Address     Name        Size     Type
-------     --------    ------   ------
000000                  000400   Interrupt Vector
000400                  000100   ROM Communication Area
000500                  000200   DOS Communication Area

000700      IO          000A80   System Data
                CON                System Device Driver
                AUX                System Device Driver
                PRN                System Device Driver
                CLOCK$             System Device Driver
                A: - C:            System Device Driver
                COM1               System Device Driver
                LPT1               System Device Driver
                LPT2               System Device Driver
                LPT3               System Device Driver
                COM2               System Device Driver
                COM3               System Device Driver
                COM4               System Device Driver

001180      MSDOS       0014F0   System Data
002670      IO          001920   System Data
              HIMEM     0004A0    DEVICE=
                XMSXXXX0            Installed Device Driver
                        000820    FILES=
                        000100    FCBS=
                        000200    BUFFERS=
                        0001C0    LASTDRIVE=
                        000740    STACKS=
003FA0      MSDOS       000040   System Program

003FF0      COMMAND     000940   Program
004940      MSDOS       000040   -- Free --
004990      COMMAND     000100   Environment
004AA0      MSMOUSE     000070   Environment
004B20      MSMOUSE     001AE0   Program
006610      GRAB        000070   Environment
006690      GRAB        005C30   Program
00C2D0      MEM         000070   Environment
00C350      MEM         0135A0   Program
01F900      MSDOS       0806F0   -- Free --

  655360 bytes total conventional memory
  655360 bytes available to MS-DOS
  605344 largest executable program size

 3145728 bytes total contiguous extended memory
       0 bytes available contiguous extended memory
 3080192 bytes available XMS memory
         MS-DOS resident in High Memory Area

C:\>
```

APPLICATIONS

The MEM command gives you an accurate way to evaluate the memory in your system and tells you where programs are loaded and how large they are. The memory addresses and file sizes are given in hexadecimal values.

TYPICAL OPERATION

You can perform this activity if you have DOS version 4.01. If you are using an earlier version, proceed to Module 35 to continue the learning sequence. Otherwise, use the MEM command to check your system's memory.

1. From the DOS prompt, type **MEM** and press **Return**. Review the display.
2. Type **MEM /PROGRAM** and press **Return**. Review this display to see where your programs are loaded and how big they are.
3. Type **MEM /DEBUG** and press **Return**. Review this final display, paying particular attention to device and install driver names.
4. Turn to Module 35 to continue the learning sequence.

Module 41
MIRROR (5.00+)

DESCRIPTION

The MIRROR command became available in DOS 5.00. This command is used with the UNFORMAT command, which was also released in DOS 5.00. MIRROR is an external command, while UNFORMAT is internal. These commands work together to restore a local hard disk or floppy disk after it has been formatted. These commands are valuable if you accidentally format a disk containing important information.

The MIRROR command creates a secondary file allocation table (FAT) that is used by the UNFORMAT command to recover files from a specified disk. The MIRROR command can also be used by the UNDELETE command. The MIRROR command is normally loaded in the AUTOEXEC.BAT file so that it is automatically run each time you start your computer.

Typing MIRROR and pressing Return installs the program for the current drive. A record of deleted files is maintained in the root directory once MIRROR is loaded. You can also install the program to track file deletions on another drive or on multiple drives. Some command forms are provided in the following list.

MIRROR C: Saves a copy of the file allocation table and root directory of drive C.

MIRROR /1 Maintains only the most recent information about the disk without making a backup copy (with the extension BAK) of the previously saved disk information file.

MIRROR C: /tc /ta Saves a copy of the file allocation table and root directory of drive C and installs delete tracking for drives C and A. The delete tracking information is maintained in the file PCTRACKR.DEL.

MIRROR /tc-50 Installs delete tracking for drive C limiting the file deletion list to 50 entries. A table of the default number of file entries follows.

Disk Size	*Entries*	*File Size*
360K	25	5K
720K	50	9K
1.2MB	75	14K
1.44MB	75	15K
20MB	101	18K
32MB	202	36K
Over 32MB	303	55K

MIRROR /U	Unloads delete tracking from memory. This command may not unload delete tracking if another memory-resident program has been loaded subsequent to delete tracking.
MIRROR /PARTN	Saves hard disk partition information, used by the UNFORMAT command, to a floppy disk. The assigned filename is PARTNSAV.FIL. Be sure to have a formatted floppy disk handy before entering this command. You are prompted for a disk drive letter.

FILES CREATED BY MIRROR The following files are created by the MIRROR program.

MIRROR.FIL	System information for each disk. UNFORMAT uses this file to unformat an unintentionally formatted disk.
MIRROR.BAK	The previous system information file; this file contains the contents of the last MIRROR.FIL created.
PARTNSAV.FIL	The hard disk partition information saved to a specified floppy disk and used by UNFORMAT to reconstruct a hard disk partition table.
PCTRACKR.DEL	A list of deleted files maintained by MIRROR's delete tracking program.

This command makes a tracking record of all files deleted from drive C. The tracking program, which is loaded in memory, writes a list of deleted files to the root directory of the specified disk. The filename assigned to the tracking file is PCTRACKR.DEL.

You can create multiple tracking records for each disk in use using the form

```
MIRROR /tc /ta
```

Here, a record is maintained for both drives C and A.

You can also limit the number of files maintained in the tracking record using a command like

```
MIRROR /tc-100
```

This command limits the number of entries to 100.

PRECAUTIONS

You should not load MIRROR for a drive that is using the JOIN or SUBST commands. You should not use the ASSIGN command after MIRROR is started.

UNFORMAT The UNFORMAT command is used to restore hard and floppy disks. This command uses the image files created by the MIRROR command. A description of this command is in Module 64.

APPLICATIONS

The MIRROR command is important for restoring unintentionally formatted disks. Perhaps the most dangerous DOS command is FORMAT. Almost all long-time PC users have experienced the trauma of accidentally issuing the FORMAT command using the wrong drive specifier. "I wanted to format the disk in drive B and accidentally entered A" is a common complaint. Now MIRROR, working with UNFORMAT, is available to help you recover from such situations.

Although UNFORMAT will operate without the files produced by the MIRROR command, having these files adds a substantial level of reliability to the UNFORMAT process. Therefore, if you or your colleagues are vulnerable to FORMAT accidents, you should put the MIRROR command in your AUTOEXEC.BAT file for insurance.

TYPICAL OPERATION

In this activity you use the MIRROR command to create a partition file that is automatically copied to a floppy disk in drive A. Begin at the DOS prompt of your hard drive (assumed to be C).

1. Insert a formatted floppy disk in drive A.
2. Type **MIRROR /PARTN** and press **Return** to create a save file on the floppy disk.
3. Respond to the MIRROR command prompt by pressing **Return**.
4. After the MIRROR image file is copied to drive A, type **DIR A:** and find the PARTNSAV.FIL file created by MIRROR.
5. Turn to Module 64 to continue the learning sequence.

Module 42
MODE (2.00+)

DESCRIPTION

The MODE command is an external utility available on DOS versions 2.00 and later. With the introduction of DOS version 3.30, a set of code page switching commands was introduced. This module first describes the traditional uses of the MODE command. At the end of this section, those MODE commands associated with code page switching are presented.

TRADITIONAL MODE COMMAND USES The MODE command is used to control several of the outputs of your computer including:

- Display output
    - Width (40 or 80 characters per line)
    - Monochrome or color (Color commands require a color board.)
    - Horizontal alignment (shift left or right)
    - Test pattern display

Examples:

MODE 40	Displays 40 characters per line.
MODE 80	Displays 80 characters per line.
MODE BW40	Displays 40 characters per line in monochrome.
MODE BW80	Displays 80 characters per line in monochrome.
MODE CO40	Displays 40 characters per line in color.
MODE CO80	Displays 80 characters per line in color.
MODE MONO	Switches display output to the monochrome board.
MODE 80,R	Displays 80 characters per line and shifts output two characters to the right.
MODE 80,L	Displays 80 characters per line and shifts output two characters to the left.
MODE 80,R,T	Displays 80 characters per line, shifts output two characters to the right, and displays a test pattern.

You can also use the MODE command to specify the number of displayed lines and columns. This form of the MODE command is valid only on some EGA or VGA monitor and compatible adapters. The general form of the command is:

```
MODE display COLS=m LINES=n
```

where: Valid column values *m* are 40 and 80
Valid line values *n* are 25, 43, or 50

Before running the command, the ANSI.SYS device driver should be loaded in the CONFIG.SYS file at system turn-on. Two command examples follow.

```
MODE CON LINES=43 COLS=80

MODE CON COLS=40
```

The first command example calls for 43 lines and 80 columns. The second example puts the monitor in the 40-column display mode. If your system does not support this command, a message to that effect is displayed.

- Typematic control

The typematic parameter was added to the MODE command in DOS version 4.01. This command lets you control the speed at which the cursor advances when a key is pressed and held. This form of the MODE command uses the CON (console) device with RATE= and DELAY= parameters. The RATE parameter uses a value of 1 through 32. The rate, in repetitions per second, is included in the following table. The DELAY parameter uses values of 1 through 4, which correspond to .25, .5, .75, and 1 second. The delay is the amount of time required after a keypress for the typematic action to begin.

Rate Value	*Rep's per Sec*	*Rate Value*	*Rep's per Sec*	*Rate Value*	*Rep' s per Sec*	*Rate Value*	*Rep's per Sec*
1	2.0	9	4.0	17	8.0	25	16.0
2	2.1	10	4.3	18	8.6	26	17.1
3	2.3	11	4.6	19	9.2	27	18.5
4	2.5	12	5.0	20	10.0	28	20.0
5	2.7	13	5.5	21	10.9	29	21.8
6	3.0	14	6.0	22	12.0	30	24.0
7	3.3	15	6.7	23	13.3	31	26.7
8	3.7	16	7.5	24	15.0	32	30.0

An example of the typematic command follows.

```
MODE CON RATE=24, DELAY=2
```

This command yields 24 repetitions per second, with an initial delay of .5 seconds before the typematic action begins.

- Printer output
  - LPT1, LPT2, or LPT3
  - Print width (such as 80 or 132)
  - Parallel or serial selection (LPTn: or COMn)
  - Automatic print retry (P)
  - Lines per inch (6 or 8)

Examples:

MODE LPT2:	Uses parallel printer 2.
MODE LPT1:,132,8	Uses parallel printer 1, 132 columns, 8 lines per inch.
MODE LPT1:,80,6	Uses parallel printer 1, 80 columns, 6 lines per inch.
MODE LPT1:=COM1,P	Changes printer output to COM1 (serial port 1); the P turns on automatic print retry.
MODE LPT1:=COM3	Changes printer output to COM3 (serial port 3).

- Asynchronous communications output
  - COM1, COM2, COM3, or COM4
  - Baud rate (speed) – 110, 150, 300, 600, 1200, 2400, 4800, or 9600
  - Parity (N = none, E = even, or O = odd)
  - Databits (7 or 8)
  - Stopbits (1 or 2)
  - Retries (P sets retries for interface to a serial printer)

Examples:

MODE COM1:12,N,8,1,P	Data output configured to 1200 baud, no parity, 8 databits, 1 stopbit; the P turns on automatic retry for printers. Note that some versions of DOS require the baud rate to be fully written, i.e., 1200 instead of 12.
MODE COM2:300,E,7,1	Data output configured to 300 baud, even parity, 7 databits, 1 stopbit, no printer retries.

CODE PAGE SWITCHING COMMANDS With the introduction of DOS 3.30, code page switching was expanded for use with many countries and their corresponding national language. The MODE command was expanded to prepare, select, display the status, and refresh code pages. Look at the following four forms of the MODE command:

```
MODE device CODEPAGE PREPARE=(nnn) filename
MODE device CODEPAGE SELECT=(nnn)
MODE device CODEPAGE /STATUS
MODE device CODEPAGE REFRESH
```

where:

device is a DOS output device including CON, PRN, LPT1, LPT2, LPT3.

nnn is one or more code page numbers, such as 437, 850, 860, 863, or 865. Code page numbers are ordinarily separated by spaces, as in the series (437 850 863). You can also insert a "place holder" by inserting a pair of commas at the location of a previously specified code page number and device. For example, if a previous MODE command prepared code pages (437 850 865) for LPT1, you can retain 850 for LPT1 and introduce new code pages using a series such as (437, ,863). Note that the effect is restricted to your LPT1 device.

filename is a device driver having the extension .CPI. Four such files supplied with DOS 3.30 are:

4201.CPI	For the IBM Model 4201 Proprinter
5202.CPI	For the IBM Model 5202 Quietwriter III Printer
EGA.CPI	For systems using enhanced graphics adapter devices
LCD.CPI	For LCD display devices such as the IBM Convertible LCD

Code Page Prepare Some code page preparation commands are provided to illustrate their form and function.

```
MODE CON CP
PREP=(850) EGA.CPI
```

This command prepares your console for use with the multilingual code page (850) and an enhanced graphics adapter. Note that CP and PREP are optional short forms for the words CODEPAGE and PREPARE.

```
MODE LPT1 CP
PREP=(850 863)
4201.CPI
```

This command prepares your LPT1 printer device for use with the multilingual or French Canadian code page and an IBM Model 4201 Proprinter.

```
MODE LPT1 CP
PREP=(850, ,437)
4201.CPI
```

Assuming that this command is used sometime after the preceding one, your LPT1 printer device is prepared for use with the multilingual, French Canadian, and U.S. code pages. The comma pair retains the previous code page position for LPT1, which was 863.

Code Page Select The MODE device CP SELECT=*nnn* command form is used to select one of the prepared code pages. When entered, the named devices (CON and LPT*n*) are set up for operation with the selected code page number. The following command illustrates code page selection for LPT1, as prepared in the preceding MODE command example.

```
MODE LPT1 CP SELECT=850
```

Code Page Status A list of prepared code pages for a specified device is displayed using a command similar to the following one.

```
MODE LPT1 CP /STATUS
```

A list of devices is displayed. An error message is displayed if code pages have not been properly prepared. Therefore, this is a good way to determine whether or not you have properly prepared a device for use with code page switching.

Code Page Refresh The code page refresh command is used to reestablish your code page settings. If you turn your printer off and back on, you can use the refresh option to reload the active code page. Continuing with the preceding code page select illustration, assume that you turned off your Model 4201 Proprinter. You can use the code page refresh option to restore code page 850.

```
MODE LPT1 CP REFRESH
```

APPLICATIONS

The MODE command has a number of important applications. It is used to control the width and color of your display. It is used to change from parallel to serial printer output or to change between printer output ports. Finally, it is used to establish communications protocol parameters, i.e., speed, parity, databits, and stopbits.

With the introduction of code page switching, the MODE command became an integral part of the code page preparation and selection scheme. It now gives you the ability to prepare one or more code pages for several devices. You can use multiple entries of the MODE command to set up a variety of devices. For example, any of the following command pairs might be placed in your AUTOEXEC.BAT file or entered at the DOS prompt.

```
MODE LPT1 CP PREP=(850) 4201.CPI
MODE CON CP PREP=(850) EGA.CPI

MODE LPT1 CP SELECT=850
MODE CON CP SELECT=850

MODE LPT1 CP /STATUS
MODE CON CP /STATUS
```

TYPICAL OPERATION

In this activity you use the MODE command to set your display width and then to set up a communications protocol. Begin at the DOS prompt.

1. Type **MODE 40** and press **Return**. Notice that the prompt looks twice as large in the 40-character mode.
2. Type **MODE 80** and press **Return** to return to the 80-character mode.

NOTE

If you have a serial output port on your computer (COM1), perform the remaining steps. Otherwise, this completes this activity.

3. Type **MODE LPT1:=COM1** and press **Return** to reroute your computer's output to your serial communications port.
4. Type **MODE COM1:1200,N,8,1,P** and press **Return**. Data output through COM1 (the serial port) is now set up as follows:

```
Baud rate - 1200
Parity - None
Databits - 8
Stopbits - 1
Automatic retry - On
```

5. Turn to Module 28 to continue the learning sequence.

Module 43
MORE (2.00+)

DESCRIPTION

The MORE command is a filter command, like the FIND and SORT commands, introduced in DOS version 2.00. The MORE command is used to pause vertical scrolling on the display screen. After each screenful, the display pauses and the message —More— appears. Pressing any key displays the next screenful. A few examples of MORE filter command lines follow.

MORE <FILE1.TXT	Displays one screenful of the text file FILE1.TXT at a time. Pressing any key displays the next screen.
DIR ¦ MORE	Pauses the directory display; similar to using the /P parameter of the DIR command.

APPLICATIONS

The MORE filter is frequently used with the TYPE, DIR, and CHKDSK /F commands. For example, when a large file is displayed using the TYPE command, the MORE filter conveniently pauses each screenful of text so you can read it. Without MORE, you have to use Ctrl-S to pause the display.

TYPICAL OPERATION

In this activity use the MORE command in combination with the DIR command to pause scrolling. This activity assumes that your DOS commands are on a subdirectory named C:\DOS. If these files are on another directory, use the subdirectory name in place of C:\DOS. Begin at the DOS prompt.

1. Type **DIR C:\DOS ¦MORE** and press **Return**.
2. Notice the directory display pauses and — More — is displayed at the bottom of the screen.
3. Press any key to see the rest of the directory listing.
4. Turn to Module 57 to continue the learning sequence.

Module 44
NLSFUNC (3.30+)

DESCRIPTION

The NLSFUNC command is an external DOS command used to support extended country information introduced in DOS version 3.30. The command name, NLSFUNC, is an acronym for National Language Support Function. The NLSFUNC command operates with the CHCP command, used to change code pages, and is always loaded before CHCP is used.

The general form of the NLSFUNC command is

```
NLSFUNC filename
```

where the filename is either the COUNTRY.SYS file or one that performs the same function. If the filename is omitted, the COUNTRY = command line within your CONFIG.SYS file is used. The purpose of the COUNTRY.SYS file is described in the Configuration File and KEYB modules.

The command

```
C:\DOS\NLSFUNC C:\COUNTRY.SYS
```

uses the COUNTRY.SYS file in the root directory of drive C as the country information file.

APPLICATIONS

The primary purpose of the NLSFUNC command is to enable use of the CHCP command. It is always loaded prior to using CHCP. The CHCP command is described in Module 9.

TYPICAL OPERATION

There is no activity required for the NLSFUNC command, as it is used in conjunction with a number of other commands associated with code page switching. You may wish to refer to Module 12, which describes its role in the code page switching scheme. Turn to Module 9 to continue the learning sequence.

Module 45
PATH (2.00+)

DESCRIPTION

The PATH command is an internal command available on DOS versions 2.00 and later. It is used to provide access to files located in other directory paths or other disks. The PATH command is usually entered as a line in an AUTOEXEC.BAT (or batch) file, which most often contains one or more DOS commands. The AUTOEXEC.BAT file is automatically executed upon system turn-on to establish desired parameters. Other batch files are executed upon command. When used, each command executes as it is encountered in the file. The creation and use of batch files is described in Module 7.

To illustrate the PATH command, assume you have a program named GATOR.COM that is located in a subdirectory. You are not sure if it is on disk C or disk A, so you want to search both disks and execute the command when found. To complicate matters, you are not sure if the program is in the SWAMP subdirectory or the MUD subdirectory.

Here is where the PATH command comes to your rescue. To set up a search for GATOR.COM, you can specify the disk and directories using the PATH command. While logged on disk C, assuming that you have a fixed disk system, type:

```
PATH\SWAMP;\MUD;B:\SWAMP;B:\MUD
```

When you type GATOR to run your program, DOS first searches the C:\SWAMP subdirectory, then the C:\MUD subdirectory. Next, it searches the B:\SWAMP subdirectory. Finally, it searches the B:\MUD subdirectory where GATOR.COM is found and executed.

You also can use the PATH command to display the path setup. To do this, type PATH and press Return. A display similar to the following is displayed.

```
A:\>PATH
PATH=\SWAMP;\MUD;B:\SWAMP;B:\MUD

A:\>
```

To cancel the path settings, type PATH; and press Return. The semicolon is the critical agent in this PATH command. Now when you check your paths with the PATH command, the message "No Path" is displayed.

APPLICATIONS

As you may suspect, a primary use of the PATH command is to provide access to programs located in multiple subdirectories. Experienced fixed disk users almost always provide a path to the subdirectory containing their DOS commands, in addition to other file utility directories.

For example, if you have three subdirectories on a fixed disk system that are frequently used with the pathnames \DOS, \SK, and \UTIL, a PATH command line is desirable in your AUTOEXEC.BAT file. Here is a practical way to create your AUTOEXEC.BAT file containing the desired PATH command line. Beginning at the root directory, perform the following procedure.

1. Type COPY CON: AUTOEXEC.BAT and press Return.
2. Type the following lines of text ending each with Return. On the last line following the CLS (clear screen) command, press Ctrl-Z (represented by ^Z) and then press Return to save the file to disk.

```
ECHO OFF
DATE
TIME
PATH \DOS; \SK; \UTIL
CLS^Z
```

3. Notice that the file is copied to your disk when you press Return.
4. Run the file by typing AUTOEXEC and pressing Return.
5. Your paths are now established; the DOS, SK, and UTIL subdirectories are automatically searched whenever you require access to a program.

TYPICAL OPERATION

In this activity you use the PATH command to establish a directory search and then use it to display the established routing. Finally, the paths are canceled. Begin at the DOS prompt.

1. Type **PATH \SWAMP;\SWAMP\MUD** and press **Return.**
2. Type **PATH**, press **Return**, and notice the following display.

```
A:\>PATH
PATH=\SWAMP;\SWAMP\MUD

A:\>
```

3. Cancel the path by typing **PATH;** and pressing **Return**.
4. Type **PATH** and check for the following display.

```
A:\>PATH
No Path

A:\>
```

5. Turn to Module 23 to continue the learning sequence.

Module 46
PIPING COMMANDS (2.00+)

DESCRIPTION

DOS versions 2.00 and later introduced a powerful internal utility that lets you redirect data input and output. This utility is called piping. Why piping? Because it is like redirecting the flow in a garden hose from one bucket to another. In more precise terms, data input and output are redirected to your computer's various devices. For example, you can pipe a screen display to a designated disk file or to your printer.

The greater than (>) and less than (<) symbols direct (or pipe) data input and output. One illustration of this is when you want to save a directory listing of the logged disk drive to a file named DIR.LST. This is achieved with the following command line:

```
DIR>DIR.LST
```

Listing a directory reveals the DIR.LST file, which contains a complete directory listing. You can alphabetize (or sort) the directory listing by including the SORT filter command. Use the command DIR ¦ SORT >DIR.LST to obtain a sorted directory file.

If you want to pipe the directory listing to your printer, use DIR >PRN. Be sure your printer is turned on and loaded with paper to avoid a printer error.

You can establish program control using pipes. The following example illustrates this capability. Here, EDLIN is used to create a list control file for displaying text on the screen. Once displayed, control returns to DOS. If you wish, you can perform the following steps:

1. Type EDLIN LISTER and press Return.
2. Type i and press Return.
3. Type L on line 1 and press Return.
4. Type e on line 2 and press Return.
5. Press Ctrl-C on line 3; your file should resemble the following illustration:

```
A:\>EDLIN LISTER
New file
*i
        1:*L
        2:*e
        3:*^C
```

6. Type e and press Return to save the file and exit EDLIN.
7. Now type a sample text file (called "SAMPLE") as follows:
   a. Type EDLIN SAMPLE and press Return.
   b. Type i, press Return, and type the following two lines; end each line with Return.

      ```
      This is a sample file.
      It was prepared with EDLIN.
      ```

   c. Press Ctrl-C to stop text entry; then type e and press Return to save the file and exit EDLIN.
8. From the DOS prompt, use piping with the LISTER file and EDLIN to display the SAMPLE file by typing the following command line:

   ```
   EDLIN SAMPLE <LISTER
   ```

9. Notice the following display:

```
A:\>EDLIN SAMPLE <LISTER
End of input file
*L
        1:*This is a sample file
        2: It was prepared with EDLIN.
*e

A:\>
```

When piping is used, DOS creates temporary piping files that contain the involved input and output data. These files appear on your directory as %PIPEx.$$$.

DOS filter commands, SORT, FIND, and MORE, are also used with the piping commands. For example, if you wish to print a sorted directory, you can type

```
DIR |SORT >PRN
```

If you want to place a sorted directory in a file named DIRFILE on the disk in drive B, you can type:

```
DIR |SORT >B:DIRFILE
```

Be sure to read about DOS filter commands in modules 31, 43, and 57, as mixing piping and filter commands offers many powerful variations.

APPLICATIONS

You can use piping commands to save directories to files, send program output to your printer, control program operation with a prepared control file, or to add text from one file to the end of another.

One particularly useful command combines piping with the SORT filter to obtain an alphabetized list. For example, if you are preparing an index, you can type each entry and its page number using an ASCII word processor. Assume your index source file is named INDEX. It includes several hundred entries similar to the following:

Radiation, 24
Argon, 15
Lithium, 8
Mercury, 11

When the source file is saved, you can use the following command to alphabetize it and save the result to a file named INDEX.SRT.

```
SORT <INDEX >INDEX.SRT
```

If the file is large, give your computer time to complete the job. The sorting process occurs in memory and sometimes takes several seconds, depending upon the size of your source file.

TYPICAL OPERATION

In this activity you use piping commands to redirect output to files. Begin at the DOS prompt.

1. Type **DIR >DIRFILE** and press **Return**.
2. Type **DIR** and press **Return**. Notice the filename DIRFILE is displayed. You have piped the directory listing to the file. (You may use TYPE DIRFILE to verify that it is a copy of the disk directory.)
3. If you have a printer, check to see that it is ready for printing.
4. Type **TYPE DIRFILE >PRN** and press **Return**. Notice that the file DIRFILE is directed to your printer.
5. Type **TYPE DIRFILE >NEWFILE** and press **Return**.
6. Type **DIR** and press **Return**. Notice that you have piped the screen output of the TYPE command to the file NEWFILE. (You can verify the contents of NEWFILE using the TYPE command.)
7. Delete the practice files DIRFILE and NEWFILE from your disk.
8. Turn to Module 43 to continue the learning sequence.

Module 47
PRINT (2.00+)

DESCRIPTION

The PRINT command is available in DOS versions 2.00 and later. This command prints one or more files while you are performing other operations. When the PRINT command is in use, it uses approximately 3200 characters (bytes) of memory. To print, the files must be standard text (or ASCII) files containing characters compatible with those used by your printer. The general form of the PRINT command is

```
PRINT FILENAME
```

Pressing Return displays the following prompt:

```
A:\>PRINT FILE1
Name of list device [PRN]:
```

If you have a standard parallel printer, just press Return since PRN is a good device name for a parallel printer. The following information is displayed; then the printer starts printing.

```
Resident part of PRINT installed

  A:\FILE1 is currently being printed

A:\>
```

If you do not have a standard parallel printer (PRN or LPT1) connected to your printer, you can type the device name for your printer (like COM1, LPT2, or AUX) and then press Return.

While your document prints, you can perform other operations. This process is called print spooling or concurrent printing.

The PRINT command lets you enter a list of filenames. For example, if you want to print NOTE1, MOMS.LTR, and a file on the disk in drive B called MYSTERY.TXT, the command is

```
PRINT NOTE1 MOMS.LTR B:MYSTERY.TXT
```

When you press Return the following information is displayed and printing starts, beginning with NOTE1.

```
A:\>PRINT NOTE1 MOMS.LTR B:MYSTERY.TXT


  A:\NOTE1 is currently being printed
  A:\MOMS.LTR is in queue
  B:\MYSTERY.TXT is in queue

A:\>
```

While NOTE1 is printing, you can go about your computing business, except for printing. If you try to print while the PRINT command is active, DOS tells you that you are out of paper. When NOTE1 finishes printing, a form feed occurs at the end of the file and then MOMS.LTR starts printing at the top of a new page. As you might suspect, B:MYSTERY.TXT is printed last.

The PRINT command offers several command options. These are:

/T Terminate all queued files. To clear out your print queue, use the command

```
PRINT /T
```

The print queue is emptied, and the message "PRINT queue is empty" is displayed.

/C Cancel the named file(s) from the print queue. To cancel B:MYSTERY.TXT from your print queue, you can type the command

```
PRINT B:MYSTERY.TXT/C
```

/P Add the named file(s) to the print queue. For example, if you want to add DADS.LTR and B:SIS.LTR to the print queue, you can type the command

```
PRINT DADS.LTR/P B:SIS.LTR
```

You can simultaneously add and cancel files by using /P and /C on the same command line. For example, the command

```
PRINT BROTHER.LTR/P UNCLE.LTR MOMS.LTR/C B:MYSTERY.TXT
```

adds BROTHER.LTR and UNCLE.LTR to the print queue and removes MOMS.LTR and B:MYSTERY.TXT.

As you can see, the PRINT command /C and /P options let you add and cancel files in the same command line. These options act as switches. For example, /C cancels the preceding filename and all following filenames until a filename with a /P switch is encountered. This and following filenames are added to the print queue until a filename with a /C is encountered. Therefore, you can cancel and add filenames to the print queue by typing /C and /P as needed.

APPLICATIONS

The PRINT command is a time-saving utility if you want to print one or more large text files while performing other computer operations. For example, if you want to print a long program listing while you work on an electronic spreadsheet, use PRINT. While the program is being listed on your printer, you can work with your spreadsheet program.

You also can queue up a large list of files for printing. While they are being printed, you can work on other things around the office or home. However, check that you have enough paper and ribbon in your printer before leaving printing unattended.

TYPICAL OPERATION

In this activity you use the PRINT command to queue up three files for printing. However, your printer should remain turned off. The exercise is designed to let you experiment with the command without actually wasting paper. Begin at the DOS prompt.

1. Check to see that your printer is off, unless you wish to actually print the named files.
2. Create a practice file as follows:
   a. Type **COPY CON FILE1** and press **Return**.
   b. Type **This is a test file**, press **Ctrl-Z**, and press **Return**.
3. Copy the practice file to two other files with the following commands:
   a. Type **COPY FILE1 FILE2** and press **Return**.
   b. Type **COPY FILE1 FILE3** and press **Return**.
4. Type **PRINT FILE1 FILE2 FILE3** and press **Return**.
5. Notice the following display.

```
A:\>PRINT FILE1 FILE2 FILE3
Name of list device [PRN]:
```

6. Press **Return** and notice the following display:

```
  A:\FILE1 is currently being printed
  A:\FILE2 is in queue
  A:\FILE3 is in queue

A:\>
```

7. Type **PRINT /T** to terminate the print queue, and notice the following message:

```
A:\>PRINT /T
Errors on list device indicate that it
may be off-line. Please check it.
PRINT queue is empty

A:\>
```

8. Delete the practice files from your disk by typing **DEL FILE?** and pressing **Return**.
9. Turn to Module 20 to continue the learning sequence.

Module 48
PRINTING OPERATIONS (1.00+)

DESCRIPTION

All versions of DOS let you print text-type (ASCII) files and the information displayed on a screen in several ways. You can:

1. Print displayed text by pressing Shift-PrtSc.
2. Display and print information concurrently by pressing Ctrl-P and:
   a. Using a command (like DIR) to display information.
   b. Using the TYPE command to display a text file on the screen.

   Concurrent printing is switched off by pressing Ctrl-P a second time.
3. Use the COPY command to copy a file to PRN, LPT1, LPT2, or LPT3 for parallel-type printers or COM1 or COM2 for serial-type printers.
4. Use the PRINT command (DOS versions 2.00 and later) followed by a filename and the printer device name.
5. Use the DOS TYPE and piping commands to redirect the screen display to a printer device port.

USING THE PrtSc KEY The PrtSc key is used by DOS to send files to your printer. On most computers, you first press and hold Shift; then press PrtSc and whatever is displayed on the screen is sent to your printer. If you have a graphics printer and the displayed information contains graphics material, such as a pie chart, load the GRAPHICS command prior to printing.

USING CTRL-P Pressing and holding the Ctrl key while typing P "toggles" DOS' simultaneous print mode on. When on, lines of text are displayed and simultaneously printed. To stop simultaneous printing, just press Ctrl-P again. Assume that you want to make a hard copy of a file named NOTE on the disk in drive B. You can type:

```
TYPE B:NOTE        (Don't press Return yet.)
```

Press Ctrl-P; then press Return. Your file is displayed and printed at the same time. When printing is finished, the DOS prompt is redisplayed. Press Ctrl-P to turn off simultaneous printing.

You can also cause text that you type from the keyboard to be printed as you type. If you want to print a few lines on paper, such as an address or telephone number, press Ctrl-P, type ECHO, and then press Ctrl-J to force a line feed. Type the information ending each line with Ctrl-J. When you finish typing the note, press Ctrl-J several times to advance the paper. Finally, press Return to end the file. To turn off simultaneous printing, press Ctrl-P again.

USING THE COPY COMMAND You can copy a text file from disk to your printer with the COPY command if you use a printer device name as a target name. To illustrate, assume that you want to copy your NOTE file from the disk in drive B to your printer. Just type COPY B:NOTE LPT1: and press Return to print the file.

USING THE PRINT COMMAND The PRINT command has several options that are described in detail in Module 47. For now, you should know that the PRINT command lets you put one or more designated files into a list (or print queue). Once listed, the files are printed in the order listed as you perform other operations. Some people call this print spooling, while others call it concurrent printing. If you try to print while the PRINT command is active, DOS simulates an out-of-paper condition.

USING THE DOS TYPE AND PIPING COMMANDS DOS versions 2.00 and later feature piping commands that permit redirection of screen output to a device of your choice. This is described in detail in Module 46. To redirect screen output to your printer, the command TYPE filename >PRN redirects the typed file from screen output to printer output.

APPLICATIONS

Having all of the many DOS printing options available lets you print files and obtain paper copies (sometimes called hard copy) of display screens in a number of ways. You should know that many printing methods are available. Once you experiment with them, you should find the techniques that best satisfy your personal needs. Then, you can easily produce quick notes and reproduce displayed screens on paper.

TYPICAL OPERATION

In this activity you use the three different DOS printing techniques. Begin at the DOS prompt.

1. Check to see that your printer is properly connected and turned on.
2. Type **ECHO** and press **Ctrl-J** a few times to advance your paper.
3. Press **Ctrl-P**, type **This is a note to myself.**, and then press **Ctrl-J** three times to advance the paper.
4. Press **Ctrl-P** to turn off printing.
5. Press **Return** to redisplay the DOS prompt, and check the printed results on your printer.
6. Type **DIR** and press **Return** to display a disk directory.
7. Press **Shift-PrtSc**; notice that the displayed text is printed.

8. Type **DIR >PRN** and press **Return** for a hard copy of your directory.
9. Experiment with these and other print options to expand your familiarity with DOS printing operations.
10. Turn to Module 47 to continue the learning sequence.

Module 49
PROMPT (2.00+)

DESCRIPTION

The PROMPT command is an external DOS command available in DOS versions 2.00 and later. You can use this command to configure a DOS prompt to your liking. Many computer users want to display more information than a simple disk drive designator, such as A> or C>. People who are inexperienced in the use of a DOS-based computer may be confused by this cryptic display. The PROMPT command gives you the ability to make the prompt more meaningful. For example, you may wish to display a prompt that says "Command?."

When entering the PROMPT command, it is followed by a space and either text or a dollar sign ($) followed by a special character. The dollar sign must precede the special character to have the desired effect. Special characters that are used with the dollar sign are contained in the following list:

$(x)	*Description*
-	Moves the cursor to the next line (carriage return/line feed)
$	Displays $ (dollar sign)
b	Displays ¦ (vertical bar)
d	Displays the system date
e	The Escape character (^[)
g	Displays > (greater than)
h	Back spaces (and erases) the previous character
l	Displays < (less than)
n	Displays the default drive letter
p	Displays the default drive and directory path name
q	Displays = (equal sign)
v	Displays the DOS version number
t	Displays the system time

The only way to appreciate what the PROMPT command does is to try a few examples. The following list illustrates commands and resulting prompts. Notice that examples are shown for subdirectories as well as main directories.

Command	*Displayed Results*
PROMPT	A> (Disables special characters)
PROMPT Command?	Command?
PROMPT pq	
Main directory prompt	A:\=
WP subdirectory prompt	A:\wp=
PROMPT pg	
Main directory prompt	A:\>
DB subdirectory prompt	A:\db>
PROMPT pdtg	
Main directory prompt	A:\Fri 10-21-1990 11:05:32:09>
SS subdirectory prompt	A:ss\Fri 10-21-1990 11:06:16:74>
PROMPT lp$g	
Main directory prompt	<A:\>
DB subdirectory prompt	<A:\db>
PROMPT $p:Command?	
Main directory prompt	A:\:Command?
123 subdirectory prompt	A:\123:Command?

If the character following $ is unrecognized, it is ignored and not displayed.

APPLICATIONS

Being able to design a prompt of your own is a convenient tool. Some experienced DOS users like to display the directory path ($p) and time ($t). Knowing the present subdirectory is particularly helpful when using a fixed disk system. It is easy to get lost in the subdirectory maze. However, by using the PROMPT $p command form, the subdirectory path designator is always displayed as part of the DOS prompt. The author uses PROMPT pg as a line in his AUTOEXEC.BAT file.

TYPICAL OPERATION

In this activity you use the PROMPT command to design a few prompts of your own. Begin at the DOS prompt.

1. Type **PROMPT $p?** and press **Return**. Your prompt should look like this:

```
A:\?
```

2. Type **PROMPT pd$t?** and press **Return.** Now check your prompt:

```
A:\Tue 02-26-199116:06:56.97?
```

3. Type **PROMPT pg**, press **Return**, and check the resulting prompt.

```
A:\>
```

4. Turn to Module 15 to continue the learning sequence.

Module 50
RECOVER (2.00+)

DESCRIPTION

The RECOVER command is an external command available on DOS versions 2.00 and later. It is used to recover one or more files from a defective disk.

FILES Use of RECOVER is best revealed through a common illustration of its use. Assume that you are experiencing problems reading or copying a file named LETTER. TXT in drive B. You suspect data errors. You may be able to recover the file using the command RECOVER B:LETTER.TXT.

The bad data is often omitted by eliminating a bad disk sector from the file. If recovery is successful, you may be able to recreate the discarded data, which is preferable to having to recreate an entire file. You should be aware that recovered files often have extra data at the end. This can be deleted using a standard ASCII word processor. Be sure to check the end of the file and eliminate any added "garbage" as required.

The RECOVER command works on one file at a time. Therefore, if you use a wild card in your filename, only the first file encountered is recovered.

DIRECTORIES There are also times when a directory is damaged. The RECOVER program attempts to repair a damaged directory. Another illustration is in order. You suspect a bad directory on a disk in drive B. From your DOS directory (in either drive A or C), you may attempt repair using the command RECOVER B:.

The RECOVER program scans the file allocation table (often referred to as the FAT) on the specified disk and creates a new directory that uses sequential numbers for filenames. Even hidden files are placed in the directory. A typical list of recovered filenames resembles the following list. The REC file extension reveals the source of filename creation.

```
FILE0001 REC
FILE0002 REC
FILE0003 REC
FILE0003 REC
    :      :
```

APPLICATIONS

The RECOVER command is a last resort when you have a problematic file. Before attempting to recover a file, you want to try to copy it to another disk. If the copy process encounters data errors, you are often given the opportunity to abort, retry, or ignore the problem. If you type I to ignore the data error, you may be able to copy most of the file. If you cannot copy the file, then you may wish to resort to the RECOVER command.

Another application for the RECOVER command is to remove the hidden DOS files from a blank disk that has been prepared for use with the FORMAT /S command. After the RECOVER command displays the hidden files, use the DEL (or ERASE) command (Module 26) to remove them from the disk. Would it not be easier to reformat the blank disk? Possibly, but the alternative does exist using the RECOVER and DEL commands, and it is usually quicker than having to format the disk. This procedure is illustrated in the Typical Operation section of this module.

TYPICAL OPERATION

In this activity you use RECOVER to restructure the directory of a scratch disk. Begin at the DOS prompt.

1. Place a scratch disk in drive B. (Use A if you have a fixed disk system.)
2. Format the disk in drive B by typing **FORMAT B:/S** and pressing Return twice. Then type **N** and press **Return** at the prompt "Format another (Y/N)."
3. Copy three files to the diskette in drive B by typing the following commands. Follow each command by pressing **Return**.

   COPY C:AUTOEXEC.BAT B:
   COPY C:CONFIG.SYS B:
   COPY C:
4. Type **RECOVER B:** and press **Return**. Then type **Y**. Notice the following display:

```
A:\>RECOVER B:
The entire drive will be reconstructed,
directory structures will be destroyed.
Are you sure (Y/N)? Y
Press any key to begin recovery of the
file(s) on drive B:
```

5. Press any key and notice the following message:

```
3 file(s) recovered

A:\>
```

6. Type **DIR B:** and press **Return**; notice the filenames in the directory listing:

```
A:\>DIR B:

 Volume in drive B has no label
 Volume Serial Number is 0E58-16FB
 Directory of B:\

FILE0001 REC     33280 02-27-91   3:58p
FILE0002 REC     37888 02-27-91   3:58p
FILE0003 REC     46592 02-27-91   3:58p
        3 file(s)      117760 bytes
                      1339904 bytes free

A:\>
```

7. Delete the files on the disk in drive B: by typing **DEL B:*.REC** and pressing **Return**. The disk in drive B is now blank.
8. Turn to Module 42 to continue the learning sequence.

Module 51
RENAME (1.00+)

DESCRIPTION

The RENAME command is an internal command available on all versions of DOS. It is used to change the name of one or more files. The RENAME command is straightforward and easy to use. The general form of the RENAME command is:

```
REN oldname.ext newname.ext
```

Either the entire word RENAME or the short form REN is permitted. Most users prefer the short form.

Several examples are provided to illustrate several forms of the RENAME command:

REN B:OL'NAME NEWNAME	This changes the file OL'NAME located on the disk in drive B to NEWNAME.
REN *.CMD *.PRG	This changes the extension CMD to PRG on all filenames located on the disk in the default drive.
REN LETTER *.FRM	This changes the filename LETTER to LETTER.FRM.

If you have DOS version 2.00 or later, you can include subdirectory pathnames. The following examples illustrate the use of pathnames with RENAME.

REN C:\WS\BOOK\ CHAPT1.TXT CH1.BK	The filename CHAPT1.TXT in the second-level directory C:\WS\BOOK is changed to CH1.BK.
REN C:\DB*.DAT *.PRG	This changes the extension DAT to PRG on all filenames in the DB subdirectory of drive C.

APPLICATIONS

The RENAME command is a frequently used utility. It is called upon whenever you wish you had used a different name for a file. Although a long, descriptive name like "CHAPTER1.TXT" is easy to remember, you may regret having to type an eight-character filename every time you use it. It is both faster and less error prone to type something like "CH1." The RENAME command is helpful when a name change is called for.

The RENAME command is also useful when you want to change an entire series of filenames. A real-world example of this is when you convert command files used with

Ashton-Tate's dBASE II program from CP/M operating system files to DOS-compatible program files.

The CP/M extension for dBASE II program files is .CMD, while DOS-based dBASE programs use the extension .PRG. You can use the RENAME command to make the change from .CMD to .PRG in a single pass. The command REN *.CMD *.PRG does the trick.

There are instances when you want to use several versions of the same program configured for different printers or help levels. You can use RENAME to provide descriptive names for each version of a program file. However, never modify the extension .COM, as this renders the file inoperable until it is changed back to a .COM file.

TYPICAL OPERATION

In this activity you use the RENAME command to rename a file temporarily. You will check the directory to verify the change, and then change it back again. Begin at the DOS prompt.

1. List a directory of your DOS files by typing **DIR** and pressing **Return**. Notice the filename CHKDSK.COM.

```
A:\>DIR

 Volume in drive A has no label
 Volume Serial Number is 0F66-14F7
 Directory of A:\

AUTOEXEC BAT       128 02-26-91    4:58p
COMMAND  COM     46246 12-13-90    4:09a
FORMAT   COM     32285 12-13-90    4:09a
UNDELETE EXE     13666 12-13-90    4:09a
DOSKEY   COM      5693 12-13-90    4:09a
HLPFILES     <DIR>     01-01-91   10:20a
MEM      EXE     22104 12-13-90    4:09a
SYS      COM     13200 12-13-90    4:09a
SMARTDRV SYS      8005 12-13-90    4:09a
HIMEM    SYS     11120 12-13-90    4:09a
DRIVER   SYS      5384 12-13-90    4:09a
ANSI     SYS      8868 12-13-90    4:09a
DISPLAY  SYS     15682 12-13-90    4:09a
CONFIG   SYS       165 02-21-91    9:42a
       14 file(s)     182546 bytes
                       96256 bytes free
```

2. Rename the CHKDSK.COM file to CHK.COM by typing **REN CHKDSK.COM CHK.COM** and pressing **Return**.
3. List the directory to verify the filename change by typing **DIR** and pressing **Return**. Notice the filename CHK.COM has replaced CHKDSK.COM.

```
A:\>DIR

 Volume in drive A has no label
 Directory of A:\

COMMAND  COM     46246 12-13-90   4:09a
ANSI     SYS      8868 12-13-90   4:09a
FORMAT   COM     32285 12-13-90   4:09a
CHKDSK   EXE     16328 12-13-90   4:09a
SYS      COM     13200 12-13-90   4:09a
FIND     EXE      6642 12-13-90   4:09a
CHK      COM     17787 10-06-88  12:00a
        7 file(s)     141356 bytes
                      218112 bytes free

A:\>
```

4. Change the name back to CHKDSK.COM by typing **REN CHK.COM CHKDSK.COM** and pressing **Return.**
5. Turn to Module 11 to continue the learning sequence.

Module 52
REPLACE (3.20+)

DESCRIPTION

The REPLACE command, introduced in DOS version 3.20, is an external command used to selectively replace files on the target disk with files having the same name on the source disk. The selection process is controlled by typing a switch, represented by /X in the following example. The command form is:

```
REPLACE A:\pathname C:\pathname\filename /X
```

The value of X controls the way REPLACE operates. Each of the available values are described in the following list.

- /A Copies specified files that are not present on the target disk. This prevents overwriting files that exist on the target drive. The /A is never used with /S, described below.
- /P Prompts you as each file is encountered on the target drive.
- /R Replaces read-only files on the target drive.
- /S Searches all directories on the target drive for filenames that match those on the source drive.
- /W Displays the prompt "Press any key to begin copying file(s)." This option is used to let you insert a diskette before REPLACE begins its file search. If both /W and /A are used, the prompt takes the form "Press any key to begin adding file(s)."
- /U Added to DOS version 4.01 to automatically replace only those files having dates and times later than the matching files on the target disk.

The following REPLACE command examples are provided for clarification and for use as models.

REPLACE A: B:	Replaces all files on disk B with those files on disk A having the same filename.
REPLACE A: B: /S	Replaces all files in all subdirectories on disk B with those files on disk A having the same filename.

REPLACE A: B: /S/P	Replaces selected files in all subdirectories on disk B with those files on disk A having the same filename. Selection is made by typing Y or N in response to a (Y/N)? (or "Yes"/"No") prompt.

APPLICATIONS

The REPLACE command is particularly valuable for ensuring that all files on one disk are copied to another. Any file or series of files that is updated can be copied from one disk to another without adding unwanted or unnecessary files to the target diskette. For example, if you wish to maintain a selection of text or data files on a backup diskette, you can use REPLACE to ensure that the latest versions of all files are copied from one disk to another. The REPLACE command eliminates the need for you to have to make a list of the selected filenames and copy them individually with the COPY command.

TYPICAL OPERATION

In this activity you copy two files to a destination diskette and then use REPLACE to see how the files are selectively copied. In addition, you use the /P option to display each filename before it is copied. Begin by formatting a floppy diskette for use as the destination disk. If you have a hard disk system, place the formatted floppy diskette in drive A. If you are using a system with two diskette drives, place the formatted diskette in drive B. The following procedure uses C as the source disk and A as the target disk. If you have two floppy diskettes, substitute A: for C: and B: for A:.

NOTE

The following steps assume your DOS files are in the C:\DOS subdirectory.

1. Log the DOS directory.
2. Use the COPY command to copy the FORMAT.COM and DISKCOPY.COM files as follows:
   a. Type **COPY C:\DOS\ FORMAT.COM A:** and press **Return**.
   b. Type **COPY C:\DOS\ DISKCOPY.COM A:** and press **Return**.
3. Type **REPLACE C:\DOS *.* A: /P**. Notice that each of the two filenames are displayed and you are prompted for a copy decision. Type **N** to not copy each of the files.
4. Experiment with other forms of the REPLACE command until you are satisfied that you understand its operation.
5. Turn to Module 68 to continue the learning sequence.

Module 53
RESTORE (2.00+)

DESCRIPTION

The RESTORE command is an external command available on DOS versions 2.00 and later. RESTORE copies files back to a fixed disk after they have been copied to floppy disks using BACKUP (Module 8).

Like the BACKUP command, RESTORE offers many options. It copies files from floppy disks to a fixed disk. You can use RESTORE to copy one or more files from a single directory, all files within a directory, or all files in all directories.

Some forms of the RESTORE command are:

RESTORE A: C:\/S	This command copies every file in every directory from the floppy disk(s) in drive A to the fixed disk (drive C). The /S designates all subdirectories. This command form normally means that you are restoring all files back to your fixed disk from several floppy disks.
RESTORE A: C:* .TXT	This command form copies all files from the active directory having the extension TXT to the fixed disk.
RESTORE A: C:/P	The /P parameter causes the program to prompt you before copying files that have changed since they were last backed up. You also are prompted if a file is marked "read-only." The prompt allows you to selectively prevent files from being restored.

```
C:\>RESTORE A: C:\PATH1\PATH2\*.EXE
```

Here, the "C:\>" represents the fixed disk DOS prompt and is not part of the command. This command causes the system to prompt you to insert the backup disk in drive A that contains the file(s) you want to restore. In this case, the files are those with the extension EXE. When the disk is inserted, pressing any key restores the files to the designated subdirectory.

RESTORE A: C: \WP\WS*.*	This command assumes a subdirectory WP for word processing and one or more filenames within that subdirectory that begin with WS. These files are restored from the floppy disk in drive A to the fixed disk.

APPLICATIONS

The primary application of the RESTORE command is to restore backed up files to a fixed disk. You can restore all files or selected files depending on the form of the command you use. Many DOS users choose to back up and restore individual directories rather than entire fixed disks because of the time it takes to restore several million characters to a large fixed disk.

TYPICAL OPERATION

In this activity you use RESTORE to restore selected files. The procedure assumes you have a fixed disk designated drive C. If the drive is E, then substitute E for C. Check to see that a disk containing the BACKUP.EXE program is on the logged (active) drive.

1. Assuming you have a fixed-disk system, place the backup disk created in Module 8 in drive A.
2. Type **RESTORE A: C:*.EXE** and press **Return.**
3. Check for a prompt that resembles the following illustration:

```
C:\>RESTORE A: C:*.EXE

Insert backup diskette 01 in drive A:
Press any key to continue . . .
```

4. Press any key; notice the "CHECKING MATCH #" message and then watch the filenames appear on the screen as they are copied.
5. Notice the "Restore completed" message after all files are restored.
6. Turn to Module 6 to continue the learning sequence.

Module 54
SELECT (3.00 - 4.01)

DESCRIPTION

The SELECT command was introduced with DOS version 3.00 and expanded with the introduction of DOS version 3.30. In these versions of DOS the SELECT command is used to define (or "select") a number of operational parameters that correspond to a specified country. These include:

- keyboard layout
- date and time format
- collating sequence
- capitalization

The SELECT command was discontinued with the introduction of version 5.00.

DOS 4.01 The SELECT command received extensive changes in DOS version 4.01, where it became a menu-driven utility used to prepare working copies of DOS or to replace older DOS versions. The DOS 4.01 SELECT program is started by placing the DOS 4.01 Install diskette in drive A and booting your computer. Upon start-up, a DOS SELECT screen is displayed. Pressing Return takes you to a series of installation menus. Because the DOS 4.01 version of SELECT uses menus, it is never used from the DOS prompt as in earlier versions.

DOS 3.00 THROUGH 3.3 These versions of the DOS SELECT command are used to install the DOS configuration or your choice in support of a selected national language and keyboard layout. During the operation of SELECT, the target disk is first formatted. Then the DOS system files and all other files on the source disk are copied to the target disk. Finally, CONFIG.SYS and AUTOEXEC.BAT files are created that correspond to the selected country and keyboard codes.

Versions 3.00 through 3.20 of SELECT formatted a disk and transferred all files using DISKCOPY. The XCOPY command is used by SELECT with versions 3.30 and 4.01 of DOS.

The CONFIG.SYS file contains the line COUNTRY=nnn, where nnn is a country code. A resulting CONFIG.SYS file prepared for Germany resembles the following:

```
COUNTRY=049,437
```

The AUTOEXEC.BAT file includes the following lines. To continue the preceding illustration, notice that the keyboard code (yy) and country code (nnn) values on the KEYB command line also correspond to Germany. The KEYB values vary with the values supplied in the SELECT command.

```
PATH \;
KEYB GR 437
ECHO OFF
CLS
DATE
TIME
VER
```

When used to configure a partition on a fixed disk, the disk must have been formatted with DOS 3.30 or later.

The general form of the SELECT command is:

```
SELECT A: d:\path\nnn yy
```

where: A: (or B:) is the source drive designator. If you do not enter a source drive, drive A: is assumed. Only A: and B: are valid source drives. When you enter a source drive, a target drive designator is also required. If only one drive is entered, it is used as the target drive.

d:*path*\ is the destination drive letter and pathname (if applicable) where the DOS files are copied. The default destination drive value is B when no destination drive is specified.

nnn is a three-character country code. (See the following table.)

yy is a two-character keyboard code that selects a keyboard layout corresponding to a specific country. Country and keyboard codes and their availability by DOS version are:

DOS Versions 3.00+			*DOS Versions 3.30-4.01*		
Country	*nnn*	*yy*	*Country*	*nnn*	*yy*
United States	001	US	Arabic	785	None
Canada (Eng)	001	US	Australia	061	US
France	033	FR	Belgium	032	BE
Spain	034	SP	Canada (Fr)	002	CF
Italy	039	IT	Denmark	045	DK
United Kingdom	044	UK	Finland	358	SU
Germany	049	GR	Hebrew	972	None
			Latin America	003	LA
			Netherlands	031	NL
			Norway	047	NO
			Portugal	351	PO
			Sweden	046	SV
			Switzerland (Fr)	041	SF
			Switzerland (Gr)	041	SG

DOS 4.01 added country codes for Korea, Japan, The People's Republic of China, and Taiwan. (See Module 12.) Due to space limitations, avoid the use of file paths on diskettes with less than 720K capacity.

Because SELECT uses DISKCOPY to create a new disk, be sure that only those files you want included on the new system (target) disk are available on the source disk. Once the files are transferred, the CONFIG.SYS and AUTOEXEC.BAT files are created to include the selected country and keyboard codes.

To illustrate what happens on early versions of SELECT when using a system with two removable disk drives (A and B), you can type SELECT 034 SP and press Return to display the following prompt:

```
A:\>SELECT 034 SP

SELECT is used to install DOS the first
time.  SELECT erases everything on the
specified target and then installs DOS.
Do you want to continue (Y/N)?  Y
```

Typing Y and pressing Return at the prompt formats a new disk in drive B with the country and keyboard codes for Spain. DOS 3.00 displays the message:

```
Copying 40 tracks
9 Sectors/Track, 2 Side(s)
```

Later versions of DOS display Head and Cylinder locations. The actual display corresponds to the version of the FORMAT command being used.

As the disk is copied, a CONFIG.SYS file containing the selected COUNTRY device driver (see Module 14) is created on the target disk. In addition, an AUTOEXEC.BAT file containing the appropriate KEYB command is prepared on the target disk so that the proper keyboard code is present.

The SELECT command can also configure fixed disk partitions for use with a selected language.

APPLICATIONS

The SELECT command is used to configure DOS for use in a country or with a language of your choice. If you or others in your office or home are using several different national languages, you may wish to use SELECT to prepare a DOS system diskette for each language used. Once prepared, you can supply a copy of DOS to each user that fits their personal language needs. As each disk is used to boot a microcomputer, the keyboard, display, date and time format, capitalization, and collating sequence that satisfies individual needs is produced.

TYPICAL OPERATION

In this activity you use the SELECT command to format a disk for use with either the French or German language, depending upon which version of DOS you are using. If you have DOS 4.01 or a DOS version prior to 3.00, you cannot perform this activity.

Begin by inserting a scratch disk into drive B. Log the DOS directory that contains the SELECT command.

Activity using DOS version 3.00:

1. Type **SELECT 033 FR** and press **Return**. Notice the following prompt:

```
A:\>SELECT 033 FR

Insert SOURCE Diskette in Drive A :

Insert TARGET Diskette in Drive B :

Press any key when ready . . .
```

2. Press any key; notice the screen message:

```
Copying 40 tracks
9 Sectors/Track, 2 Side(s)
```

3. Type **N** in response to the "Copy another (Y/N)?" prompt.
4. Turn to Module 37 to continue the learning sequence.

Activity using DOS version 3.10 to 3.31:

1. Type **SELECT B: 049 GR** and press **Return**. The following message is displayed:

```
A:\>SELECT B: 049 GR

SELECT is used to install DOS the first
time.  SELECT erases everything on the
specified target and then installs DOS.
Do you want to continue (Y/N)?  Y
```

2. Type **Y** to begin the formatting process.
3. After formatting is complete, type **N** in response to the "Format another..." prompt.

4. Upon completion of the format and copy process, type **DIR B:** and press **Return** to verify that the CONFIG.SYS and AUTOEXEC.BAT. files have been created. You should see the following two entries.

```
CONFIG   SYS          18     02-20-91    4:43p
AUTOEXEC BAT          56     02-20-91    4:43p
```

5. Type **TYPE B:AUTOEXEC.BAT** and press **Return** to display the contents of the AUTOEXEC.BAT file on the screen. It should match the AUTOEXEC.BAT file shown in the Description section of this module.
6. Type **TYPE B:CONFIG.SYS** and press **Return** to display the contents of the CONFIG.SYS file on the screen. It should contain "COUNTRY=049,437."
7. If you wish, experiment with other country and keyboard codes and examine the results.
8. Turn to Module 37 to continue the learning sequence.

Module 55
SET (2.00+)

DESCRIPTION

The SET command is an internal command available on DOS versions 2.00 and later. When SET is typed as a command without following text, in the form

```
SET
```

the SET command displays the current DOS "environment." For example, typing SET and pressing Return displays the following:

```
C:\>SET
COMSPEC=C:\DOS5\COMMAND.COM
PROMPT=$p$g
TEMP=C:\WINDOWS\TEMP
DIRCMD=/O:-GN/P
PATH=C:\;C:\DOS5;C:\WINDOWS;C:\TC\BIN
```

You can use SET to redirect use of an alternate command processor (or COMMAND.COM file). For example, if you are using a hard disk system under DOS 3.3 and wish to run DOS 4.01, it is not necessary to install DOS 4.01 on your hard disk. You can boot from a floppy drive containing the DOS 4.01 system. Then, assuming you have all DOS 4.01 commands in a subdirectory named C:\DOS4, you can issue the command

```
SET COMSPEC=C:\DOS4\COMMAND.COM
```

Now your programs are directed to the DOS command processor located in the C:\DOS subdirectory. This gives you the ability to run a version of DOS that differs from what is installed on your system's root directory.

You can set a parameter using a command similar to

```
SET PATH=\DB
```

When you use the SET command to display DOS environment settings, PATH=\DB is displayed. To cancel the path setting, type

```
SET PATH=
```

Displaying the settings now shows PATH=. Of course, the path setting can be changed using the PATH command itself.

You can use SET to assign a string to a variable in the form:

```
SET variable=string
```

An example of this would be if you wanted to assign the pathname C:\WINDOWS to the variable WD. This is accomplished by typing

```
SET WD=C:\WINDOWS
```

Now you can use the line DIR %WD% in place of DIR C:\WINDOWS in a batch file. The DIR %WD% command must be in a batch file; it does not operate as anticipated if you type it at the DOS prompt. You can verify that the variable is set by typing SET. The line WD=c:\windows is displayed.

APPLICATIONS

One of the most convenient uses of the SET command is reviewing the setup of the DOS environment. If you wish to view the current active directory paths and the PROMPT command form, you can use the SET command to see all of the DOS settings in a single display.

As previously described, SET COMSPEC lets you run alternate versions of DOS on the same computer.

TYPICAL OPERATION

In this activity you use the SET command to view the DOS environment, to change the prompt parameters, and then to cancel the prompt parameters. Begin at the DOS prompt.

1. Type **SET** and press **Return**. Check for a display similar to the following illustration.

```
C:\>SET
COMSPEC=C:\DOS5\COMMAND.COM
PROMPT=$p$g
TEMP=C:\WINDOWS\TEMP
DIRCMD=/O:-GN/P
PATH=C:\;C:\DOS5;C:\WINDOWS;C:\TC\BIN
```

2. Type **SET PROMPT=$p:** and press **Return**.
3. Check the DOS environment again by typing **SET** and pressing **Return**. Notice that the PROMPT command form is displayed.

```
C:\>SET
COMSPEC=C:\DOS5\COMMAND.COM
PROMPT=$p:
TEMP=C:\WINDOWS\TEMP
DIRCMD=/O:-GN/P
PATH=C:\;C:\DOS5;C:\WINDOWS;C:\TC\BIN
```

4. Cancel the prompt setting by typing **SET PROMPT=** and pressing **Return**.
5. Type **SET** and press **Return** again to check the DOS environment; notice that the canceled PROMPT setting is no longer displayed.

```
C:\>SET
COMSPEC=C:\DOS5\COMMAND.COM
PROMPT=
TEMP=C:\WINDOWS\TEMP
DIRCMD=/O:-GN/P
PATH=C:\;C:\DOS5;C:\WINDOWS;C:\TC\BIN
```

6. Type **PROMPT pg** and press **Return** to reset the prompt display.
7. Turn to Module 16 to continue the learning sequence.

Module 56
SHARE (3.00+)

DESCRIPTION

The SHARE command was introduced with DOS version 3.00 to support networking. This command is normally used by system programmers to allocate disk space for file sharing. To allocate 1024 bytes of space, use the command

```
SHARE /F:1024
```

If you fail to specify /F: followed by a value, DOS uses 2048 bytes.

In addition to the /F parameter, SHARE also uses a /L:nn parameter, where nn is the number of locks. If no value is specified, DOS establishes 20 locks.

To verify that SHARE is installed, you can type SHARE and press Return. Notice this message:

```
SHARE already installed
```

APPLICATIONS

SHARE allocates file space for recording the necessary information to enable sharing disk space with other users on a local area network. The lock function lets you lock selected files to prevent unauthorized access.

TYPICAL OPERATION

In this activity you use SHARE to set up 2048 bytes of disk space for file sharing information. Next, you check to see if SHARE is installed. Begin at the DOS prompt.

1. Type **SHARE** and press **Return**. The default value of 2048 bytes is reserved.
2. Type **SHARE** and press **Return** again to verify that the SHARE command reserved the disk space. Notice this message:

   ```
   SHARE already installed
   ```

3. Turn to Module 18 to continue the learning sequence.

Module 57
SORT (2.00+)

DESCRIPTION

The SORT command is another DOS filter command introduced in DOS version 2.00. Filter commands are used to intercept, rearrange, and output selected data. Three filter commands are: SORT, FIND, and MORE. This module deals with the SORT command. However, examples include combining this command with other DOS commands and filters.

The SORT filter intercepts text data and organizes (or sorts) it in alphanumeric order. The general form of the SORT command is:

```
SORT source file >target file
```

This command sorts each line in the source file and copies it to the target file in sorted order.

The normal SORT operation arranges data in ascending (0 - 9, A - Z) order. If you require a descending (or reverse) order sort, add /R to the end of the command line. This puts data in a Z - A, 9 - 0 order.

Another parameter (/+n) is used to start the sort at a specific column within the specified source file. For example, you can start sorting on column 6 by typing /+6 at the end of the SORT command line.

A few examples of how to use the SORT filter is shown below. Some examples include piping commands. The greater than symbol (>) is a destination pipe; the less than symbol (<) is a source pipe.

DIR ¦ SORT	This command alphabetizes the directory listing and then displays it on your screen.
DIR ¦ SORT /R	This command is identical to the one above except that it places the directory in descending (reverse) order.
DIR ¦ SORT >DIRFILE	This command alphabetizes the directory listing and directs (pipes) it to a file named DIRFILE.
SORT <FILE1 >FILE2	This command alphabetizes the lines of text in FILE1 and places it in FILE2.

SORT /+10 <FILE1 > FILE2 — This command is identical to the one above except that the sort begins with the 10th character in each line of text.

DIR ¦ SORT >PRN — This command routes a sorted directory to the selected system printer.

The following SORT commands are used to sort a directory into an intermediate file (SORT1.DIR), which is then sorted again into a final file (SORT2.DIR) to provide a directory that is sorted by file creation date.

1. Type DIR ¦ SORT /+14 >SORT1.DIR and press Return to sort the directory by month into the file SORT1.DIR.
2. Open the file with an editor and delete all characters following the year to prevent the file from being sorted by time. Then save the file.
3. Finally, type SORT /+30 <SORT1.DIR >SORT2.DIR and press Return to sort the SORT1.DIR file by year.

APPLICATIONS

The filter commands are useful in many ways. The SORT filter is excellent for alphabetizing large directories. If you wish, you can sort disk directories to your printer and then store the printed copy of the directory with the disk.

TYPICAL OPERATIONS

In this activity you use the SORT filter in two ways. First, you use it to sort a directory display. Next, you use it to sort file entries. Begin at the DOS prompt.

1. Type **DIR ¦SORT /R** and press **Return**; notice that your directory is listed in reverse alphabetical order.
2. Type **COPY CON TEMP1** and press **Return**; then type the following lines ending each with **Return**. Finally, press **Ctrl-Z** and **Return** on the last line to save the file to disk.

```
A:\>COPY CON TEMP1
Zebras
Bears
Whales
Alligators
Birds
^Z
        1 file(s) copied

A:\>
```

3. Type **SORT <TEMP1 >TEMP2** and press **Return**. Wait for the DOS prompt display before performing step 4.
4. Type **TYPE TEMP2** and press **Return**; notice that the lines within this file are sorted in alphabetical order.

```
A:\>TYPE TEMP2
Alligators
Bears
Birds
Whales
Zebras

A:\>
```

5. Type **DEL TEMP?** and press **Return** to delete the TEMP1 and TEMP2 files.
6. Turn to Module 31 to continue the learning sequence.

Module 58
SUBST (3.10+)

DESCRIPTION

The SUBST command was introduced in DOS version 3.10. The command word SUBST is an abbreviation for substitute. It is an external command that lets you assign a disk drive designator to a drive and file path of your choice. If you have a subdirectory designated as C:\DOS\UTIL, you can use SUBST to shorten this notation to a single disk drive letter. For example, the command

```
SUBST E: C:\DOS\UTIL
```

lets you use E: as a shorthand form for the notation "C:\DOS\UTIL."

Typing SUBST alone displays

```
E: => C:\DOS\UTIL
```

This shows you current substitution settings. You can see a file directory of C:\DOS\UTIL with DIR E:.

You can have several substitutions in effect at a time. The normal range of drive letters available is A - E. However, you can add the line LASTDRIVE = Z to your CONFIG.SYS file (see Module 14) and restart your system (with Ctrl-Alt-Del) to use drive designators A through Z. Never use a drive designator, such as A or B, that presently exists.

A substitution setting is disconnected with SUBST E:/D. This cancels the drive and/or pathname relationship associated with E:.

APPLICATIONS

The SUBST command is convenient in a few important ways. First, it lets you establish a shorthand form for drive and subdirectory access. Using E: instead of C:\DOS\UTIL saves keystrokes and reduces typos. Another convenient application is when you use programs that do not support file paths in program calls. WordStar version 3.3 and earlier is a good example of this. However, the program operates with other subdirectories using a substitute drive designator. For example, you can read and write files to drive E: when SUBST E: C:\DOS\UTIL is active.

TYPICAL OPERATION

In this activity you make a subdirectory and use SUBST to establish a relationship between that subdirectory and drive E:. This activity assumes you are using a fixed disk system and are logged to drive C.

NOTE

If you have drive E, use another designator, such as F, in place of E. It may be necessary to place LASTDRIVE=F in your CONFIG.SYS file and warm boot (Ctrl-Alt-Del) your computer before this activity works properly.

1. From the root directory, type **MD TEMP** and press **Return.**
2. Type **SUBST E: C:\TEMP** and press **Return.**
3. Type **DIR E:** and press **Return**; look at your display.

```
C:\>DIR E:

 Volume in drive E is DISK1_VOL1
 Volume Serial Number is 1458-047A
 Directory of E:\

.            <DIR>      02-28-91  11:07a
..           <DIR>      02-28-91  11:07a
        2 file(s)           0 bytes
                      7225344 bytes free

C:\>
```

4. Type **SUBST E: /D** and press **Return** to cancel the substitute drive.
5. Turn to Module 5 to continue the learning sequence.

Module 59
SYS (1.00+)

DESCRIPTION

The SYS command is an external DOS program available on all versions of DOS. This command transfers the DOS system files (BIO.COM and DOS.COM) to a specified target disk. Only diskettes that have an empty directory or that have been formatted with the /S or /B can be used with the SYS command.

DOS 4.01 added the capability to specify an optional source drive and file path or the current default drive to simplify installation of DOS on networks.

Recall from the FORMAT module that the /S parameter transfers the system during the formatting process. The /B parameter reserves system space during formatting. A disadvantage of the /B parameter is that it creates a smaller capacity, eight-sector diskette.

The SYS command has the form:

```
SYS C:
```

When DOS is successfully transferred, the message "System transferred" is displayed.

The following command is now possible in DOS 4.01.

```
SYS B:\DOS C:
```

This command transfers the operating system from the B:\DOS subdirectory to drive C.

The SYS command transfers the BIO.COM and DOS.COM system files, which are hidden files (not displayed with DIR). For more information about these files, see Module 3. The SYS command does not transfer the COMMAND.COM file. Use the COPY command to transfer this file to the target disk. If you are using DOS 4.01, SYS transfers the volume serial number with the system files. The SYS command does not write to a network drive or drives designated with the ASSIGN or SUBST commands.

APPLICATIONS

You should be aware that DOS is licensed to you when it is purchased. When you buy a new program, the manufacturer often instructs you to write the system on the program disk using the SYS command. This makes the disk bootable, that is, it will start your computer.

If you give someone a disk with DOS on it, you have violated your license agreement. Therefore, if you wish to sell a program you have written, you should format the disk on which you plan to put the program with the /B parameter. Then, you can copy your program onto the formatted disk. The recipient of your program can use the SYS command to transfer the system from his own copy of DOS.

TYPICAL OPERATION

In this activity you use the FORMAT /B and SYS commands to format a new (or used) disk and transfer the system. Begin at the DOS prompt.

NOTE

In the following step, a scratch disk is one that you can use for practice. It should either be a new, blank disk or an old one containing obsolete data files that you no longer want.

1. Place a scratch disk in drive B and close the load lever.
2. Type **FORMAT B:/B** and press **Return**.
3. Once the disk is formatted, type **N** in response to the "Format another (Y/N)?" prompt.
4. Type **SYS B:** and press **Return**. When DOS is transferred, check the display:

```
A:\>SYS B:
System transferred

A:\>
```

5. Turn to Module 67 to continue the learning sequence.

Module 60
TIME (1.00+)

DESCRIPTION

Like the DATE command, the TIME command is also one of DOS' internal commands, and therefore is not seen when a directory of disk files is displayed. The system time uses a 24-hour clock. If you are using DOS 3.3 or earlier, you must enter 1:30 p.m. as 13:30. If you are using DOS 4.01+, you can use 12-hour notation. This is described in the last paragraph of this section.

The TIME command is run automatically after the DATE command when you insert the DOS disk and turn on your computer. Automatic execution of the TIME command is suppressed if your system is configured with a hardware clock-calendar device or uses an AUTOEXEC.BAT file that excludes a TIME command line.

RUNNING TIME MANUALLY You can run the TIME command manually by typing TIME and pressing Return at the DOS prompt. When the TIME command runs, a prompt similar to the following is displayed.

```
A:\>TIME
Current time is  2:39:48.94p
Enter new time:
```

The time expression is given in:

hours:minutes:seconds.hundredths of a second

DOS 4.01 and later display a and p for am and pm.

Type the current hour and minute in the form 10:45 and press Return. The time is recorded by DOS. You may use a period in place of a colon to separate the hours, minutes, and seconds. Seconds and hundredths of a second may be omitted. However, if you wish to enter the time to this level of accuracy, separate seconds and hundredths with either a period or a comma. If the time is not important to you, you can respond to the TIME prompt by pressing Return. This sets the system clock to 00:00.

You can also type TIME, the current time notation, and press Return to set the time. This command form inputs the time without displaying the DOS time prompt.

DOS 4.01+ AND 12-HOUR TIME NOTATION The DOS 4.01 TIME command was changed to support 12-hour time notation. To use 12-hour times, times are entered with an a or p or a.m. or p.m. Look at the two following examples.

```
TIME 10:30a
TIME 10:30p
```

Both of these are valid time entries. If you wish to use the 24-hour time notation, use 22:30 in place of 10:30p and 10:30 in place of 10:30a.

APPLICATIONS

As in the DATE command, it is much easier to press the Return key than to enter the time notation. However, files that are saved to disk are tagged with the time and date. This lets you examine a directory to determine which files are most current. Therefore, it is best to set the clock to the current time. This is particularly true if you intend to use commands that are time and date sensitive, such as XCOPY or REPLACE. In addition, some programs use the system time to display a clock on the screen.

Although it may seem like a waste of your time to enter the system time and date every time you turn on your computer, it is strongly recommended.

If entering the time becomes a nuisance, you can obtain a clock-calendar option board to eliminate the need to type the date and time every time you turn on your computer. Many computers come standard with a hardware clock-calendar. These systems use a battery to maintain clock and calendar operation. Even when the computer is turned off or disconnected from the wall outlet, the clock and calendar continue to operate.

TYPICAL OPERATION

In this activity you use the TIME command to enter the current time. Check to see that your computer is properly connected and that your DOS diskette is properly inserted in drive A.

1. If your computer is already turned on and the DOS prompt is displayed, go to step 3 below. Otherwise, turn on your computer.

NOTE

In the following step, you normally respond to the DATE and TIME prompts at system turn-on. However, to illustrate use of the TIME prompt by itself, ignore these prompts for the time being.

2. Press **Return** twice in response to the DATE and TIME prompts. The A> prompt is now displayed as shown here:

```
A:\>
```

3. Type **TIME** and press **Return**; notice the TIME prompt.

```
A:\>TIME
Current time is  2:39:48.94p
Enter new time:
```

4. Type the current time in the indicated form (separate the hour and minute with a colon) and press **Return**.
5. The current time is now recorded. To verify the current time, you can repeat step 3. If you do not want to change the time, press Return to redisplay the DOS prompt. Pressing Return leaves the system time unchanged.
6. If you are using DOS 4.01, experiment with the 12-hour time notation by following the time with an a or p.
7. Turn to Module 65 to continue the learning sequence.

Module 61
TREE (2.00+)

DESCRIPTION

The TREE command was introduced in DOS version 2.00. TREE is an external DOS command that displays all directory pathnames on the specified disk. An optional /F parameter is available to let you display filenames. DOS 4.01, which displays the file tree using block graphics, added the /A parameter which displays an alternate graphic character set.

A few examples of the TREE command are provided for clarification. If you wish to view all directories contained on drive C, you can type:

```
TREE C:
```

A screen similar to the following is displayed.

```
A:\>TREE C:

DIRECTORY PATH LISTING FOR VOLUME ???????????

Path: \BILL
Sub-directories: LILBILL
                 WMJR

Path: \BILL\LILBILL
Sub-directories: None

Path: \BILL\WMJR
Sub-directories: None

Path: \TOM
Sub-directories: None

Path: \MARY
Sub-directories: None

Path: \JOAN
Sub-directories: None
```

If you are using DOS 4.01, your display resembles the following:

```
A:\>TREE C:
Directory PATH listing for Volume RUSS_STULTZ
C:.
├───BILL
│   ├───LILBILL
│   └───WMJR
├───TOM
├───MARY
└───JOAN
```

The DOS 5.00 TREE /A command uses an alternate set of characters in place of the block graphic characters.

```
A:\>TREE C:/A
Directory PATH listing for Volume RUSS_STULTZ
C:.
+---BILL
|   +---LILBILL
|   \---WMJR
+---TOM
+---MARY
\---JOAN
```

You can pause the display by pressing Ctrl-S. To resume the display, press any key. Another way to pause the display automatically is to add the MORE filter to the TREE command line by typing:

```
TREE C: |MORE
```

If you want to view all of the filenames within each directory, you can type the TREE command followed by /F in the form:

```
TREE C:/F            (or TREE C:/F |MORE)
```

A screen similar to the following is displayed.

```
A:\>TREE C:/F

DIRECTORY PATH LISTING FOR VOLUME ???????????

Path: \BILL
Sub-directories: LILBILL
                 WMJR

Files:           EDLIN   .COM

Path: \BILL\LILBILL
Sub-directories: None

Path: \BILL\WMJR
Sub-directories: None

Files:           None
```

```
Files:            None

Path: \TOM
Sub-directories: None

Files:            None

Path: \MARY
Sub-directories: None

Path: \MARY
Sub-directories: None

Files:            MEMO    .BAK
                  MEMO    .#01

Path: \JOAN
Sub-directories: None

Files:            DEPT    .LTR
```

You can also route (or pipe) the tree display to a file using the following form of the command.

```
TREE /F >CTREE
```

The display is routed to the file CTREE rather than being displayed.

APPLICATIONS

It is often important to know all pathnames and filenames within file paths. The TREE command is an indispensable tool for determining the organization of your disk, particularly if it is a large fixed disk.

TYPICAL OPERATION

In this activity you use the TREE command to determine which pathnames and filenames exist on your DOS disk. Before issuing the TREE command, you first make a temporary directory. After using the TREE command, the temporary directory is removed. Begin at the DOS prompt.

1. Make a directory by typing **MD FANG** and pressing **Return.**
2. Type **TREE** and press **Return**; notice the display.

```
A:\>TREE
Directory PATH listing
Volume Serial Number is 0F66-14F7
A:.
├───HLPFILES
└───FANG
```

3. Remove the FANG pathname by typing **RD FANG** and pressing **Return.**
4. Turn to Module 49 to continue the learning sequence.

Module 62
TYPE (1.00+)

DESCRIPTION

The TYPE command is an internal command that is available on all versions of DOS. This command displays the contents of standard text (ASCII) files on your screen. The general form of the TYPE command is

```
TYPE filename
```

The named file is displayed on the screen. If it is longer than the screen, it scrolls upward until the last line of the file is displayed. Then the DOS prompt is redisplayed. The typed (or displayed) file moves upward so rapidly it is difficult to read. However, you can pause the movement by pressing Ctrl-S. When you are ready, press any key to resume scrolling.

If you have DOS 2.00 or later, you can use the MORE filter command to freeze each screen full of information. Using TYPE LETTER.001 ¦ MORE freezes each screen full of information, and prompts you to strike a key to display the next screen.

If you want to display and print a file simultaneously, you can press Ctrl-P (or Ctrl-PrtSc) prior to pressing Return at the end of the TYPE command line. You should also check your printer for proper connection and power before you press Return.

The DOS piping commands (See Module 42) also provide a means to route a typed file to your printer. Look at the following illustration.

```
TYPE filename >PRN
```

This command routes (or pipes) the named file to your printer.

APPLICATIONS

The TYPE command offers a convenient way to examine files by displaying them on your screen. For example, if you are trying to find a certain file and cannot remember what name you used, the TYPE command can come to your rescue. Just TYPE the files to the screen until you recognize the one you need.

As mentioned above, TYPE also offers a quick way to print a file. By turning on printing (with Ctrl-P), you can dump a file to your printer to obtain a fast paper copy. You can also use the piping or filter commands described above. These operations eliminate the need to use word processing software to print a standard text file. Be aware, however, that you cannot TYPE (and print) binary or other non-ASCII format files; if you try, only garbage is displayed. This is because your printer is unable to process nonprintable characters.

TYPICAL OPERATION

In this activity you use the TYPE command to display a file on your screen. Begin at the DOS prompt.

1. Create a temporary file using the COPY command as follows:
   a. Type **COPY CON: A:TESTFILE** and press **Return**.
   b. Type **This is a test file.** and press **Return**.
   c. Press **Ctrl-Z**; then press **Return** to write the file to disk. (Ctrl-Z inserts an end-of-file marker.)
2. Type **TYPE TESTFILE**, press **Return**, and notice the following display.

```
A:\>TYPE TESTFILE
This is a test file.

A:\>
```

3. Type **DEL TESTFILE** and press **Return** to delete the file from your disk.
4. Turn to Module 10 to continue the learning sequence.

Module 63
UNDELETE (5.00+)

INTRODUCTION

The UNDELETE command is an external command that is used to recover deleted files. It is important to undelete as soon as possible, as new files occupy the space formerly occupied by deleted files. Therefore, if you create new files after deleting, you may never be able to undelete the desired file.

When files are deleted, the first character of the filename is removed from the directory file. The UNDELETE command either replaces the missing character with one of its own, or you may be prompted to furnish a beginning character. The parameters used with UNDELETE control the replacement process.

If you delete files and then remove a directory, it will be difficult to undelete files in the removed directory. You may be able use the UNFORMAT command to restore the directory and then try UNDELETE. Bear in mind that the more you change a disk, the more unlikely it is that you can recover a file.

UNDELETE COMMAND FORMS The most elementary form of the UNDELETE command is to type UNDELETE and press Return. There are also a number of parameters available to give you flexibility in the way the command operates. These are described in the following list.

UNDELETE	This command form recovers all deleted files in the current directory one at a time. You are prompted as each file is displayed. If the file is unrecoverable, the system tells you so.
UNDELETE C:\WP\FILES*.WPF	This command undeletes all files having the extension .WPF in the \WP\FILES directory. The files are undeleted one at a time, as you are prompted as each file is displayed. If the file is unrecoverable, the system tells you so.

UNDELETE C:\ /ALL	This command automatically undeletes all files. The first character of the filename is replaced with one of the following characters in the indicated order: # % & - 0 1 2 3 4 5 6 7 8 9. The # sign is used unless there is another file having the same name. If this occurs, % is used as the first character of the filename, then &, and so on.
UNDELETE /DOS	This command undeletes files in the DOS directory.
UNDELETE C:\ /LIST	This command lists all files that are available for undeletion.
UNDELETE C:\DB /ALL	This command automatically undeletes all files in the specified directory.
UNDELETE /DT	This command uses the filenames found in the delete tracking file PCTRACKR.DEL. This file is created by the MIRROR program.

THE MIRROR COMMAND The MIRROR command, described in Module 41, can be used by the UNDELETE command. Typing MIRROR and pressing Return installs the program. A record of deleted files is maintained in the root directory of the current drive. You can also install the program to track file deletions on multiple drives. Use MIRROR /tc to track deletions on drive C. Use MIRROR /tc /ta to track deletions on both C and A.

APPLICATIONS

Almost all users occasionally delete files unintentionally. When this happens, the UNDELETE command comes to the rescue. For example, using a wild card to delete multiple files might include a file you wanted to keep. You might want to display a list of recently deleted files using the UNDELETE /LIST command. If the file you want to recover is displayed, use UNDELETE *.*ext*, where *ext* is the file extension of the file you want to recover.

TYPICAL OPERATION

In this activity you create a temporary subdirectory named TEMP and a few files within that directory. Then you delete them and use the UNDELETE command to restore them. Finally, you delete them again and remove the directory.

1. Type **CD** and press **Return** to move to the root directory.
2. Make a directory named TEMP by typing **MD TEMP** and pressing **Return.**

3. Create two temporary files in the TEMP directory as follows:
   a. Type **HELP DIR > \TEMP\TEMP1.TXT** and press **Return**.
   b. Type **HELP MIRROR > \TEMP\TEMP2.TXT** and press **Return**.
4. Type **CD\TEMP** and press **Return** to log the TEMP directory.
5. Type **DIR** and press **Return** to display a directory. Notice that the new files are listed.
6. Type **DEL TEMP?.*** and press **Return** to delete these files.
7. Type **DIR** and press **Return** to verify that the files are gone.
8. Type **UNDELETE /LIST** and press **Return** to list the deleted files. Notice the following display.

```
A:\TEMP>UNDELETE /LIST

Directory: A:\TEMP
File Specs: *.*

    Delete Tracking file not found.

    MS-DOS Directory contains    2 deleted files.
    Of those,    2 files may be recovered.

Using the MS-DOS Directory.

      ?EMP1     TXT        23  2-27-91  9:17a  ...A
      ?EMP2     TXT       696  2-27-91  9:18a  ...A

A:\TEMP>
```

9. Now restore the files by typing **UNDELETE** and pressing **Return**. Notice the following display.

```
A:\TEMP>UNDELETE

Directory: A:\TEMP
File Specs: *.*

    Delete Tracking file not found.

    MS-DOS Directory contains    2 deleted files.
    Of those,    2 files may be recovered.

Using the MS-DOS Directory.

      ?EMP1     TXT        23  2-27-91  9:17a  ...A
Do you want to undelete this file? (Y/N)
```

10. Type **Y** in response to the first prompt and notice the next prompt "Enter the first character of the filename." Respond by typing **T**.
11. Repeat step 10 to restore the second file.

12. Type **DIR** to display the restored filenames.
13. Delete the files and remove the TEMP directory by typing the following commands, pressing **Return** after each.

    DEL *.*
    Y
    **CD **
    RD TEMP
14. Turn to Module 51 to continue the learning sequence.

Module 64
UNFORMAT (5.00+)

DESCRIPTION

The UNFORMAT command, which is an internal DOS command, became available with the release of DOS 5.00. This command restores the directories and files on a disk after it has been formatted. UNFORMAT uses files created by the MIRROR command (Module 41) if they are available.

UNFORMAT COMMAND FORMS Following are forms of the UNFORMAT command.

UNFORMAT C: /J	Verifies that the MIRROR image files are available for drive C and agree with system information on the disk. This parameter does not perform the actual unformatting operation. If the MIRROR image file is valid, the message "The system area of drive C has been verified to agree with the image file."
UNFORMAT A: /P	Unformats the disk in drive B and simultaneously sends listed information to the connected printer; do not use the /P switch if you want UNFORMAT to use the MIRROR image file.
UNFORMAT B: /L /P	Unformats the disk in drive B. The /L switch lists all files and subdirectories. The /P switch simultaneously sends the listed information to the connected printer. The /P parameter does not use MIRROR image files. Use Ctrl-P to pause the display.
UNFORMAT B: /P /PARTN	When /P is used with /PARTN, only fragmented files and subdirectories are listed. Use Ctrl-S to pause the display.
UNFORMAT B: /TEST	Determines if drive B can be unformatted without the use of a MIRROR image file.
UNFORMAT A:	Unformats the disk in drive A. Uses the MIRROR image file if available. Otherwise, proceed without it.
UNFORMAT C: /PARTN	Rebuilds the disk partition table using the MIRROR-generated PARTNSAV.FIL file.

EXCEPTION: If the target disk was formatted using FORMAT /U, UNFORMAT cannot restore it.

USING UNFORMAT WITH MIRROR If you plan to use UNFORMAT, the following steps are advisable.

1. Copy your CONFIG.SYS file and all pertinent device drivers (SYS files) to a bootable floppy disk. This disk is used as a boot disk before using the UNFORMAT command.
2. You should also have run the MIRROR command to create a file containing the file allocation table and root directory. UNFORMAT prompts you for this file during the restoration process.

NOTE

The /P, /L, and /TEST parameters prevent the use of the MIRROR-generated files.

3. During the rebuilding process, UNFORMAT displays the date and time of the most recent MIRROR file. A prompt asks for a Y or N entry. Typing Y uses the indicated file; N displays the date and time of the next prior MIRROR file. You might use an older file if you used the MIRROR command after you accidentally formatted the disk.

APPLICATIONS

The UNFORMAT command is used to recover unintentionally formatted disks. Perhaps the most dangerous DOS command is FORMAT. Thousands of users have issued the FORMAT command and accidentally specified the wrong drive designation. Now UNFORMAT is available to restore an accidentally formatted disk. Although UNFORMAT operates best with the files produced by the MIRROR command, it may produce satisfactory results without these files if the formatted disk has not been used.

TYPICAL OPERATION

In this activity you format a floppy disk in drive A. Then you create a subdirectory and create three files. Next, you format the floppy disk. Finally, you use the UNFORMAT command to recover the disk and its contents. Begin at the C: DOS prompt.

1. Insert a floppy disk in drive A, type **FORMAT A:**, and press **Return** twice.
2. Type **MD A:\TEMP** and press **Return** to create a TEMP subdirectory on the disk in drive A.

3. Copy three files to the disk in drive A as follows:
   a. Type **HELP DIR > A:TEMP1.TXT** and press **Return**.
   b. Type **UNDELETE /? > A:\TEMP\FILE1.TXT** and press **Return**.
   c. Type **HELP FORMAT > A:\TEMP\FILE2.TXT** and press **Return**.
4. Type **DIR A: /s** and press **Return**. Check the directory listing.

```
A:\>DIR A: /S

 Volume in drive A has no label
 Volume Serial Number is 3464-10F4

Directory of A:\

TEMP         <DIR>     02-28-91   9:49a
TEMP1    TXT      1028 02-28-91   9:49a
        2 file(s)       1028 bytes

Directory of A:\TEMP

.            <DIR>     02-28-91   9:49a
..           <DIR>     02-28-91   9:49a
FILE1    TXT       362 02-28-91   9:50a
FILE2    TXT       955 02-28-91   9:50a
        4 file(s)       1317 bytes

Total files listed:
        6 file(s)       2345 bytes
                      352256 bytes free

A:\>
```

5. Format the disk in drive A by typing **FORMAT A:** and pressing **Return** twice.
6. Type **UNFORMAT A: /TEST** and press **Return** twice to test recovery. Type **Y** in response to displayed prompts to see what can be recovered.
7. When the DOS prompt is redisplayed, type **UNFORMAT A:** and press **Return** twice to actually recover the files. Read the information and type **Y** in response to the prompt.
8. When the operation is completed, type **DIR A: /S** and press **Return** to display the files on the unformatted disk.
9. Turn to Module 55 to continue the learning sequence.

Module 65
VER (2.00+)

DESCRIPTION

The VER command was introduced in DOS version 2.00. It is an internal DOS command that displays the version of DOS you are using. To run the VER program, type VER and press Return.

APPLICATIONS

Because several different versions of DOS are available, you may wish to determine which version you are using. This is accomplished with the VER command. Knowing the installed DOS version is important, because different versions of DOS have different command forms. In addition, some programs are specifically designed to operate with specific versions of DOS.

TYPICAL OPERATION

In this activity you use the VER command to see which version of DOS you are using. Begin at the DOS prompt.

1. Type **VER** and press **Return**.
2. Notice a display similar to the following screen illustration.

```
A:\>VER

MS-DOS Version 5.00

A:\>
```

3. Turn to Module 40 to continue the learning sequence.

Module 66
VERIFY (2.00+)

DESCRIPTION

The VERIFY command is an internal DOS command that is available on DOS versions 2.00 and later. The command verifies that data is recorded properly when written to a disk. The default setting is for VERIFY to be off. To turn VERIFY on, type VERIFY ON and press Return. When on, all disk write operations are verified for accuracy. To determine whether or not VERIFY is on, you can type VERIFY and press Return. The message "VERIFY is on" is displayed when it is active. When VERIFY is on, file operations take slightly longer because of the extra time it takes to check the data as it is written.

To turn VERIFY off, type VERIFY OFF and press Return. Now when you type VERIFY and press Return, the message "VERIFY is off" is displayed.

APPLICATIONS

You can use the VERIFY command when the integrity of data transfer is critical. In addition, turning on the VERIFY function eliminates the need to use the /V parameter during file copying operations (see Module 15).

TYPICAL OPERATION

In this activity you use the VERIFY command to turn on verification, then examine the VERIFY status, and finally, turn VERIFY off. Begin at the DOS prompt.

1. Type **VERIFY ON** and press **Return**.
2. Type **VERIFY** and press **Return**; notice the following display.

```
A:\>VERIFY
VERIFY is on

A:\>
```

3. Type **VERIFY OFF** and press **Return**.
4. Type **VERIFY** and press **Return**; notice the following display.

```
A:\>VERIFY
VERIFY is off

A:\>
```

5. Turn to Module 45 to continue the learning sequence.

Module 67
VOL (2.00+)

DESCRIPTION

The VOL command is an internal DOS command that displays the volume label (or name) of the specified disk. This command is available in DOS versions 2.00 and later. You may recall from Module 32, which describes the FORMAT command, that an optional 1- to 11-character volume name may be assigned to a disk by typing the FORMAT command with the /V parameter. The VOL command is used to check the name of a volume.

Typing VOL A: and pressing Return displays a message similar to the following screen illustration.

```
A:\>VOL A:

 Volume in drive A has no label
 Volume Serial Number is 0F66-14F7

A:\>
```

All DOS versions beginning with 2.00 and prior to version 3.00 require that a volume name be assigned during the disk formatting process. DOS 3.00 introduced the LABEL command (Module 38). This command lets you assign or change a volume name after a disk has been formatted.

APPLICATIONS

It is sometimes a good idea to assign volume names to disks for identification purposes. By giving a disk a meaningful volume name, you can examine the volume name to determine disk contents. Even if the paper label is separated from the disk, having an embedded, meaningful volume name lets you identify the disk quickly.

TYPICAL OPERATION

In this activity you use the FORMAT /V and VOL commands to assign and then check the volume name of the disk in drive B. Begin at the DOS prompt.

1. Place a scratch disk in drive B: and close the load lever.
2. Type **FORMAT B:/V** and press **Return**.

3. Once the disk is formatted, notice the following prompt.

```
Volume label (11 characters, ENTER for none)?
```

4. Type **SCRATCH** and press **Return**.
5. Type **N** in response to the "Format another (Y/N)?" prompt.
6. Type **VOL B:** and press **Return**; notice the following display.

```
A:\>VOL B:

 Volume in drive B is SCRATCH
 Volume Serial Number is 3168-16D4

A:\>
```

7. Turn to Module 38 to continue the learning sequence.

Module 68
XCOPY (3.20+)

DESCRIPTION

The XCOPY command is an external command introduced with DOS version 3.20. It is used to selectively copy files from one disk to another, or those files that have been created or modified since the last backup. The general form of the XCOPY command is

```
XCOPY A: C:\path\filename
```

This form of the command operates like the COPY command. There are a number of options that are added after the target filename to control file selection. The option letters, represented by /x in the following command line example, are quite useful.

```
XCOPY A: C:\path\filename/x
```

The value of /x controls the way XCOPY operates. Each of the available values are described in the following list.

/A Copies files that have the archive bit, which is set with the BACKUP and ATTRIB commands, set to a value of one.

/D Copies all files that are the same or later than a specified date. The date is added to the command as shown:

```
XCOPY A: C:/D:06-21-88
```

The date is entered in the format mm-dd-yy, dd-mm-yyy, or yy-mm-dd.

/E Creates subdirectories on the target disk even if the new subdirectories are empty. This happens when the command option used prevents the transfer of files within the subdirectory because they do not meet selection criteria.

/M Copies files having an archive bit value of one. When copied, the archive bit is reset to zero on the source file. This lets you use XCOPY in backup operations. An archive bit value of one indicates that the file was created or modified since the last BACKUP or XCOPY /M operation.

/P Displays a (Y/N)? prompt before copying a file to allow selection.

/S Copies files from the source disk that are within and subordinate to the active (or logged) directory. This can include a number of directory paths, as XCOPY searches through the directory tree. This option does not create new directory paths on the target disk unless the /E option is also used. If /S is omitted, XCOPY works only within the named directory.

/V As in COPY, this option verifies that data is written properly. As in the COPY command, the /V option slows the copy process.

/W Displays the prompt "Press any key to begin copying file(s)." This option is used to let you insert a diskette before XCOPY begins its search for source files.

A few important XCOPY features include:

- The default value of filenames is *.*.
- XCOPY creates file paths on the target diskette if they do not exist.
- You can specify target filenames as with COPY.
- The maximum number of characters for a disk, path, and filename is 63.
- XCOPY does not copy hidden or deny-read files.

The following XCOPY command examples are provided for clarification and should serve as models.

```
XCOPY C:\ E:\ /S
```

Copies all files from drive C:\ to drive E:\ including all files in subordinate directory paths. Drive E may be another disk or a tape device.

```
XCOPY C:\ E:\ /S /P
```

This command form performs the same operation as the preceding example except that each filename is displayed and you are prompted for a copy decision.

```
XCOPY C:\WP E:\ /S
```

Copies all files from the C:\WP file path to the E:\WP file path. Any file paths that are subordinate to \WP are also copied from drive C to drive E.

```
XCOPY C:\ E:\ /S/M
```

Copies all files in all subdirectories from drive C:\ to drive E:\. The /M option resets the archive bit of the source files to zero. The value zero indicates that the file has been modified (or created) since the last backup operation. This lets you substitute XCOPY for the BACKUP command.

APPLICATIONS

The XCOPY command provides a convenient way to copy multiple files without having to copy each individually. The available options let you copy only those files that were created or modified after: 1) the last backup operation, or 2) a specified date. It also gives you an alternate way to perform a backup procedure without using the BACKUP command.

You can also use XCOPY to reset file attributes within a selected directory. This provides an alternate to the ATTRIB command.

The /P option displays a (Y/N)? prompt before a file is copied. This is a convenient way to copy several files from a directory without having to type the filename of each. The /W option reminds you to insert a disk before beginning the copy process. This helps prevent "Abort, Retry, Ignore" messages.

TYPICAL OPERATION

In this activity you use XCOPY to selectively copy files with the filename extension COM in all subdirectories. In addition, you use the /P option to display each filename before it is copied. Begin by formatting a floppy diskette for use as the destination disk. If you have a hard disk system, place the destination disk in drive A. If you are using a system with two diskette drives, place the formatted diskette in drive B. The following procedure uses C as the source disk and A as the target disk. If you have two floppy diskettes, substitute A: for C: and B: for A:.

1. Log the DOS directory.

NOTE

In the following step, select three files to copy. Omit the rest by typing N in response to the (Y/N)? prompt. This will keep you from exceeding the capacity of the target diskette.

2. Type **XCOPY C:*.COM A: /S/P** and press **Return**. Notice that a filename is displayed and you are prompted for a copy decision.
3. Type **Y** to copy some files and **N** to omit others.
4. You may experiment with other forms of the XCOPY command until you are satisfied that you understand its operation.
5. Turn to Module 50 to continue the learning sequence.

Appendix A
TERMS AND DEFINITIONS

ASCII file	A file consisting of characters that conform to the American Standard Code for Information Interchange. This is the standard code used by most computer systems. It is comprised of a 7-bit code that represents 128 characters and control codes.
Applications program	A computer program designed to perform a common application such as word processing, accounting, or database management.
Assembler	A program used to convert a file containing instructions recognizable by programmers into machine language recognizable by the microprocessor in use.
Assembly language	An instruction set comprised of mnemonics that are recognizable by an assembler program such as the IBM Macro Assembler.
Asynchronous	A communications format that is independent of instructions (or synchronization) from another computer with which it is communicating.
Binary file	A file made up of binary digits (bits) that is more space efficient than the 7-bit ASCII code.
Bisynchronous	A computer communications format that relies on interaction (or synchronization) with another computer with which it is communicating.
Bit	Binary digit; its value is either 1 or 0.
Branching	A decision point or branch in the flow of a program, process, or structure.
Breakpoint	A forced interruption within a computer program at a predetermined location or event.
Byte	A computer character made up of eight binary digits.
Calls	A program instruction that either fetches or sends one or more control codes or characters to a device or memory location within the computer.
Chains	A sequence of location pointers that connect (or chain together) the parts of a disk file.

Code Page	A table containing characters and symbols that correspond to specific countries. Code page switching was introduced with DOS version 3.3.
Command	An instruction that is recognized by a computer program.
Compiler	A computer program used to convert a program written in a high-level programming language, like FORTRAN or Pascal, into machine-recognizable code.
Concatenate	To collect separate elements into one. An example is when separate files are combined into one.
Cursor	A flashing rectangle or bar that designates where characters are entered on a computer's display screen.
DOS	The acronym for Disk Operating System.
Diagnostic	A program used to evaluate the condition of a computer or computer device.
Directory	A list of filenames contained on a disk.
Dummy device	A device name used to simulate program operations. DOS uses NUL as a dummy device name.
Extension	One to three optional characters that are added to the end of a filename for increased clarity.
File	A program or data file residing on disk.
File allocation table	Part of the DOS directory in which statistical information about each file is kept.
File control block	A file control block exists for each file on a disk. Here, information about the file's name, location, and size is maintained.
Filename	A 1- to 8-character name used to identify a computer file; an optional 1- to 3-character extension may be used.
Flag	A digit used to indicate an occurrence or state.
Format	The way in which media (usually a disk) is organized.
Global	Applies to an entire file or disk.
Handshaking	The interaction between two devices, as in bisynchronous communications, where the transfer of information between two computers requires a continuous exchange of signals between them.
Hexadecimal	The base 16 number system consisting of the digits 0 1 2 3 4 5 6 7 8 9 A B C D E F.
I/O device	A computer input/output device. Your keyboard is an input device; your display screen and printer are output devices. Your disk drive is both an input and output device.

Initialization	Setting a device to its beginning (or initial) state.
Interface	The interconnection between two devices.
Landscape mode	A wide presentation. In printing, this refers to printing so that the printout is horizontal on the paper.
Library	A collection of utility programs used by certain high-level programming languages. Having a library of common utilities eliminates the need for programmers to write commonly used routines.
Logged disk	The active (or default) disk drive.
Logical device	A portion of memory or disk that is named and treated by software (or a program) as a physical device.
Macro assembler	An assembler that interprets an instruction set made up of mnemonics (abbreviated instructions) and converts them into machine language.
Object file	A file created by an assembler.
Overhead	Extra space used by system files.
Parallel	A computer connection scheme in which data elements are transmitted simultaneously (or in parallel) over multiple conductors or signal paths.
Parent directory	The top level directory for a specified directory path. Can be the top level (or root) directory, but usually refers to a pathname one level below the root directory.
Partition	A portion of a fixed disk that is reserved for a group of files that operate under control of a common operating system, like Xenix or CP/M-86.
Pathname	The name of a directory path within a tree-structured directory system. Introduced in DOS version 2.00.
Portrait mode	The vertical (or normal) printout mode.
Ports	Input/output connectors on a computer.
Prompts	A message displayed by a computer program to encourage a user response.
Protocol	A computer communication specification defining software and hardware configurations.
Queue	A series of events waiting to be executed.
RAM	Random access memory; a memory structure that allows the direct access of any part of computer memory, regardless of physical location.
ROM	Read-only memory; a preprogrammed device that cannot be altered.

Register	A storage location within a digital computer device designed to store data, instructions, or location or status information.
Root directory	The top-level, or main, directory within a tree-structured directory system.
Scratch disk	A working disk normally used for experimentation or practice.
Scroll	The vertical or horizontal movement of characters on a computer screen.
Serial	A computer connection scheme in which data elements are transmitted in a sequential stream (or in serial) over an electrical conductor.
Strings	A continuous series (or string) of characters. A text string can be any unique sequence of letters.
System	Often used as a short form for Disk Operating System.
Utilities	A program that performs a commonly used task.
Volume name	The name (or label) given to a disk when it is formatted. With DOS version 3.00, the LABEL command lets you create, change, or delete a volume name.
Warm boot	Reinitialization of the computer and disk operating system without turning the power off. With DOS, this is achieved by simultaneously pressing Ctrl-Alt-Del.

Appendix B
MS-DOS EXERCISES

1. About This Book
   a. Describe the purpose of an operating system.
   b. What is a DOS command?
   c. How is the "Recommended Learning Sequence" used?
   d. What does <CR> mean?
2. A Sample Session With DOS
   a. How are disk drives designated?
   b. What is the left-hand diskette drive normally designated?
   c. What is the difference between a floppy disk and a hard (or fixed) disk?
   d. List five ways to damage a floppy disk.
   e. What is the purpose of the write protect notch?
   f. What is a distribution disk?
   g. What is a working copy?
   h. What is a prompt?
3. System Overview
   a. List five things that DOS can do for you.
   b. Compare a magnetic tape to a disk.
   c. Draw a diagram of a disk showing tracks and sectors.
   d. What is a computer term for character?
   e. What does the term boot strap a computer mean?
   f. What is the difference between an internal and external program?
   g. What is a device?
   h. What keys are pressed to reset your computer?
4. APPEND
   a. What command is similar to APPEND?
   b. What is the purpose of APPEND?
   c. What command is used to append C:\DB and C:\WS?
   d. How do you cancel the APPEND command?
   e. Describe two parameters added to APPEND in DOS 4.01.
5. ASSIGN
   a. Write the command line for redirecting drive A commands to drive B.
   b. Write the command line that disables the ASSIGN command.

6. ATTRIB
   a. What is the purpose of the ATTRIB command?
   b. Write the command that makes MYPROG.COM a read-only file.
   c. Write the command to verify that MYPROG.COM is a read-only file.
   d. Write the command that returns the file to read/write.
7. Automatic File Execution (Batch Commands)
   a. What is a batch file?
   b. In what order are commands within a batch file executed?
   c. What key sequence is pressed to stop batch file operation?
   d. Why might you use the REM command?
   e. Give two good reasons for creating and using automatic batch files.
8. BACKUP
   a. What is the purpose of the BACKUP command?
   b. What is the command to backup all files in all directories from disk drive C to disk drive A?
   c. What is the command to backup those files in the WP subdirectory on drive C to a disk in drive A?
   d. What is the command to backup only those files that have been modified since the last time BACKUP was used?
   e. What does the command BACKUP C: A: /S /D:10-21-89 accomplish?
9. CHCP
   a. Is CHCP an external or internal DOS command?
   b. What does the CHCP command change?
   c. What command must be used before CHCP takes effect?
   d. What is displayed if the COUNTRY.SYS file is missing?
10. CHKDSK
    a. What is the purpose of the CHKDSK command?
    b. How are hidden files displayed with CHKDSK on DOS versions 2.00 and later?
    c. Why might you use the /F parameter with CHKDSK?
    d. What is meant by the message "Contains 2 non-contiguous blocks"?
11. Clear Screen (CLS)
    a. What versions of DOS feature the CLS command?
    b. Why might you use the CLS command?
    c. Where is the prompt displayed after the CLS command is used?
12. Code Page Switching
    a. What is the primary purpose of code page switching?
    b. Describe how the CONFIG.SYS and AUTOEXEC.BAT files are used with code page switching.
    c. Describe the use of the MODE command in the preparation of code page switching.
    d. Write the MODE command that prepares your system for use with an EGA display.
    e. Write the COUNTRY command that prepares your system for use with the Spanish language.

13. COMP
    a. What is the COMP command used for?
    b. You want to compare a:file1 to b:file1. Give the command line.
    c. If the files are different in size, what message is displayed?
14. Configuration Commands
    a. What is the filename of a configuration file?
    b. How can a configuration file be created?
    c. What effect does BREAK = ON have on DOS operation?
    d. How can you reassign the value of one key with another?
    e. What is a Set Mode code; how is it used?
    f. What does the command FILES = 8 do?
    g. What is a virtual disk? Which driver installs a virtual disk?
    h. Describe the LASTDRIVE command.
    i. Describe a buffer.
15. COPY
    a. Give four uses of the COPY command.
    b. What does the term concatenate mean?
    c. Define sourcefile and targetfile.
    d. What is the result of the command COPY FILE1+FILE2 FILE3?
    e. What does the command COPY CON: MYFILE do?
    f. What does Ctrl-Z do relative to the above question?
16. CTTY
    a. What is the CTTY command used for?
    b. If you issue the CTTY command without having a terminal connected to your computer, what happens?
17. DATE
    a. When do you first encounter the DATE command?
    b. Show how the date is typed in response to the date prompt.
    c. How can you bypass your response to the date prompt?
    d. Why is it important to type the date?
18. DEBUG
    a. Who usually uses the DEBUG utility?
    b. What command line is used to DEBUG the file MYPROG.COM?
    c. How do you move DEBUG's pointer to a specific memory address?
    d. What command displays (or dumps) the contents of memory address 3C4?
    e. Memory address 0105 contains 31 hex and you wish to replace it with 39 hex. What command lets you enter 39 hex in place of 31?
    f. What is the command for displaying all the registers of your microprocessor?
    g. What command writes the changed contents to disk?
    h. What command is used to quit the DEBUG program?

19. Directory Commands (DIR, MKDIR, RMDIR, CHDIR, DIRCMD)
    a. What is the purpose of the DIR command?
    b. Describe two ways to pause the directory display.
    c. How are subdirectories created?
    d. Describe the directory "tree" structure.
    e. What must be done before a subdirectory can be removed from disk?
    f. Describe the purpose of MD, CD, and RD.
    g. What is the purpose of SET DIRCMD?
20. DISKCOMP
    a. Describe the purpose of the DISKCOMP command.
    b. Write the command to compare disk A to disk B.
    c. Write the command to compare an 8-sector disk to a 9-sector disk.
    d. What message is displayed if the disk comparison is okay?
21. DISKCOPY
    a. Describe the purpose of the DISKCOPY command.
    b. Write the command to copy the contents of disk A to disk B.
    c. What might be a problem when using DISKCOPY?
    d. Write the command to copy all files on disk A to disk B using the COPY command instead of the DISKCOPY command.
22. DOSKEY
    a. Which version of DOS introduced the DOSKEY command?
    b. Where are DOS commands kept?
    c. What does the command DOSKEY /INSERT do?
    d. How do you adjust the number of commands stored by DOSKEY?
    e. Write a command that assigns the string DIR /P to the macro *DP*.
23. DOSSHELL
    a. What version of DOS introduced the DOSSHELL utility?
    b. Which version of DOSSHELL introduced *task switching*?
    c. What does task switching do?
    d. How do you access DOSSHELL menus (or *action bar*)?
    e. What kind of operations are performed with the File System?
    f. Explain how you would add a program to an existing group in the Main menu window.
24. EDIT
    a. What is a *full-screen editor*?
    b. What are some of the advantages of EDIT over EDLIN?
    c. What program must be present for EDIT to run?
    d. How is a block of text *marked*?
    e. How is a block of text *cut*?
    f. How is a block of text *pasted*?

25. EDLIN
    a. How does EDLIN differ from a full-screen editor?
    b. What are some uses of EDLIN?
    c. Write the command to create a file named MY.BAT using EDLIN.
    d. How do you start entering text into MY.BAT?
    e. Once several lines are typed, how do you return to the EDLIN prompt?
    f. How is the file displayed (or listed) to the screen?
    g. What does the command 5i do?
    h. What does the command 4,6,1m do?
    i. What command is used to save the file and return to DOS?
26. ERASE (or DELETE)
    a. Describe uses for the DEL command.
    b. Write the command to delete all files having the extension DAT.
    c. How can all files on a disk be simultaneously deleted?
27. EXE2BIN
    a. Where did this command get its name?
    b. Write the EXE2BIN command for converting PROG.EXE to PROG.COM.
28. FASTOPEN
    a. What is the purpose of the FASTOPEN command?
    b. Where does it store path and filenames?
    c. What is the default number of filenames maintained by FASTOPEN?
    d. What is the maximum number of filenames that can be maintained by FASTOPEN?
29. FDISK
    a. Describe the purpose of the FDISK command.
    b. After a fixed disk is partitioned, what must be done?
    c. Write the command to format hard disk drive C and simultaneously transfer the operating system.
    d. Describe two differences between the DOS 4.01 FDISK display screens and earlier versions.
30. Filenames
    a. What is the purpose of a filename?
    b. What kind of filenames should you use?
    c. What is an extension?
    d. How many characters can you have in a filename? In an extension?
    e. What do the extensions EXE and COM normally indicate?
    f. What is a wild card?
    g. Write the command to list all filenames beginning with "G."
31. FIND
    a. Describe the concept of filtering a command.
    b. Name three filter commands.
    c. What can the FIND filter be used for?
    d. Write three DOS commands that include the FIND filter.

32. FORMAT
    a. What does the FORMAT command do to a new disk?
    b. What happens if you format a disk containing files?
    c. What are some compatibility considerations between DOS versions 1.xx and 2.xx?
    d. Write the command to format the disk in drive B with a system.
    e. Write the command to format the disk in drive B with 8 sectors.
    f. How do you assign a volume name to a disk when it is formatted?
33. GRAFTABL
    a. What characters are accessed using GRAFTABL?
    b. What is a common use for these characters?
    c. Write the command form for displaying the GRAFTABL status.
34. GRAPHICS
    a. When does the GRAPHICS program take effect?
    b. How is a screen printed in the 640 x 200 color graphics mode?
    c. What DOS 4.01 GRAPHICS command parameter reverses black on white?
    d. What DOS 4.01 GRAPHICS command parameter is used with an LCD display?
    e. What is defined within the GRAPHICS.PRO file?
35. HELP, /?
    a. What is the purpose of the HELP command?
    b. What version of DOS introduced the HELP command?
    c. Explain two ways that you can display help information about the CHKDSK command.
36. JOIN
    a. What is the first step in using the JOIN command?
    b. What directory may not be used with the JOIN command?
    c. What five commands are avoided when JOIN is in use?
    d. When JOIN is in use, what is displayed when you type JOIN and press Return?
37. KEYB
    a. What is the purpose of the KEYB command?
    b. Where is the KEYB command normally found?
    c. When is the KEYBOARD.SYS file used?
    d. What are the keyboard and country codes for Germany, Denmark, and the Netherlands?
38. LABEL
    a. What is the purpose of the LABEL command?
    b. Write the command to change an existing label to DISK #1.
    c. Write the command to change DISK #1 to DISK #2.
39. LINK
    a. List four functions performed by the LINK command.
    b. Who normally uses the LINK command?
    c. How is the file VM.TMP created?
    d. What is meant by compiling and linking?

40. MEM
    a. What version of DOS introduced the MEM command?
    b. What is displayed with the MEM command?
    c. What does the /PROGRAM parameter display?
    d. When is expanded memory displayed?
41. MIRROR
    a. What other DOS commands work with the files produced by the MIRROR command?
    b. What are the names of two files created by the MIRROR command?
    c. Describe the effect of the command MIRROR C: /tc /ta.
    d. Describe the effect of the command MIRROR /tc-50.
    e. How can you unload delete tracking from memory?
42. MODE
    a. What outputs are controlled with the MODE command?
    b. Write the command to redirect printing from LPT1 to LPT2.
    c. Write the command to set the following communications parameters:

```
Output port - COM1
Transfer speed - 1200 baud
Parity - None
Data bits - 8
Stop bits - 1
```

    d. What is typematic control?
    e. Write a MODE command to prepare your console for use with the multilingual code page (850) and an enhanced graphics adapter.
43. MORE
    a. When might you use the MORE filter?
    b. Write a command that pauses a directory display.
    c. What does the command TYPE MYDOC ¦ MORE do?
44. NLSFUNC
    a. What does the term NLSFUNC stand for?
    b. What command is used with NLSFUNC?
    c. What is the purpose of this command pair?
45. PATH
    a. What does the PATH command achieve?
    b. Write the path command to access program files in the root (main) directory from a subdirectory.
    c. How are established directory paths canceled?
    d. Write a PATH command to access multiple file directories named C:\WP, C:\DB, and C:\DOS.
46. Piping Commands
    a. What is meant by piping?
    b. Write the command to pipe a directory to the file B:NAMES.LST.
    c. Write the command to pipe a directory listing to your printer.
    d. Describe the result of TYPE MYFILE >PRN.

47. PRINT
    a. Describe the purpose of the PRINT command.
    b. What do the terms concurrent printing or print spooling mean?
    c. Write the command to print MYFILE.TXT with the PRINT command.
    d. Write the command to add the file DADS.LTR to the print queue.
    e. Write the command to terminate printing of all queued files.
48. Printing Operations
    a. How can you print text that is displayed on the screen?
    b. How can lines of text be simultaneously printed as they are displayed?
    c. Write the COPY command to print A:MYFILE.TXT.
    d. Write the piping command to print A:MYFILE.TXT on your printer.
49. PROMPT
    a. Why might you use the PROMPT command?
    b. Write the command to display the time as part of the DOS prompt.
    c. Write the command to display the path name as part of the DOS prompt.
50. RECOVER
    a. Describe the purpose of the RECOVER command.
    b. Write the command to recover the file A:MYTEXT.DAT.
    c. What may exist at the end of a recovered file?
    d. What is the filename FILE0001.REC?
51. RENAME
    a. Why might you wish to rename a file?
    b. Write the command to rename MYFILE.BAK to MYFILE.OLD.
    c. Write the command to rename all files with the extension CMD to PRG.
52. REPLACE
    a. What is the purpose of the REPLACE command?
    b. What is the purpose of the /A option?
    c. What is the purpose of the /P option?
    d. Describe the operation of the command REPLACE A: B: /S/P.
53. RESTORE
    a. What is the purpose of the RESTORE command?
    b. Write the command to restore all files from floppy disks in drive A to a hard disk in drive C.
    c. Write the command to restore all files with the extension TXT from floppy disks in drive A to a hard disk designated drive C.
54. SELECT (Questions a. through d. apply to DOS versions 3.00 through 3.3.)
    a. What is the purpose of the SELECT command?
    b. What command is used by the SELECT utility?
    c. How is the time and date format influenced by the SELECT command?
    d. What is a country and keyboard code?
    e. What function does the DOS 4.01 SELECT command perform?

55. SET
    a. What is displayed when SET is typed from the DOS prompt?
    b. What is COMSPEC?
    c. Give a practical use for the SET COMSPEC command.
    d. Write the command to cancel path settings.
56. SHARE
    a. Write the form of the SHARE command to set aside 1024 bytes of disk space.
    b. Under what circumstances would you use the SHARE command?
    c. What does SHARE do for you?
57. SORT
    a. What is the purpose of the SORT filter?
    b. How might you combine SORT and a pipe to save an alphabetized directory listing to a file?
    c. Write the SORT command that sorts a shopping list file named SHOPLIST to a new file named SHOPLIST.SRT.
58. SUBST
    a. What is the function of the SUBST command?
    b. Describe the operation of the command SUBST E: C:\DOS\UTIL.
    c. How can you display the current status of the SUBST command?
59. SYS
    a. Describe the purpose of the SYS command.
    b. Why might SYS not work on a disk containing files?
    c. What FORMAT parameters must be used to reserve space for system files?
    d. What capability was added to SYS with DOS 4.01?
60. TIME
    a. When do you first encounter the TIME command?
    b. Show how the time is typed in response to the time prompt.
    c. How can you bypass your response to the time prompt?
    d. Why is it important to type the time?
    e. What additional feature was added to the TIME command with the release of DOS 4.01?
61. TREE
    a. Describe the use of the TREE command.
    b. How can you pause the display when using the TREE command?
    c. Write the command for displaying all files within directories.
    d. How did DOS 4.01 change the TREE command display?
62. TYPE
    a. Describe the purpose of the TYPE command.
    b. What is meant by scrolling?
    c. How can you pause and resume scrolling?
    d. How can you type and print a file simultaneously?

63. UNDELETE
    a. What is the purpose of UNDELETE?
    b. Why might you not be able to recover a deleted file?
    c. What is the command for automatically undeleting all files on the logged drive?
    d. What is the command for deleting all files having the extension .DOC in the subdirectory C:\WP?
    e. What is the command for listing all files that are available for undeletion?
64. UNFORMAT
    a. What version of DOS first included the UNFORMAT command?
    b. What other DOS program helps improve the integrity of the UNFORMAT command?
    c. Describe the purpose of the command UNFORMAT C: /J.
    d. Which UNFORMAT parameter prints information as it is listed?
    e. What is the purpose of the UNFORMAT A: /TEST command?
    f. What FORMAT command parameter prevents the UNFORMAT command from restoring a disk?
65. VER
    a. Describe the purpose of the VER command.
    b. Write the command to display the version of your DOS system.
66. VERIFY
    a. Describe the purpose of the VERIFY command.
    b. What is the default state of the VERIFY command?
    c. How is automatic verification turned on?
67. VOL
    a. Describe the purpose of the VOL command.
    b. How is a volume name initially created?
    c. How many characters are allowed within a volume name?
    d. Write the command to display the volume name of the logged disk.
68. XCOPY
    a. Compare the XCOPY and REPLACE commands.
    b. Which files are copied from one disk to another using the command XCOPY C:*.PRG A:/D:10-21-89?
    c. What is the effect of the command XCOPY A: B:/P?
    d. Describe the XCOPY /M and /W options.
    e. What two file types are not copied with the XCOPY command?

Index